Lonely planet

BEST BIKE RIDES
ITALY
BEST DAY TRIPS ON TWO WHEELS

AMY MCPHERSON, MARGHERITA RAGG AND ANGELO ZINNA

Contents

DOWNLOADABLE DIGITAL RIDE MAPS

Download GPX or KML files of the
rides in this book so you can take
the route with you on your ride.

Welcome to Italy

Cycling is a way of life for many Italians, young and old. Here you are just as likely to see Lycra-clad road racers battling up the twisting roads of a mountain as you are to spot a local pedalling through narrow village streets with bags of groceries on a rusty old bike.

A bike ride in Italy is rarely just a bike ride. It is rather an opportunity to see regional culture, take in the landscapes, both bucolic and urban, and experience the Italianness of exploring on two wheels. Choose an itinerary that follows a dedicated cycleway, along rivers and seafronts, through forests and historic centres, or around scenic mountain loops.

And with the increasing popularity of e-bikes, many of the great rides have become more accessible to cyclists of all abilities. So go on, go for a ride!

Cycling near Arezzo (p164)
UMOMOS/SHUTTERSTOCK ©

My Perfect Bike Ride

Amy McPherson

CICLOVIA
ACQUE-
DOTTO
PUGLIESE

P198

Cycling anywhere in Italy induces different kinds of happiness, but for me, no place matches the kind of joy I feel when I am among the *trulli* (traditional stone huts with a conical roof) and olive groves of Puglia. There's something uplifting about riding through this arid landscape peppered by cone-shaped roofs and whitewashed houses, tracing the stone walls lining the quiet country roads, and having the wind push me along past the turquoise water of the Adriatic coast.

Margherita Ragg

SENTIERO
DELLA
BONIFICA

P164

My ideal bike ride includes three elements: good roads, hills and great views. I love cycling on roads or cycle paths – I'm not a fan of gravel or mountain-bike riding – so nice smooth surfaces are a must. I also enjoy cycling around hills and mountains because these paths usually come with views! I like cycling itineraries known as *'mangia e bevi'* in Italian – a combination of short climbs and descents, exactly the kind you find in Tuscany (pictured).

Angelo Zinna

ASINARA
ISLAND

P208

Heading to Sardinia in the middle of winter was a wonderful way to explore some of the coastal wonders of the island without the crowds. Cycling uninhabited Asinara under the February sun allowed me to discover this stretch of land, once closed off to the public, at its rawest state – in the company of wild horses, donkeys and goats that roam freely between sandy beaches, abandoned architecture and shrub-covered hills.

Trulli (p201) in Puglia

Top 5 Scenic Rides

1 Sentiero della Bonifica
A quiet ride through Tuscany along a canal.

2 Lago Arvo Loop
Circumnavigate the lake in Sila National Park in Calabria.

3 Asinara Island
Pristine beaches and abundant wildlife on a quiet island.

4 Via Panoramica del Parco del San Bartolo
The sea backdrops a long scenic ride.

5 Ciclovia del Toce
Enjoy views to the Alps in Piedmont's Lake District.

Montecchio castle (p167), Tuscany

Our Picks

BEST COASTAL ROUTES

Surrounded by five seas of the Mediterranean, Italy has about 7500km of coastline, including those of its beautiful islands, with waters coloured turquoise to midnight blue. Along the rugged cliffs and beautiful beaches are coastal villages and towns that often have distinct characters and traditions, not to mention picture-perfect postcard scenery. All can be admired on the numerous cycle routes along the coast.

TOP TIP

You can cycle the Italian coastline on the Ciclopista del Sole and Via Adriatica.

LIBERO_MONTERISI/SHUTTERSTOCK ©

Costa dei Trabocchi

Visit Abruzzo's traditional fishing piers and many quiet beaches along the coast on this beautiful ride.

P44

Costa degli Etruschi

Starting and ending in Cecina, this Tuscan coastal ride with forest bathing and wild sand dunes is for everyone.

P138

Ciclovia Adriatica: Bari to Polignano a Mare

From Bari, explore the wild coastline of Puglia before visiting dreamy Polignano a Mare.

P178

Alghero to Punta Giglio

A seaside cycling path in Sardinia that enters a natural reserve with exceptional views of both the city and Capo Caccia.

P214

Riviera dei Fiori

A leisurely ride along the Ligurian coast, offering some of the region's most spectacular views.

P74

SIMONA ABBONDIO/ALAMY STOCK PHOTO ©

Above: Riviera dei Fiori (p74) near Sanremo; Right: Polignano a Mare (p183)

8   BEST BIKE RIDES: ITALY

TOP TIP

Lampedusa of the Pelagic Islands is Italy's southernmost island; it's actually closer to Tunisia than it is to anywhere in Italy.

TOP TIP

The word 'tiramisu' means 'pick me up' – it was originally created in 1971 as a dessert to help customers wake up after a heavy meal!

Our Picks

BEST FOODIE ROUTES

If there is one thing that defines passion in Italy (other than the bicycle), it is the pride Italians express for their cuisine. Across dining tables, around bar corners and through the deli storefronts, someone, somewhere, will always be discussing food. There is no single Italian food – something as simple as pasta is different throughout Italy. What better way to experience each region's produce and specialities than on one of these great foodie rides.

TOP TIP

Not all pasta is made equal! Pasta shapes and what they are cooked with differ from region to region.

Through the Hills of Barolo

For those who enjoy pairing scenery with world-class wines, truffles and cheese, this ride in the Langhe region is for you.

P60

Through Trapani's Salt Pans to Marsala

Enjoy Sicilian street food in Trapani before arriving at one of Sicily's most renowned wine regions, where a sweet reward awaits.

P218

Ciclabile del Conca

A great choice for wine lovers, this route passes right through a vineyard, where you can park your bike and go wine tasting!

P112

Fritto misto di mare

Ciclopista del Trammino

The marina area of Pisa is fantastic for a seafood lunch. Make sure to try the *fritto misto di mare,* a local favourite!

P156

Costa dei Trabocchi

As well as being a great coastal ride, many of the fishing piers along the route are now seafood restaurants serving the local seafood the local way.

P44

Vineyards in the Langhe region of Piedmont (p60)

Our Picks

BEST WILDLIFE ROUTES

From the mountains to the sea, Italy is a land of natural beauty and rich biodiversity. The country's many nature reserves and oases are home to an abundance of wildlife, in particular water birds, which can be spotted all along the coast, in marshlands and lagoons. On average, more than 1,500,000 birds call Italy home, and the country is an important route for migratory birds coming from Africa via the Mediterranean Sea.

TOP TIP

Be a responsible wildlife spotter: observe, don't disturb. Watch from a distance and never actively approach wildlife, and never attempt to feed them.

LUCIANO SALVATORE/SHUTTERSTOCK ©

 1

Pista Ciclopedonale del Lago di Varese

The wetlands around Varese are important as the breeding grounds for the ferruginous duck.

P98

 2

Ciclabile del Conca

Cycle through a part of the wildlife oasis of the Conca Valley known for sightings of rare bird species.

P112

 3

Asinara Island

The worst traffic you'll encounter here will be from the indigenous donkeys that roam the island.

P208

 4

Orbetello Lagoon & Flamingos

Loop around the Orbetello lagoon in search of its flocks of migrating pink flamingos.

P160

 5

Giro Laguna

Discover the lesser-known side of the Venetian lagoon and admire a unique ecosystem home to several species of herons.

P120

ELISA LOCCI/SHUTTERSTOCK ©

Above: Donkeys, Asinara Island (p208); Right: Flamingos, Orbetello (p160)

TOP TIP

Seeing flamingos in Italy is more common than you think. Other than Orbetello, you can spot them on your rides in Sardinia, the Venetian lagoon and Sicily.

Our Picks

BEST HISTORIC ROUTES

Italy's ancient Roman history is well known throughout the world, as is its more recent WWI and WWII histories. Less known is the multi-layered past from pre-Roman settlements, eras of foreign conquest, the triumph of the Renaissance, and the industrial heritage found in hidden corners all around the country. Be reminded of these historical anecdotes and learn the stories on a bike ride through the past.

TOP TIP

Before the Romans, four powerful civilisations ruled Italy: Etruscans, the Nuragic, the ancient Greeks of Magna Graecia and the Celts of Cisalpine Gaul.

Roman Pozzuoli & Lago d'Averno

Discover this 'hidden gem' of the Roman Empire on a bike ride around Pozzuoli and Lake Averno.

P194

Sentiero della Bonifica

Tuscany's reclaimed lands make a great bike ride with information boards along the way to learn about the canal's history.

P164

Via Appia Antica & Parco degli Acquedotti

From important Roman highway to impressive aqua engineering, this is a ride back to ancient Rome.

P34

Pista Ciclabile del Mincio

Learn about this Italian region under various conquests, from Austrian to Veronese Scaligers, on this excellent cycleway.

P90

Carbonia to Sant'Antioco

Old mining towns and ancient tombs – this is a ride through the fascinating and lesser-known history of Sardinia.

P224

MAURO TOCCACELI/ALAMY STOCK PHOTO ©

Parco degli Acquedotti (p39)

Our Picks

BEST ART & CULTURE ROUTES

Since its ancient beginnings, Italy's arts and culture scene has been at the forefront of its identity and a great influence around the world, from the opera to its many styles of architecture and fine arts. From old masters to new-age art, traditional festivals to modern sporting events, there's always something to admire and celebrate in the plethora of museums, galleries, palaces, theatres and heritage sites throughout the country.

TOP TIP

With 58 world heritage locations, there are more Unesco World Heritage Sites in Italy than anywhere in the world.

MART, Rovereto (p131)

Ciclopedonale Puccini

This bike route following the Serchio river is part of the Puccini bikeway, named after the town's famous son, composer Giacomo Puccini.

P142

Florence: Parks, Michelangelo & Football

Two Italian greats in one ride: find Michelangelo all over Florence and drop by the National Football Museum.

P150

Ciclovia del Sole

Ride across a territory home to artists, songwriters and food lovers, so iconic it's been called 'Italy in miniature'.

P108

Ciclabile dell'Adige

A scenic itinerary that ends at MART, one of Italy's most important contemporary art galleries.

P128

San Giuliano & La Cripta del Peccato Originale

A chance to visit the impressive religious frescoes in the Crypt of the Original Sin, by an unknown artist nicknamed 'flower painter'.

P188

When to Go

In Italy, there's always a good place for a bike ride, no matter the season.

BIG EVENTS

Most people know **Carnival** as a major festival for Venice, although different versions are celebrated all over Italy. Traditionally held 40 days before Easter, it's a good time to observe the local tradition and culture. **February**

Italy's national day, **Festa della Repubblica**, is celebrated with much military gusto, particularly in Rome, but you'll notice displays of patriotism everywhere, with the Italian flag and its colours decorating buildings and landmarks. **2 June**

International bike race **Giro d'Italia** is the biggest cycling event on the Italian sporting calendar for cycling fans. **June**

Fiera Internazionale del Tartufo Bianco d'Alba is an international festival dedicated to Alba's white truffles held every weekend between October and mid-November.

The country's elongated geography and varying climates make Italy a potential year-round destination for cycling. But it is in spring and autumn when you're likely to get the best weather to explore by bike – during these months, the colours of nature are intensified, the range of festivals make it better for cultural experiences and tourist crowds are less intense.

Summer is a favourite for holidaymakers, when deep-blue skies, plenty of sunshine and balmy evenings are almost guaranteed. As alluring as this may be, the heat of summer can be challenging for cyclists and the risk of heat stroke and dehydration high. If you are riding on a warm day, set out early and carry plenty of water.

NADIR BALMA/SHUTTERSTOCK ©

Giro d'Italia

Weather Watch

JANUARY	FEBRUARY	MARCH	APRIL	MAY	JUNE
Avg daytime max: **12°C**	Avg daytime max: **13°C**	Avg daytime max: **16°C**	Avg daytime max: **19°C**	Avg daytime max: **23°C**	Avg daytime max: **27°C**
Days of rainfall: 7	Days of rainfall: 7	Days of rainfall: 7	Days of rainfall: 7	Days of rainfall: 6	Days of rainfall: 4

Cyclists with vintage bikes, L'Eroica

TOP TIP

After the skiing crowds have left and the snow melts away to sprouting flowers, many snow tracks in northern Italy become accessible for cyclists and hikers.

Accommodation

During summer it will be busy everywhere you go in Italy. It's when most Europeans take their annual holidays so accommodation prices will be at their peak and availability limited. This also accounts for the ski season in the mountains during winter. For better rates, travel outside school and public holidays, especially in July and August.

LOCAL FESTIVITIES

L'Eroica is an event dedicated to the tradition of cycling along the Strade Bianche (White Road) in the province of Siena, where participants must ride on historic bikes built in 1987 or earlier and dress in vintage cycling kits. **June**

The **Feast of San Gennaro** (St Januarius in English) is observed in Naples with the miracle of liquefaction of the saint's blood from the crypt of the cathedral. **19 September**

Lanciano in Abruzzo returns to medieval times for **Mastrogiurato**, a week where locals parade and dance, and feast on suppers called *panarde* of 40 dishes. **August/September**

St Joseph's Day is celebrated with bread, fava beans and baked goods across Sicily to thank St Joseph for providing food during a time of a severe drought in the Middle Ages. **March**

OLIVE HARVEST IN PUGLIA

Between late autumn and early winter, the weather in Puglia remains pleasant for a bike ride. During the olive harvest, watch as families gather and share the intense labour required to produce the region's superb olive oils and to celebrate this ancient tradition.

JULY	AUGUST	SEPTEMBER	OCTOBER	NOVEMBER	DECEMBER
Avg daytime max: **31°C** Days of rainfall: **3**	Avg daytime max: **31°C** Days of rainfall: **3**	Avg daytime max: **27°C** Days of rainfall: **7**	Avg daytime max: **22°C** Days of rainfall: **8**	Avg daytime max: **17°C** Days of rainfall: **9**	Avg daytime max: **13°C** Days of rainfall: **8**

Get Prepared for Italy

Useful things to load in your bag, your ears and your brain

▶ WATCH

The Talented Mr Ripley
(Anthony Minghella; 1999) Psychological thriller with scenes filmed almost entirely in locations in Italy.

Pane e tulipani
(Silvio Soldini; 2000) A heart-warming Italian comedy about life, family and love.

Il Postino (The Postman)
(Michael Radford/ Massimo Troisi; 1994) A simple love story to the backdrop of Procida and Salina.

Life is Beautiful
(Roberto Benigni; 1997) Bittersweet and heart-wrenchingly real.

Clothing

Italians are famous for their 'style first, comfort second' approach to clothing. Having said that, it will do you good to ensure you have a set (or two) of loose, non-restrictive shirts and trousers or shorts for days you want to spend on the bike.

Cycling jerseys and padded shorts: If you already own these, then bring them along – they will make you more comfortable, especially on longer rides.

T-shirts and shorts: For warm summer days, a T-shirt with stretch and non-restricting shorts will suffice. Bring along a light jacket if the weather looks to be shifty.

Gloves and sunglasses: These are optional, but you'll find them useful to protect your eyes from road dust and glare, and your hands from blisters from your bike handles.

Closed-toe footwear: For safety, proper footwear is always better than sandals; cycling in flip-flops is never a good idea.

Layers: For spring and autumn, combine a T-shirt and a thin, long-sleeved top for changes in temperatures across the day, and carry a light rain jacket (not a heavy-duty ski jacket!). Consider a neck warmer (tube), which can also act as a head covering under the helmet.

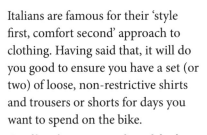

GORILLAIMAGES/SHUTTERSTOCK ©

Lake Garda (p132)

Greetings & Basics

Buongiorno Good morning, good day

Buona sera Good evening

Ciao! Hi! / Bye!

Si Yes

No No

Per favore Please

Grazie Thank you

Prego You're welcome

Parla Inglese? Do you speak English?

Road Signs

Incrocio pericoloso Dangerous junction

Rallentare Slow down

Curva pericolosa Dangerous bend

Strada chiusa Rad closed

Deviazione Diversion

Bici a mano Cyclists dismount

Discesa ripida Steep descent

Vietato Forbidden

Vietato appoggiare biciclette Do not leave/park bikes here

LISTEN

Cycling Europe Podcast
(2009–present) Dedicated to travel and adventures by bike in Europe; several episodes on Italy are worth listening to.

Tutto Modugno
(Domenico Modugno; 1972) A series of albums from the popular Italian singer from Polignano a Mare.

Eurovision Song Contest: Turin
(2022) The album of Eurovision finalists who performed for the event held in Turin.

READ

Gironimo! Riding the Very Terrible 1914 Tour of Italy
(Tim Moore; 2015) One man attempting to ride the course of the first ever Giro d'Italia.

Pedalare! Pedalare!
(John Foot; 2012) A history of a nation's relationship with the bicycle and the importance of cycling.

Giro d'Italia: The Story of the World's Most Beautiful Bike Race
(Colin O'Brien; 2017) Everything you wanted to know about the professional bike race Giro d'Italia.

EMILIA-ROMAGNA

Imola

Ravenna

Faenza

Forlì

Cesena

Rimini

SAN MARINO

Cattolica

Parco Nazionale delle Foreste Casentinesi, Monte Falterona e Campigna

SAN MARINO

Pesaro

02

Urbino

Senigallia

Ancona

Jesi

Adriatic Sea

CROATIA

Arezzo

Tuoro

Arno

Tevere

Fabriano

Macerata

Civitanova Marche

01

Lago Trasimeno

Perugia

Assisi

LE MARCHE

UMBRIA

Foligno

Parco Nazionale dei Monti Sibillini

Orvieto

Lago di Corbara

Spoleto

04

Ascoli Piceno

Giulianova

Lago di Bolsena

Lago di Alviano

Tevere

Terni

Parco Nazionale del Gran Sasso e Monti della Laga

Teramo

Viterbo

Rieti

△ *Corno Grande*

Pescara

LAZIO

L'Aquila

Chieti

Ortona

05

Tarquinia

Lago di Bracciano

Tevere

Vasto

Civitavecchia

Avezzano

Sulmona

△ *Monte Amaro*

Termoli

ROME

Tivoli

03

Parco Nazionale della Majella

Lido di Ostia

△ *Monte Cavo*

ABRUZZO

Parco Nazionale d'Abruzzo, Lazio e Molise

MOLISE

Frosinone

Isernia

Campobasso

LAZIO

Tyrrhenian Sea

Latina

Parco Nazionale del Circeo

Terracina

Gaeta

Golfo di Gaeta

Caserta

Benevento

MEDITERRANEAN SEA

PIXELSHOP/SHUTTERSTOCK ©

Castello di Gradara (p33)

Rome & Central Italy

01   **Around Lago Trasimeno**

A recently completed path runs 61km around the lake and through the Umbrian countryside. **p24**

02   **Via Panoramica del Parco del San Bartolo**

Great seaside cycling through the green, hilly Parco del San Bartolo. **p30**

03   **Via Appia Antica & Parco degli Acquedotti**

Explore archaeological treasures on the old Roman road, now an open-air museum and protected nature reserve. **p34**

04   **The Spoleto–Norcia Railway**

Cycle along a disused railway track converted into an adventurous mountain-biking path. **p40**

05   **Costa dei Trabocchi**

Local culture combines with unparalled scenery on this mostly flat path linking beaches, farmland and nature reserves. **p44**

Explore

Rome & Central Italy

All roads lead to Rome, as the saying goes, but if you're visiting central Italy on a bike you might want to travel beyond the capital and explore the incredible variety of scenery that this part of the country has to offer. Stretching from the Tyrrhenian to the Adriatic Seas, across the highest peaks of the Apennine Mountains – Italy's spine – this part of the country will surprise you with breezy coastal paths, tranquil lakeside riding and challenging mountain-biking climbs. There is something for all riders here, you just have to choose your adventure.

Lazio

Rome is the epicentre of Lazio, a captivating region rich in history, culture and stunning landscapes. From the rolling hills that embrace the capital to little-visited countryside and the many historic cities that tell stories of Roman grandeur, options abound when it comes to travelling at a slow pace. Ride through charming medieval villages, visit ancient Roman ruins, and indulge in delicious local cuisine and wine. Many well-maintained cycling paths have been built in and outside of Rome in recent years, offering the chance to rediscover a region that, despite its long history, continues to evolve.

Umbria

Known as the Green Heart of Italy, Umbria doesn't see nearly as many visitors as nearby Tuscany – and that is exactly why this region is so intriguing, especially for those seeking to slow down and enjoy the rural character of this lush, hilly, landlocked territory. Discover the medieval architecture of ancient cities such as Perugia, Spoleto or Norcia, then head out of the urban centres to dive into the atmosphere of central Italy's largest lake, Lago Trasimeno. Don't skip on the local cuisine – truffles, olive oil and wine are all staples waiting to be tasted.

WHEN TO GO

Spring and autumn are the best seasons to visit central Italy. While sunny winter days can also make for great rides, the weather is typically hard to predict. From April to June and from September to November you'll get the best climate conditions, avoiding the scorching heat of the summer.

Marche

Sitting right below the lively riviera of Emilia-Romagna, Marche opens up onto the Adriatic Sea, offering a great alternative to the summer resorts of its neighbouring region. There is no shortage of sandy beaches, but Marche is more than that. With a dozen nature reserves and protected parks scattered within its borders, a long list of charming yet little-visited cities celebrated since the Middle Ages and a well-developed cycling culture, Marche will quench your thirst for adventure without skimping on some well-deserved Mediterranean relaxation.

Abruzzo

It's hard to enter wild Abruzzo and not be immediately impressed by its diversity. The tallest peaks of the Apennine Mountains dominate the heart of the region in the Parco Nazionale del Gran Sasso e Monti della Laga, while the long coast stretches along the deep blue waters of the

Mediterranean dotted with the ancient fishing platforms known as *trabucchi*. Challenge yourself on the steep inclines of the mountainous interior or ride the recently inaugurated Via Verde by the ocean, stopping along the way to refuel with some freshly caught seafood.

TRANSPORT

The starting points of the itineraries covered in this chapter can all be reached by public transport. Train stations are located close to the start of the routes and you can carry your bike on many Italian trains by paying a surcharge of €3.50. Check the schedules on trenitalia. com and look for the bicycle symbol if you're planning to take your own bike on board.

 WHAT'S ON

SpoletoNorcia in MTB

A mountain-biking festival that takes place in Spoleto in early September and sees cyclists of every level coming from different parts of Italy to ride on the path built over the former Spoleto–Norcia railway. It's the largest amateur cycling event in central Italy. Read more on p41.

Bike Marathon Gran Sasso d'Italia

Cyclists gather in L'Aquila in June for a 135km race with 3000m of elevation gain running around the tallest peak of the Apennines.

Resources

Turismo Marche (turismo. marche.it) Marche's official tourism website has an entire section dedicated to cycling itineraries, mostly on secondary roads with low car traffic.

Umbria Tourism (umbria tourism.it/bikes) The official website for the region's incoming visitors has plenty of information about exploring on two wheels.

Abruzzo Turismo (abruzzo turismo.it) Abruzzo's tourism site is also rich in resources for cycle touring.

 WHERE TO STAY

From rustic farmhouses to elegant villas, central Italy caters to every taste and budget. Most of the itineraries outlined in this chapter begin near cities where hotels, cosy B&Bs and private homes are all available. Wild camping is forbidden in Italy, but in places like Lago Trasimeno you can book a spot to pitch your tent in one of the many lakeside campgrounds. During peak season (June to August) prices increase significantly and it is recommended to book in advance. Before and after the summer, you can expect bargain prices and crowd-free sightseeing.

01

Around Lago Trasimeno

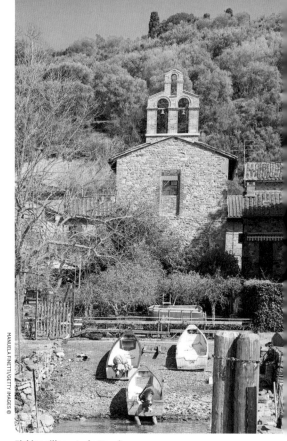

MANUELA FINETTI/GETTY IMAGES ©

Fishing village, Isola Maggiore

DURATION	DIFFICULTY	DISTANCE	START/END
4hr	Intermediate	61km	Castiglione del Lago

TERRAIN	Mostly gravel, some sections paved

Lago Trasimeno, Italy's fourth largest lake, sits in the province of Perugia, close to the border separating Umbria with Tuscany, with three tiny islands – Isola Maggiore, Isola Minore and Isola Polvese – dotting its 128-sq-metre surface. After more than a decade of work, the 61km cycle path that runs around the shallow Trasimeno waters was completed in 2023, offering the chance to explore the Umbrian countryside on a flat route that makes for an accessible day adventure amid calming waters, olive groves and lakeside hamlets.

Bike Hire

Rent a mountain bike or an e-bike at Cicli Valentini (ciclivalentini.it), located a kilometre from the train station, near the official starting point of the path in Castiglione del Lago. Staff are happy to give advice.

Starting Point

You can start anywhere around the lake, but Castiglione del Lago is ideal, due to its frequent rail connections with Rome and Florence. The train station is about 2km from the beginning of the path.

01 From the roundabout outside the Cicli Valentini bike shop, ride west on Via Firenze and take the first turn on the right, entering Viale Umbria. Cycle towards the lake past two roundabouts. After the second roundabout you'll see a gate on your left, opening onto a narrow, unpaved track. Take this route and you'll soon meet a small bridge crossing a river. Ride across the open area once occupied by Castiglione del Lago's airport and you'll soon notice the sign saying 'Itinerario Ciclabile Lago Trasimeno – Km 0'. This is where your journey around the lake begins.

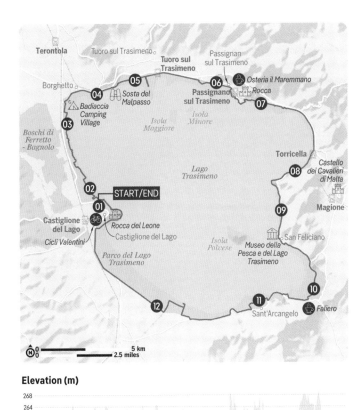

Elevation (m)

Isola Maggiore

Despite its name – literally 'greater island' – Isola Maggiore is not the largest by size of the three islands emerging from the waters of Lago Trasimeno. Its surface, 24 hectares, measures less than half that of Isola Polvese. Isola Maggiore is, however, the largest island when it comes to population – a not-so-impressive record considering that Isola Polvese and Isola Minore are uninhabited. Existing as a fishing village since the 15th century, the population of Isola Maggiore remained steadily above 200 until the 1950s, when it began declining. In 1887 the marquises Guglielmi chose the island as their summer residence, commissioning the construction of the castle that still tops the vegetation.

02 The initial section of the path doesn't run beside the lake, but stretches under the shade of maritime pine trees on a tranquil grassland. You'll start seeing Lago Trasimeno after about 2km; at the time of writing, this initial section of the route had been damaged by rain, with some large holes marking the ground. Be careful, especially if you're riding in a group.

03 Shortly after the glimmering lake appears on your right-hand side, the gravel path is interrupted by asphalt as you reach the Badiaccia Camping Village. The road will take you to Borghetto, a settlement sitting right on the border between Umbria and Tuscany with a population of less than 300; here you can spot the towering remains of a castle said to date back to the 14th century. You'll share the road with (very few) passing cars for a matter of minutes before returning to the unpaved bicycle route leading to the lake.

04 After returning on the gravel path you'll ride the whole northern side of the Trasimeno between the railway tracks and blue lake waters. A good reason to take a break will appear right after Km 11, when you'll see a solitary platform extending into the lake, offering unparalleled views of the painting-worthy scenery. Despite the idyllic atmosphere, the viewpoint called Sosta del Malpasso is known for a far-from-peaceful historic event. In June 217 BCE, Roman Consul Gaius Flaminius was moving along Trasimeno's coast with 25,000 soldiers, tracked by his archenemy, the Carthaginian general Hannibal. Wrongly

☕ Take a Break

Located on the southeastern edge of the lake, the legendary trattoria **Faliero** has built its reputation around one specific dish – the owner Maria's savoury cake, locally known as *torta d'la Maria*. This 'cake' is cooked in the traditional *testo*, a terracotta griddle heated to make crispy flatbread, which is then stuffed with a variety of delicious fillings, from pork sausage to local *pecorino* (sheep's milk cheese). Maria and her family have been making their *torta* the same way since 1969 and there's a good reason why the recipe has never changed.

believing Hannibal was still a day's march away from the lake, Gaius Flaminius left his troops exposed – the Carthaginians were hiding in the misty forests above the track and as soon as the Romans misstepped, they attacked mercilessly, slaughtering thousands.

05 Continue onwards and you'll cross the town of Tuoro, passing its small port and train station. Ride on the white path all the way to the charming centre of Passignano, about 20km in. An important junction in Roman times, connecting the Italian peninsula's north and south, Passignano is topped by its iconic Rocca, the stone-built castle marking the heart of the town, which dates back to the 6th century. Besides history, Passignano offers the most options when it comes to stopping for gelato, espresso or lunch along the way (but don't overdo it, there's still a long way to go).

06 In Passignano you have two options. From April to September a ferry connects Passignano to Castiglione del Lago via Isola Maggiore, the main island of Lago Trasimeno. With a grand total of 10 permanent inhabitants, Isola Maggiore can be visited year-round, but it's only in spring and summer that the ferry travels onwards to Castiglione del

Lago. So, if you'd rather stop cycling here, in high season you can conclude your trip by crossing the lake back to your starting point. But by continuing you'll cycle through one of the most beautiful sections of the itinerary.

07 As you continue past Passignano following the paved blue path, you will soon find yourself immersed in a landscape of small olive farms, with hills gently sloping into the lake, which will continue to offer great views of its main island. The path reaches the eastern edge of the lake; from here keep cycling south in the direction of San Feliciano. You'll see the landscape grow taller on your left as the Umbrian hills come closer to the shore, but the path will keep running evenly all the way.

08 The long curve leading to the south of the lake will separate you from the railway tracks running beside you until this point. If you're feeling ambitious, consider making a detour to Magione's town centre to Castello dei Cavalieri di Malta, a fortification dating back to the 12th century. It now houses one of the most important wineries in the area. Tours and tastings, including a visit to the chapel dedicated to St John the Baptist, are available by booking via sagrivit.it.

Passignano

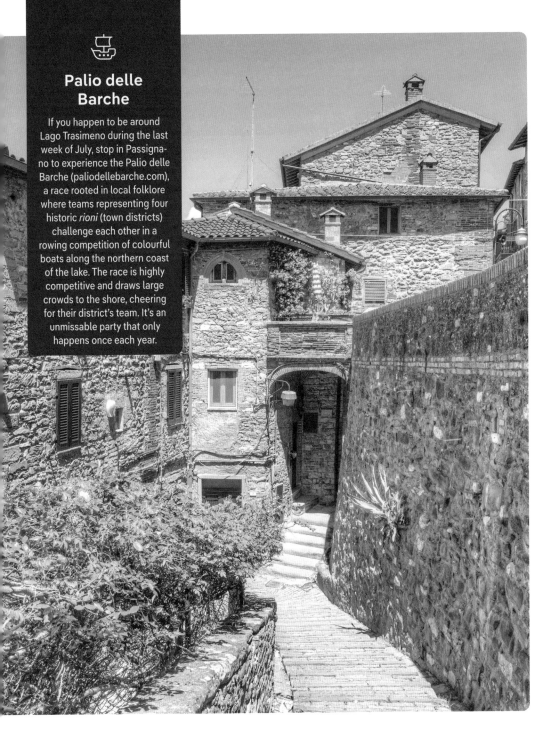

Palio delle Barche

If you happen to be around Lago Trasimeno during the last week of July, stop in Passignano to experience the Palio delle Barche (paliodellebarche.com), a race rooted in local folklore where teams representing four historic *rioni* (town districts) challenge each other in a rowing competition of colourful boats along the northern coast of the lake. The race is highly competitive and draws large crowds to the shore, cheering for their district's team. It's an unmissable party that only happens once each year.

Museo della Pesca e del Lago Trasimeno

This small museum in San Feliciano is dedicated to the fishing culture long shared by the communities living around the lake. Lock your bike and explore the museum's four halls to learn about the formation of the lake – estimated at about 1.7 million years ago – and the history and life of the people that settled along its shores, surviving thanks to the constantly evolving tools and technologies used for fishing.

09 As you pass Magione, you'll reach Punta del Lago, from where Isola Polvese will become visible. The take-off point to reach Trasimeno's largest island is San Feliciano, 3.5km south, home of the Museo della Pesca e del Lago Trasimeno (see left). San Feliciano is a great place to stop for the night if you break the trip into two days, with hotels and campgrounds open from spring to autumn.

10 From this point, the path merges with the main road from time to time, with short asphalt stretches that rejoin the gravel path regularly. Around Km 41, you'll notice a sign saying 'Biciclette a mano', meaning that you should get off your bike and push it. This section, stretching for approximately 50m, runs right next to a block of houses from which residents could exit unexpectedly. While it may be tempting to simply cycle it, given the usually quiet atmosphere around here, do as the sign says – even if you avoid an accident you may meet locals cursing at you for not abiding by the only rule you are asked to respect.

11 Before the final stretch on the southern edge of the lake, refuel in Sant'Arcangelo with some *pizza rossa* (tomato-only pizza) at the local cafe. Past Sant'Arcangelo you'll get back on the shore in Panicale, where a bird-watching walkway has been built from the cycle path all the way to the lake's water. Peek through the windows of the structure into the reed bed and you might spot mallards, pochards, garganeys as well as red and grey herons, marsh harriers and peregrine falcons resting after a long flight.

12 You're about to close the loop – the path here runs parallel to a straight, trafficked road, making the final 5km before returning to Castiglione del Lago the less pleasant part of the ride. Nevertheless, green fields and quaint, sometimes abandoned farmhouses continue to accompany you all the way to the urban centre, which you'll recognise when you see the medieval fortress known as the Rocca del Leone, staunchly looking out to the lake amid the greenery. Follow the path that runs along the shore until you see a black, electronic sign saying 'Ciclisti dall'inizio dell'anno'. Here you can check how many cyclists before you have completed the loop in the current year. Then pat yourself on the back – you've reached the end of the tour.

☕ Take a Break

Recognisable by its long green awning facing the lake, **Osteria il Maremmano** is one of Passignano's most beloved eateries. Roman-inspired pasta dishes such as the evergreen *cacio e pepe* served in the pan are on the menu, next to mouthwatering specialities you're unlikely to have tried elsewhere. The rustic decor complements the Umbrian flavours, making it perhaps too comfortable for those who had initially planned to cycle another 40km to complete the Lago Trasimeno loop.

San Feliciano

02

Via Panoramica del Parco del San Bartolo

DURATION	DIFFICULTY	DISTANCE	START/END
3.5hr	Difficult	46km	Pesaro

TERRAIN		Paved

Villa Imperiale, Pesaro

The northern Adriatic coast can appear monotonous to those coming from the shores of Emilia-Romagna, where holiday resorts line up one after the other along umbrella-dotted beaches. But enter Marche and the scenery changes. The Parco del San Bartolo is a green, hilly strip of land enclosed between the cities of Pesaro, in the south, and Gabicce Mare, in the north, allowing for great seaside cycling. While not a proper cycling path, the SP44 road that cuts through the park sees little car traffic, as newer roads have been built to connect the main urban centres.

Bike Hire

MTB Pesaro Tour rents mountain bikes from its store on Viale Giovanni Amendola 9 in central Pesaro. For those not too keen to challenge Marche's hilly coastline, e-bikes are available.

Starting Point

The SP44 runs near Pesaro's port, not far from the historic city centre. Ride along the Foglia river on Via Canale until reaching the bridge, then take a left to enter the road that will take you all the way to Gabicce.

01 Pesaro is quickly becoming one of Italy's most bike-friendly cities thanks to its Bicipolitana project. Take your bike for a spin in the charming centre, then follow the Linea 1 towards the port until meeting the SP44. From there, head north in the direction of the Parco Naturale del Monte San Bartolo.

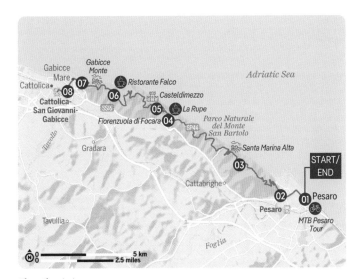

Elevation (m)

TOP TIP:

Pesaro's Bicipolitana project involves 200km of cycle paths (some sections are still being completed) that connect the different corners of the city through well-signed routes.

02 From the port of Pesaro, follow the scenic route leading to the Parco Naturale del Monte San Bartolo, a protected area boasting rich flora and fauna. The mountain, which surpasses 200m in altitude at its highest point, is reached via a scenic, wide asphalt road with several rest areas equipped with benches and picnic tables. The first 5km past the port will require some stamina, as the twisting road climbs at a constant angle around the mountain. On a weekend, you'll be sweating with groups of local cyclists tackling the incline (5% average) all the way to Santa Marina Alta, approximately 7km north of Pesaro.

03 A small church will meet you in Santa Marina Alta, one of the smallest settlements of the San Bartolo area, offering spectacular views of the hills, the Apennine Mountains and the Adriatic Sea. The descent from there has some hairpin bends that will require some attention and good brakes.

04 The next stop is the gracious hamlet of Fiorenzuola di Focara, a historic town built on a rocky outcrop overlooking the Adriatic, approximately halfway between Pesaro and Cattolica. Enter the remains of the city walls that once surrounded the settlement to take a look at the 12th-century Chiesa di Sant'Andrea and the castle, one

Villa Imperiale

As you exit Pesaro and ride through Monte San Bartolo, take a left at the Strada dei Cipressi to pay a visit to the monumental Villa Imperiale, a luxurious Renaissance-era residence. Commissioned in 1469 by Alessandro Sforza, ruler of Castelnuovo, Gradara and Pesaro, the towering structure surrounded by the thickly forested grounds of the nature reserve allows visitors to take a peek into the customs, tastes and lifestyles of the aristocratic families that inhabited the palatial complex for centuries. Villa Imperiale is open in summer only, with guided visits available by booking online.

of four defensive structures in the region dating back 700 years. An inviting beach with clear waters lies below Fiorenzuola di Focara, ideal for refreshing yourself after the route's many ups and downs. North of Fiorenzuola's main beach you can also find a naturist beach where clothing is optional.

05 Continue along the quiet SP44 for another 2km to reach another ancient fortress in the province of Pesaro, Casteldimezzo, literally 'the castle midway'. A slight descent from Fiorenzuola di Focara is followed by an incline leading into the ancient hamlet, inhabited permanently by only 14 people.

06 From Casteldimezzo, the road will take you to near the end of the park's borders in Gabicce Monte. As you arrive, take a break at the local viewpoint offering a spectacular look at the coast and the towns of Emilia-Romagna's bustling riviera. After a break, ride past Gabicce Monte for 6km and get back to sea level entering Gabicce Mare, positioned right on the regional border between Marche and Emilia-Romagna. Here you'll find a flat cycling lane stretching onto the *lungomare* all the way to Cattolica.

07 At this point you can choose whether to conclude your journey or continue cycling inland to visit the elegant fortress of Gradara. Strategically positioned on a hill overlooking the Adriatic, Gradara is one of Marche's best preserved medieval cities, known for its incredible Rocca Malatestina, built in 1150. Stepping back into the Middle Ages, however, has to be earned. Reaching Gradara from Gabicce Mare will require you to tackle the road leading up to the castle, with an inclination that reaches 7%. From Gradara you can return to Pesaro via the SS16.

08 Return to Pesaro by cycling back on the same route. Alternatively, public transport allows you to return to Pesaro from both Gabicce Mare and Gradara. The Marche region has set up a service known as Bici & Bus, allowing you to take your bike on some Adriabus coaches connecting Gabicce Mare, Gradara and Pesaro. Check the schedules at adriabus. eu. Alternatively, ride to the Cattolica-San Giovanni-Gabicce railway station, 2km from Gabicce Mare's town centre across the Emilia-Romagna border, and jump on a train back to Pesaro. Place your bike in a carriage marked with a bicycle symbol.

☕ Take a Break

The family-run trattoria **La Rupe** in Fiorenzuola di Focara makes for a great lunch spot thanks to the sunny terrace overlooking the sea. Cooking up authentic recipes since the 1960s, La Rupe offers both quick, traditional meals like stuffed *piadine* as well as a full menu of starters, first and second courses, mostly seafood-based. Pizzas are available for vegetarians. Alternatively, continue to Vigna del Mare and take a right towards the coast to reach **Ristorante Falco**, where top-notch seafood is served with a side of spectacular ocean views.

FOTOEMBER/GETTY IMAGES ©

Castello di Gradara

Castello di Gradara

The Castle of Gradara is best known as the setting of the romantic tale of Francesca da Polenta and Paolo il Bello, recounted in the 13th century by none other than Dante in his magnum opus, the *Divine Comedy*. In the fifth canto of the *Inferno*, the great poet narrates the arranged marriage that Guido da Polenta had planned for his daughter Francesca with the Lord of Pesaro, Giovanni Malatesta, despite Francesca's love for Paolo, Giovanni's brother. Francesca and Paolo eventually become lovers, maintaining an 18-year-long affair – a sin that causes them to end in Dante's hell for eternity, after being murdered by Francesca's husband Giovanni.

03

Best for

HISTORY

Via Appia Antica & Parco degli Acquedotti

DURATION	DIFFICULTY	DISTANCE	START/END
2.5hr	Easy	29km	Centro Servizi Appia Antica

TERRAIN	Paved, some sections unpaved

Villa dei Quintili (p36)

You could spend days exploring the archaeological treasures lined up on Rome's Parco Regionale dell'Appia Antica, an open-air museum and protected nature reserve stretching south of the city centre. This itinerary will take you across a section of the Via Appia Antica – the *regina viarum* that the Romans built in the 4th century BCE, originally stretching all the way to Brindisi – and then to the nearby Parco degli Acquedotti, allowing you to explore two of the most impressive feats of engineering of the ancient world in a matter of hours.

Bike Hire

Rent city bikes at EcoBike Roma (ecobikeroma.it), the service affiliated with the Parco Regionale dell'Appia Antica's official visitor centre. Discounts are available when you book your bike online.

Starting Point

The Centro Servizi Appia Antica visitor centre (housing EcoBike Roma) is near the park's northern edge. It can provide maps and detailed information about the historic sights found along the way.

01 Pick up your bike and head south. The road splits shortly after the visitor centre – on the left you have the Via Appia Antica, on the right, Via Ardeatina. Take the left and continue straight into the park. For the first 1.5km you'll be sharing the road with cars. Road traffic can be intense in this initial section, but once you enter the park only residents with a special permit are allowed to drive – luckily they are few and far between. There is an alternative route running via the Catacombe di San Callisto that allows you to avoid

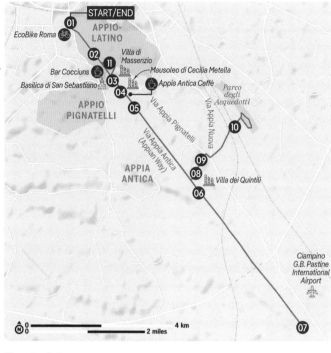

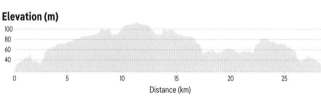

Elevation (m)

Distance (km)

Villa Capo di Bove

A short distance past the Mausoleo di Cecilia Metella, you'll notice the entrance to Villa Capo di Bove, an enviable residence that was purchased by the Italian Ministry of Culture only in 2002. Following the acquisition of the previously private estate, Rome's Archaeological Superintendence began excavating the land surrounding the villa, uncovering a series of thermal baths dating as far back as the 2nd century BCE. Well-preserved mosaics emerged from the excavation, suggesting that the thermal baths were part of a luxurious property owned by one of the richer city residents. The villa itself, built in the mid-20th century, now hosts regular art exhibitions and events.

the main road, but at the time of writing it was closed due to ongoing renovation work.

02 The first major monument you'll encounter is the white Basilica di San Sebastiano, built above the catacombs of the same name in the 4th century CE. Enter the church to admire Gian Lorenzo Bernini's *Salvador Mundi* and, if time allows, join a 30-minute tour of the catacombs. The Catacombs of San Sebastiano are among the oldest and most important in Rome, built between the 2nd and 4th centuries, and estimated to have contained the remains of thousands of early Christians.

03 You won't have to travel far past the basilica to find another reason to stop – the Villa di Massenzio is just 200m ahead, and it's a truly spectacular sight. Park your bike outside the complex and enter the archaeological area consisting of three main structures – the palace, the circus, and the mausoleum whose red-brick ruins appear to blend with the lush vegetation. Before continuing, walk across the green field amid the remains of the circus built by Emperor Maxentius (278–312 CE) – a 500m-long arena reserved for the ruler and his close circle but which could host a maximum of 10,000 guests.

04 Built between 30 and 10 BCE, the circular mausoleum dedicated to Cecilia Metella marks the end of the open road; from here onwards motorised traffic will be next to none. The massive funerary monument belonging to the daughter of a noble Roman family is one of the area's most distinctive

☕ Take a Break

Little **Bar Cocciuns** makes for an ideal breakfast spot, right beside the Basilica di San Sebastiano. The cafe has a sunny terrace hiding behind the basilica's walls, and offers tasty, freshly made jam tarts, cakes, a variety of biscuits and – obviously – espresso. Many of the major sights of the Via Appia Antica are located steps away from this typically Italian cafe. Stop by to fuel up on caffeine before starting your tour of archaeological monuments.

archaeological sights, made of massive blocks of tuff. It sits right in front of the roofless Chiesa di San Nicola, one of the few Gothic churches in Rome, dating back to the 14th century. Take some time to explore the architectural masterpieces then cross the III Miglio, the third Roman mile, and access the heart of the park.

05 You can't really go wrong here – the Appia Antica continues straight, lined with pine and olive trees, Mediterranean shrub and poplars that open up to farmland on both sides of the road. The remains of several tombstones and memorials dot the area, but the true highlight is the basalt stones that appear on the road every few hundred metres. These are the original rocks used nearly 2000 years ago to build the Roman highway – a testament to the skill and ambition of the Romans. These short sections are uneven and can be tricky to cycle on, but you can easily avoid them by riding on the side of the road.

06 When you reach Km 6 you'll see another major monument of the Appia Antica – Villa dei Quintili, a 2nd-century residential complex once belonging to the Quintili brothers, who would eventually be executed for conspiring

against Emperor Commodus. Before their arrest, the two consuls lived in one of the largest villas in southern Rome; the ruins testify to the grandeur of the home through sumptuous decorations and marble floors still visible today. In spring, you might also see an abundance of wild orchids growing around the monument.

07 After Villa dei Quintili, around Km 8, you'll see the Roman aqueducts on the horizon to your left. You'll have the opportunity to see them up close soon, but in the meantime continue riding ahead until Km 10, crossing what is typically one of the quieter sections of the park. Past a round mausoleum, Rome's second airport – Ciampino – will appear in the distance. Once you see the airport you can turn back.

08 Head back to Villa dei Quintili and turn right after the monument, taking the side road marked with a small sign saying 251. This unpaved path connects the Via Appia Antica with the busy Via Appia Nuova, from where you'll reach the Parco degli Acquedotti. This detour will add approximately 8km to your itinerary, allowing you to experience two of the richest archaeological areas outside Rome's historic centre. On road

MAURO TOCCACELI/ALAMY STOCK PHOTO ©

Via Latina

Via Latina

When visiting the Parco degli Acquedotti you might notice another ancient road made of basalt stones running not far from the Via Appia Antica. The Via Latina route is believed to have been used since Etruscan times, with the Romans developing it in the 4th century BCE to function as a primary artery connecting the heart of the Empire to Benevento, in what is now the region of Campania. It is still possible to admire a portion of the original road, with one of the best-preserved sections found in the Parco Archeologico delle Tombe di Via Latina, where 450m of the ancient route are lined with Roman funerary monuments.

Appia Antica Ruins

Many other sites where archaeological ruins blend with the natural environment are found in the vicinity of the Parco Regionale dell'Appia Antica. If time allows, consider extending your trip to explore the Valle della Caffarella or the Parco della Torre del Fiscale.

251 you'll ride past a farm housing hundreds of goats; the sight will make you question whether this is the same bustling city you came from in the morning.

09 Continue until you reach Via Appia Pignatelli and take a right – you're back on the asphalt and in the open traffic, so watch out for cars. Less than 100m ahead Via Appia Pignatelli merges with Via Appia Nuova, a major road in southern Rome that is heavily trafficked throughout the day. Here you will have to cross a busy intersection and enter Viale Appio Claudio, which will take you directly into the Parco degli Acquedotti.

10 Your first encounter with the park will be via the non-accessible golf course – cycle around it clockwise and you'll soon find yourself under the imposing aqueduct that runs through this large green patch of land. One of ancient Rome's engineering marvels, the towering structures found here, south of the Quadraro neighbourhood, are very well preserved. Emperor Caligula commissioned the construction of the first aqueduct you'll see when you enter the park – the

Acquedotto Claudio – in 38 BCE and the project was completed under Claudius in 52 BCE. The park extends for 240 hectares with endless paths connecting the remains of six Roman aqueducts. Take your time to explore, stop for a picnic, then return to the entrance of the park and head back towards the Via Appia Antica.

11 Retrace your steps along the Viale Appio Claudio, Via Appia Nuova and Via Appia Pignatelli to head back to the Via Appia Antica. Follow the same route you rode through earlier until the Villa di Massenzio. Shortly after the ruins the road splits into two one-way streets – to avoid crashing into the oncoming traffic you have to take a right and briefly return to Via Appia Pignatelli before rejoining the Via Appia Antica and returning to the visitor centre to complete your trip. A bus stop is located metres away from the visitor centre, from where you can find frequent services to the city. If you are riding your own bike you can continue for another 2km to reach another spectacular piece of Roman architecture, the Terme di Caracalla.

☕ Take a Break

A lovely garden welcomes you in the bike-friendly **Appia Antica Caffè**, ideally positioned past the Mausoleo di Cecilia Metella. Indulge in scrumptious sandwiches filled with locally sourced ingredients or keep it light with a flavourful salad. On a hot day the homemade ice cream is hard to beat. If you decide to stop here on your way back, order a refreshing *aperitivo* served with a side of appetisers. Vegetarian options available.

Parco degli Acquedotti

04

The Spoleto-Norcia Railway

DURATION	DIFFICULTY	DISTANCE	START/END
3hr	Intermediate	31km	Spoleto

TERRAIN	Unpaved, some sections paved

SALVATORE MICILLO/SHUTTERSTOCK ©

Cyclists, SpoletoNorcia in MTB

In the heart of the Umbrian countryside, a disused railroad track has been converted into a fun, adventurous mountain-biking path starting from the historic centre of Spoleto and ending in Norcia. Ride through tunnels that once allowed for the train to travel across the lower Apennines in the early 20th century, before the railway was abandoned in 1968. This itinerary will take you through the first section of the 51km track to the hamlet of Sant'Anatolia di Narco.

Bike Hire

La Spoleto Norcia MTB (laspoletonorciainmtb.it) organises mountain-bike and e-bike rentals. Book your bike online and pick it up at the bike terminal Le Mattonelle on Via Enrico Mattei.

Starting Point

The entry point to the old railway is in the north-eastern part of Spoleto, near the roundabout leading onto Via Flaminia. You'll see a vertical green and blue sign from the main road, marking the entrance.

01 Take some time to visit the historic centre of Spoleto, 60km from Perugia, before setting off on your bike to ride through the Umbrian countryside. The surprising yet little-known central Italian city is dominated by the 14th-century Rocca Albornoziana, the stone-built castle overlooking the urban core's red rooftops from its privileged position. The entry point to the cycling path is located close to the railway station, north of the city centre. From the railway station, ride south along Viale Trento e

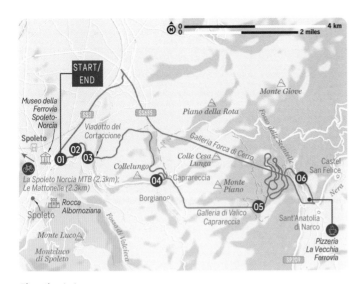

TOP TIP:

Make sure to have lights mounted on your bike, as you'll be cycling through some dark tunnels.

Elevation (m)

SpoletoNorcia in MTB

Each year at the start of September, the old Spoleto–Norcia railway sees thousands of cyclists coming together to ride the distance between the two cities during the noncompetitive SpoletoNorcia in MTB race, one of the largest mountain-biking events in central Italy. It's now in its 9th edition, and cyclists can choose from four itineraries, starting from the family-friendly 10km path from Spoleto to Caprareccia to a more technical 85km route filled with ups and downs for pro bikers. Learn more at laspoletonorciainmtb.it.

Trieste, then take a left on Via San Tommaso. Continue until you reach the roundabout leading onto Via Pietro Conti, cross Via Flaminia and you should see the gate opening onto the dirt track on your right within minutes.

02 From the beginning, the path climbs up at a steady incline of approximately 4.5%. While this can be tough on untrained legs, it is also what makes this itinerary historically intriguing. In order to adapt to the geography of this part of Italy, the Spoleto–Norcia railway had to challenge the Apennines, riding at an unusual inclination – a feat of engineering considering the times. Despite its short length

– only 51km – 19 tunnels had to be carved in the mountains and 24 bridges built to allow the train to reach Norcia. Ride in the direction of La Fornace along the white dirt track.

03 The incline is gradual and not forgiving, but the views get increasingly better as you climb up. The highlight of this section is the Viadotto del Cortaccione, which will, by itself, make the uphill cycle worth the effort. Along the first 7km of the trail you'll cross several scenic bridges and short tunnels that open up onto the surrounding greenery and the remains of a now disused power line. Keep riding until you reach the highest point of the itinerary near Caprareccia.

04 The Caprareccia viaduct precedes the now-abandoned train station where trains riding between Spoleto and Norcia used to stop. Take a moment to admire the scenery at this spectacular bridge opening up to forests known for their truffles, then continue into the longest tunnel of the itinerary. The Caprareccia tunnel extends for approximately 2km and once you reach its centre you'll find yourself in complete darkness. Make sure to have a powerful torch with you to see where you are going – the gravel here requires some attention to be navigated.

05 Once you leave the tunnel behind, you'll start descending towards the valley of the Nera river. While you might be grateful for some downhill action, some sections of the path are no joke, as the decline is as steep as the incline. It is only possible to imagine how difficult it must have been for engineers to build the infrastructure necessary for a train to ride along these slopes. Continue onwards on the path, passing three more tunnels.

06 When you descend the winding trail that runs down to the valley from Caprareccia, the cycling path will join the main road and continue beside it until the town centre. Shops selling traditional delicacies on the side of the road will welcome you into the medievel town of Sant'Anatolia di Narco, where you can refuel before returning to Spoleto. You can either retrace your steps and follow the railway track backwards, or you can take the paved SS685 road running through the town, to make a loop without having to climb up the mountain pass another time. Those willing to cycle further can also do so along the Ciclovia del Fiume Nera (p51) running south from Sant'Anatolia di Narco.

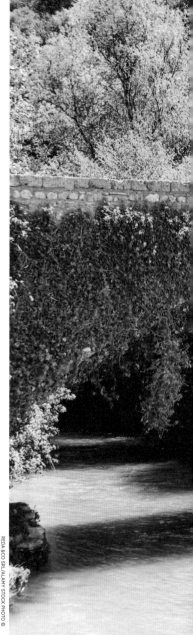

 Take a Break

Named after the railroad it sits on, the simple **Pizzeria La Vecchia Ferrovia** offers the chance to recharge with some thin-crust pizza before returning to Spoleto. Located at the entrance of Sant'Anatolia di Narco, La Vecchia Ferrovia is ideal for a quick bite on the welcoming terrace or a more sumptuous meal made of homemade pasta accompanied by a glass of local wine. Make sure to give the truffle-based dishes a try.

Nera river, Sant'Anatolia di Narco

Museo della Ferrovia Spoleto-Norcia

If you want to learn more about the previous life of this cycling itinerary, stop by Spoleto's Museo della Ferrovia Spoleto-Norcia, a municipal museum entirely dedicated to this unique railway. The museum traces the history of the project originally drafted in 1913 by Swiss engineer Erwin Thomann, with memorabilia, mechanical parts and photographs documenting the decommissioned railway. The Spoleto-Norcia railway was completed in 1926 and operated until 1968, when new roads connecting the two cities made the service obsolete. The museum is housed inside Spoleto's former station where trains destined for Norcia used to depart, steps away from the new railway station. Open on weekends only.

05

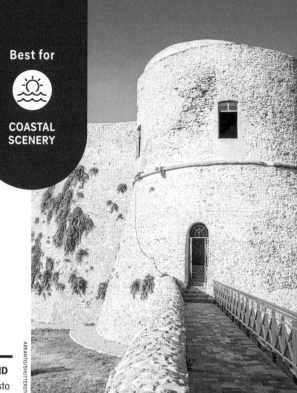

Best for

COASTAL SCENERY

Costa dei Trabocchi

DURATION	DIFFICULTY	DISTANCE	START/END
3hr	Easy	42km	Ortona/Vasto

TERRAIN		Paved

Castello Aragonese

Named after the fishing platforms that extend from the rocky beaches into the Adriatic Sea, the stretch of land known as Costa dei Trabocchi offers the chance to combine local culture with unparalleled scenery. The newly built cycling path – nicknamed Via Verde – links the town of Ortona with Vasto, crossing nine municipalities over 42km. Sandy beaches, rural hamlets and nature reserves take turns as you travel south. The path is relatively flat and both its start and end points can be reached by regional trains.

Bike Hire

Blue Bike Ortona and Officine Forti both rent bikes near Ortona's railway station. From November to March they operate at reduced hours, so make sure to book ahead if you're planning an off-season visit.

Starting Point

The aptly named Via Verde (Green Way) passes near Ortona's port and railway station – its bright colour makes it impossible to miss. Start your journey south from Via Cervana, heading towards Marina di San Vito.

01 The section of Abruzzo's coastline known as Costa dei Trabocchi begins a few kilometres north of Ortona, in Francavilla al Mare. Public transport connections, however, make Ortona the ideal take-off point. History has not been kind to this town of some 23,000 people; the town was bombed during WWII in the early 1940s and nearly wiped out. Its Castello Aragonese, built in 1452 by Alfonso of Aragon on a hill dominating the coast, was heavily damaged during the conflict but ultimately survived, standing today as Ortona's architectural icon. Pay a

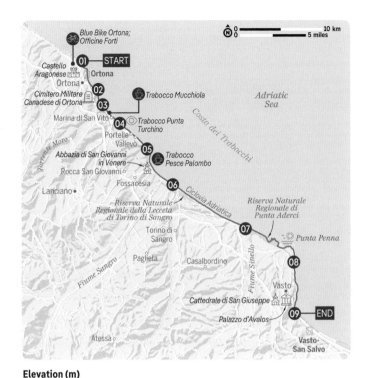

TOP TIP:

If you'd rather not take the train back but are not sure about sitting on a bike for 80-plus kilometres, consider renting an e-bike in Ortona to reach Vasto and return on the same day. With some electric pedalling power on your side you should be able to complete the whole itinerary twice in under five hours.

Elevation (m)

Distance (km)

visit to the fortress before setting off on two wheels.

 02 From central Ortona, ride in the direction of Marina di San Vito. As you exit the town's centre, a kilometre after the train station, you'll pass by the sandy Lido dei Saraceni beach and reach the cliffs of Punta Acquabella. A short detour inland between the Lido dei Saraceni and Punta Acquabella will take you to the Cimitero Militare Canadese di Ortona (Moro River Canadian War Cemetery), where the largest number of Canadian

soldiers who died during WWII in Italy are buried. Approximately 1600 Commonwealth soldiers were laid to rest here.

03 Marina di San Vito is positioned 4km past the Punta Acquabella. Here you'll start seeing the impressive *trabucchi* lining up one after the other. Many of the *trabucchi* have now been converted into restaurants that open up onto the ocean – such as the Trabocco San Giacomo, which extends from the beach at Marina di San Vito Chietino – but these suspended struc-

tures are believed to have existed in Abruzzo since medieval times, functioning as shelter for fishers as well as mechanical tools for catching fish without venturing out into the waters of the Mediterranean. From the platform, fishers would lower nets hanging from long poles directly into the sea when they saw a shoal of fish passing by. Once the fish entered the trap, two people would lock them in by raising the net.

 04 The fascinating wooden structures that appear to hover above the sea

☕ Take a Break

Dining in one of the wooden structures that have become the most recognisable feature of this part of Italy is an experience you won't be able to repeat elsewhere. Of the many *trabucchi* that have been converted into suspended restaurants, it's worth booking a table at **Trabocco Mucchiola**, near Ortona, where freshly caught seafood is cooked creatively in a hard-to-beat location. The menu is typically fixed, with prices hovering around €60.

have long functioned as a magnet for curious artists, writers and – more recently – photographers. Minutes after Marina di San Vito you'll reach Portelle, where you can find the rural home inhabited by the famous Italian writer Gabriele D'Annunzio in the summer of 1889. The brick country house – often referred to as 'the hermitage' – hosted the author, who chose the silence and sublime scenery of Abruzzo's coast to seek inspiration for his works. Near Portelle you can visit the Trabocco Punta Turchino, perhaps the best known of the region's iconic structures. D'Annunzio himself admired the Trabocco Punta Turchino in *The Triumph of Death* (1894), writing, 'At the extreme point of the right-hand promontory, on a bank of rocks the Trabocco stretched, a strange fishing machine, constructed entirely of beams and planks, like a colossal spider web'. After Marina di San Vito, urban settlements gradually become more scarce, with long stretches of pebbly beaches accompanying you on the ride.

05 Continue onwards past the settlement of Vallevò and its beaches, and approximately 10km later you will enter the area of Fossacesia, where a sign will point you to the Trabocco Pesce Palombo, one of

the best known *trabucchi* restaurants in the region. As you move along the cycle path, you should also be able to spot the evocative Abbazia di San Giovanni in Venere – a sandstone Cistercian monastery dating back to the 12th century, strategically positioned on an olive-grove-covered hill overlooking the Adriatic Sea. If you want to visit the abbey, climb the twisting Strada Statale 524 for about 15 minutes, until you'll find yourself in front of the three semicircular apses facing the ocean. From Fossacesia the *trabucchi* start to diminish, but the wilder sections of the coast make up for the lack of cultural landmarks.

06 By continuing along the coast, you'll soon reach the Marina di Torino di Sangro, where you'll have the option to dip your toes in either the pebbly or sandy beaches found a short distance from each other. Here, you will also be able to immerse yourself in the lush Mediterranean vegetation of the Lecceta Regional Natural Reserve of Torino di Sangro, a 175-hectare forest crisscrossed by hiking trails. The reserve was established in 2001 to protect one of the few forests growing right on the Adriatic coast and is home to a vast population of land tortoises that roam freely amid ancient oak

ANDREW MAYOVSKYY/SHUTTERSTOCK ©

Abbazia di San Giovanni in Venere

Abbazia di San Giovanni in Venere

Encircled by dark-green olive groves, the Abbazia di San Giovanni in Venere is an unexpected architectural wonder in this beautiful natural landscape. Blending elements of Romanesque and Gothic styles, the monastic complex was built in the 12th century by Cistercian monks on the remains of a pagan temple dedicated to Venus, believed to have existed since 80 BCE. During WWII the abbey's exterior was damaged by US bombing, but after a period of neglect the local congregation launched a series of renovation projects that were completed in 2020 and have brought the structure back to its original splendour.

Rocca San Giovanni

If your legs allow it, consider a detour to visit the hilltop hamlet of Rocca San Giovanni, a charming little stone-built settlement sitting at 115m altitude near Fossacesia. The medieval town, believed to have existed since the year 1000, is built around the charming Piazza degli Eroi, where an 800-year-old clock tower rises towards the sky, emerging from the ancient walls. The quiet, flowery alleys that intersect in the historic centre will allow you to experience Abruzzo from a different perspective, especially if you stop at one of the local eateries to enjoy a glass of Montepulciano d'Abruzzo, which is produced in Rocca San Giovanni's surroundings.

trees populated by over 60 different species of birds. It's worth temporarily leaving your bike behind and exploring the quiet walking paths that rise towards the hilly interior of this section of the itinerary, and making good use of the shaded picnic tables dotting the park.

07 The Lecceta Regional Natural Reserve of Torino di Sangro isn't the only natural wonder found in the southern section of the path – keep riding for approximately 8km and you'll be rewarded with the Punta Aderci Regional Nature Reserve. The first nature reserve to be established on Abruzzo's coast, Punta Aderci stretches across 285 hectares from the Spiaggia di Torre Sinello, near the mouth of the Sinello river, to Punta Penna, near Vasto's port. Coves, beaches, dunes, cliffs, grasslands, olive groves and hidden bays dotted with Mediterranean shrubs form the landscape of this spectacular coastal park, with opportunities for kayaking, hiking and admiring a scenery unlike any other. Punta Aderci's most revered inhabitant is the Kentish plover – known in Italian as *fratino* – a small, rare bird that populates the coastal areas of southern Europe and lays its eggs on the ground.

08 The southernmost beach of the Punta Aderci reserve is Punta Penna, a popular spot in summer for its fine, golden sand and turquoise waters. Vasto's port is found a short distance on, and from there Vasto's town centre – the end point of this itinerary – is 8km away. On this final leg of the journey you'll encounter the Trabocco Canale and the Trabocco Scoglio Schiena d'Asino. After entering Vasto proper, triumphantly positioned on a promontory overlooking the sea, it's worth exploring the historic centre – this is perhaps the most culturally intriguing town on the Costa dei Trabocchi. Take some time to visit the Cattedrale di San Giuseppe, Vasto's main religious structure, and the 16th-century Palazzo d'Avalos, which contains the local archaeological museum.

09 If you want to return to your starting point in Ortona, head to the railway station of Vasto-San Salvo, located 6km south of Vasto's historic centre near the border with Molise. From here regional trains depart regularly for Ortona and Pescara. Make sure your train allows for carrying bikes on board and always use the carriages with a bicycle sign. Check the timetable on trenitalia.com.

☕ Take a Break

The daily catch inspires the ever-changing menu of the renowned **Trabocco Pesce Palombo**, located in the middle of your cycling itinerary, near Fossacesia. Seafood-based dishes tend to dominate the menu, but ingredients obtained from nearby hills are also worth trying. While you might not know in advance what you're going to eat, you can be sure that getting up from the table will be a challenge. If you plan to visit in the high season, book a table in advance.

Old Town, Rocca San Giovanni

Also Try...

Roman ampitheatre of Amiternum

Ciclabile sul Tevere

DURATION	DIFFICULTY	DISTANCE
1.5hr	Easy	32km

The cycling path that runs parallel to the Tiber river for over 30km cuts through central Rome from the area of Saxa Rubra all the way to Tor di Valle, allowing you to view the Italian capital from a new, exciting angle.

Ride your bike along the riverfront through the heart of the city, passing under ancient bridges and avoiding the busy traffic that clogs the streets just metres above your head. Take a day off from museums and archaeological sites to admire world-class sights such as Castel Sant'Angelo and the Isola Tiberina as you move through the Eternal City on this well-maintained path loved by both locals and visitors. From central Rome you can access the path at Ponte Matteotti or Porta Portese.

Lago di Bracciano Loop

DURATION	DIFFICULTY	DISTANCE
2.5hr	Intermediate	35km

The 35km cycling route starting from the lakeside town of Bracciano, a centre dominated by its medieval fortress and one hour by train north of Rome, takes you through picturesque hamlets along secondary country roads that cross lush forests and fields.

With its gentle hills and easy terrain, cycling around Lake Bracciano is a perfect day trip for cyclists of all levels. Visit the charming town of An-guillara, make a detour to the Roman amphitheatre of Sutri and explore the Unesco-listed reserve of the Faggeta di Monte Raschio, near Oriolo Romano, before returning to your starting point under the imposing Bracciano castle.

Tiber river, Rome

Ciclovia del Fiume Nera

DURATION	DIFFICULTY	DISTANCE
2hr	Easy	28km

After reaching Sant'Anatolia di Narco on the cycling path built on the former Spoleto–Norcia railway, you can continue riding south on the Ciclovia del Fiume Nera.

The route runs along secondary roads and gravel paths all the way to the Cascata delle Marmore, the majestic 165m waterfalls found inside the homonymous nature reserve. Extending your journey on this route running along the banks of the Nera river will take you through barely inhabited hamlets of the lower Apennines.

Strada Maestra del Parco del Gran Sasso

DURATION	DIFFICULTY	DISTANCE
7hr	Difficult	76km

The road connecting L'Aquila with Teramo runs between the spectacular landscapes formed by the Gran Sasso in the south and the Laga Mountains in the north.

It passes through the archaeological site of Amiternum, where Roman ruins over 2000 years old are waiting to be explored. Cycle in the heart of the Parco Nazionale del Gran Sasso – where the tallest peak of the Apennines dominates the scenery at 2912m high – immersed in Abruzzo's unspoilt nature. This route, which follows the old SS80 road, is not for everyone; besides the distance, you'll have to face 1300m in elevation gain to reach Teramo, on the opposite side of the national park.

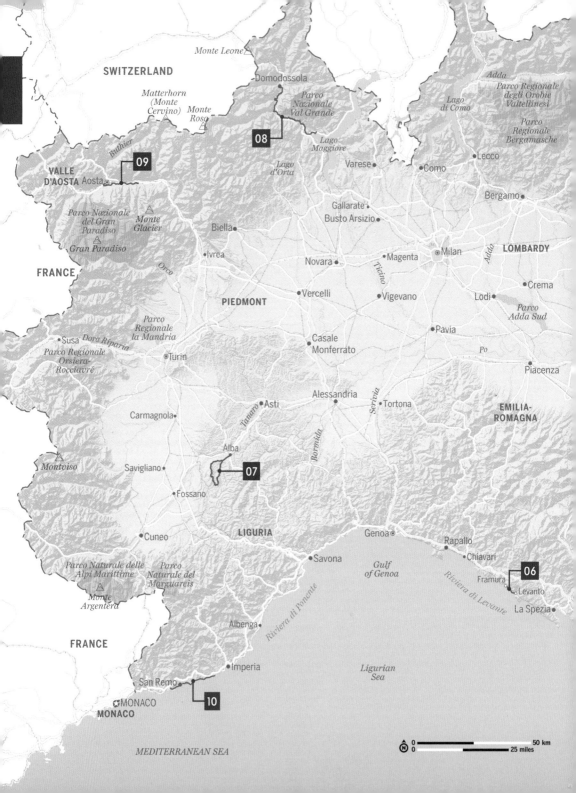

IRISPHOTO2/GETTY IMAGES ©

Roman ruins, Aosta (p73)

Northwest Italy

Explore

Northwest Italy

The scenery hardly gets more diverse than in northwestern Italy, where some of the country's tallest mountains slope down into the Mediterranean, allowing you to explore the pristine alpine landscapes of Valle d'Aosta as well as the bustling riviera of the Ligurian coast. Whether you're looking for an uphill challenge or a relaxing seaside ride, options abound. Split between Valle d'Aosta, Piedmont and Liguria, this area combines family-friendly, well-maintained cycling paths built on former railroad tracks with dirt paths criss-crossing nature reserves to be explored on a mountain bike.

Valle d'Aosta

Winding roads, high mountain passes, green valleys and spectacular peaks – these are just some of the elements picture-perfect Valle d'Aosta has to offer to those willing to challenge the majestic geography of this small, autonomous region perched in Italy's northwestern corner. The Romans had already spotted the wealth of the region as early as 2000 years ago, when they formed a settlement in the regional capital of Aosta under the orders of Emperor Augustus; the 'Rome of the Alps' sits in the heart of Valle d'Aosta combining invaluable cultural landmarks with endless options for outdoor activities. A dozen nature reserves and protected parks mark the territory, offering endless opportunities to experience the alpine scenery, get acquainted with the local wildlife and test your limits as a cyclist.

Piedmont

Italy's second-largest region is known for its refined elegance, its dedication to good food and wine, and its picturesque hilly landscapes that come to life in spring and turn red in autumn. Exit the wide streets of sophisticated Turin to explore the vineyard-covered hills of the Langhe region, a Unesco World Heritage Site that combines rich cultural heritage with spectacular scenery. Medieval castles peek out from the hamlets where some of the best wines in Italy have been produced for centuries – names such as Barolo and Barbaresco provide convincing excuses to take a break from riding and refuel with some of the products Pied-

WHEN TO GO

Covered in snow during much of the winter, Valle d'Aosta is best explored between June and September, when mild temperatures offer a pleasant escape from the heat enveloping much of the rest of the country. The same goes for Piedmont's high-altitude areas, while spring and autumn are ideal for the central hilly areas. Liguria gets packed in July and August – avoid the peak summer months.

mont is most proud of. Indulge in the truffle-based cuisine of Alba, climb the mountains bordering France, and explore the Lake District on dirt tracks.

Liguria

Liguria's rugged coastline, dotted with charming fishing villages and colourful houses, has long been a favourite summer escape for Italians and international visitors looking to make the most out of the Mediterranean sun. In the past few years, the region has invested in the development of cycling infrastructure along the coast, making Liguria the perfect backdrop for explorers on two wheels. While there's no shortage of challenging routes in the interior, the coastline is marked by flat, breezy cycling lanes that run parallel to the sea above the track of disused railways. Fuel up with some focaccia and set out to discover the dreamy beaches of the Ligurian coast on a long, effortless ride.

TRANSPORT

Northwest Italy is best explored with your own vehicle, especially if you're planning to head out to the countryside or in the more remote mountainous area. The cycling routes covered in this chapter, however, can all be reached with public transport. Trains and buses arrive at all starting points listed; check the schedules via trenitalia .com or through the Moovit app.

 WHAT'S ON

Milano-Sanremo

This professional cycling race – nicknamed the 'spring classic' – is one of Italy's most important cycling competitions, held each year in March since 1907. Exceeding 290km in length, the Milano-Sanremo is one of the toughest single-day races in the country, with 175 pro cyclists challenging each other on the roads of northwestern Italy.

Gran Fondo di Alassio

(granfondoalassio.it) An international race where athletes challenge each other on a route climbing up Monte Tirasso from Alassio. It also takes place in March.

 WHERE TO STAY

Hostels are fairly uncommon outside of major centres – of the destinations listed in this chapter, Aosta is the only city where hostels are available to budget travellers. B&Bs and private homes are the most popular type of accommodation found in the area, besides hotels. Luxurious options abound in the Ligurian Riviera, especially in the area of Sanremo, where one of the four casinos legally operating in Italy stands, while the countryside of Piedmont has a large choice of farm stays, where you can enjoy the freshest produce and culinary specialities right where they are made.

Resources

Gran Paradiso National Park (pngp.it) The park's official website has a section dedicated to cycling routes where you can browse itineraries based on difficulty level.

Cicloturismo Piemonte (cicloturismo.piemonte.it) Piedmont has developed an app for cycle touring, with dozens of routes available at your fingertips.

06

Levanto to Framura on the Ciclabile Maremonti

DURATION	DIFFICULTY	DISTANCE	START/END
30min	Easy	6km	Levanto/ Framura

TERRAIN		Paved

DELBO ANDREA/SHUTTERSTOCK ©

Via del Mare near Framura

The cycling path known as the 'Ciclabile Maremonti' connects the town of Levanto with Bonassola and Framura, extending for an easy 6km along the former railroad that once stretched along Liguria's coast. The route is completely flat, making it suitable for all abilities, and passes through a series of short tunnels lining up one after the other and opening to spectacular ocean views. Join local cyclists, runners and walkers on this seaside path completed in 2011, running next to coves and cliffs dropping into the Mediterranean waters.

Bike Hire

Well positioned on Via Giuseppe Garibaldi in Levanto, Cicli Raso rents city bikes to visitors exploring the coast. Prices start at €10 per day.

Starting Point

The cycling route starts at the Amerigo Vespucci Promenade in southern Levanto. The path is well signed – you can't miss it.

01 From Levanto's railway station, easily reached from La Spezia in under an hour, head straight towards the coast, found 1km west. As you reach the *lungomare* the sea breeze will hit your face. Turn right and continue until the first roundabout – here the Maremonti cycling path begins, running parallel to the Amerigo Vespucci Promenade towards the sandy Spiaggia Vallesanta, a few metres ahead.

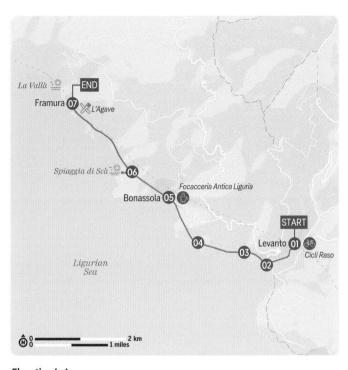

Framura's Via del Mare

With some time to spend in Framura, it's worth taking a walk on the Via del Mare, a cliffside promenade lined with Mediterranean vegetation, which takes you to some of the town's best beaches. From the Framura train station follow the sign pointing to the Via del Mare promenade and soon enough you'll reach the pebbly, open beach of La Vallà. After a short distance you'll find the beach of Arena, Framura's largest. Both beaches make for a great cooling-down swim, especially in the morning when the water is as clear as it gets.

Elevation (m)

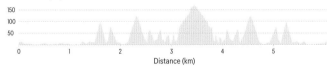

02 Follow the path along the former tracks of the old Levante Riviera railway line – completed in the late 19th century and operating until 1970 – past the beaches. The elevated bike lane spills into a lavender-scented herb garden with benches from which you can admire the sea. Within minutes you'll officially enter the municipality of Bonassola, as shown by the brown sign you should see on your right. Here you'll enter the first of a series of stone-built tunnels piercing the rocky cliffs; this

is where the train used to pass. These tunnels are lit and, if you're cycling in summer, offer some welcome respite from the sun.

03 The path runs just metres away from the water, and between the first tunnel and the second, a series of secluded coves touched by the blue waters of the Mediterranean dot the coastline. While the route couldn't be easier, pay attention when riding because the path is shared with pedestrians – pedestrians and cyclists should

technically stay on opposite sides, but the path gets busy in summer months and the boundaries become blurry. Before entering the second tunnel you will see a rocky beach on your left. As the sign indicates, this beach is dog-friendly; it was established in 2017 to welcome pet owners and their four-legged friends.

04 Spectacular panoramic views continue after the tunnel, all the way into Bonassola proper, where you'll find a large, popular beach calling you for a break. Abandon the cycling path and take some time to explore Bonassola's colourful centre. After roaming the charming streets of this quintessentially Ligurian coastal town, stop at one of Bonassola's bakeries to enjoy a slice or two of delicious *focaccia ligure*, the traditional flatbread covered with extra virgin olive oil this corner of Italy is known for.

05 Once your seaside focaccia is done with, get back on track and continue in the direction of Framura, 3km away. The remaining section of the path runs through many tunnels that follow one another at a short distance. The tunnels here have a series of large openings on one side; these panoramic windows, carved out from the walls, take away some of the cool temperature found in the previous tunnels, but offer spectacularly framed views of the ocean that you can admire as you ride along. The route cuts through a promontory that extends into the sea after Bonassola and ends minutes away from Framura.

06 As you get closer to the destination you'll pass by the seemingly hidden Spiaggia di Scà, a pebbly cove formed between vertical cliffs that turns the ocean water into a picturesque emerald pool. You can only access the beach on foot via a steep path downhill. Continue riding and you'll reach Framura's naturist beach, 1km further west.

07 Once you enter the little town of Framura, the path ends as you reach the local train station. A free, panoramic lift takes you down to the marina where you can dip your toes in the water. If you still have time, park your bike and go for a stroll on Framura's Via del Mare, an 800m-long suspended promenade leading to the beach of La Vallà. Hungry? Take a break at L'Agave, the elegant wine bar and restaurant located at the end of the cycling path overlooking the ocean, offering a variety of fresh, seafood-based local specialities. Take the same route back to Levanto if you need to drop your rental bike off at the local store.

☕ Take a Break

Bonassola's **Focacceria Antica Liguria** is a local institution, serving freshly baked breads of all kinds, including the proudly traditional *focaccia ligure* – a staple that can't be skipped around here. Just a few simple ingredients – flour, salt, water and olive oil – contribute to the creation of this local speciality, although this particular bakery will provide you with many other varieties of focaccia, if you are looking for something more sophisticated.

ANDREA BERG/SHUTTERSTOCK ©

Madonnina della Punta

Madonnina della Punta

If you're up for a walk, head up to the chapel of the Madonnina della Punta, a small sanctuary perched on top of a cliff above Bonassola. Following a path uphill you'll soon reach this spectacular lookout spot where you'll be able to admire the whole coast from above. Getting here takes about 20 minutes – pass by the Oratorio di Sant'Erasmo then take the staircase until you reach Via Roma, which leads directly to the little pink chapel. For best results, arrive during sunset – outside of peak summer season, you'll likely have the place for yourself.

07

Through the Hills of Barolo

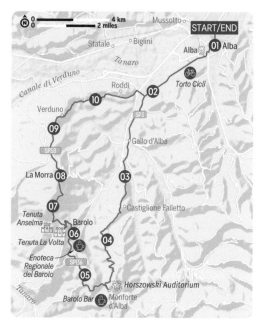

DURATION	DIFFICULTY	DISTANCE	START/END
3.5hr	Intermediate	44km	Alba

TERRAIN		Paved

Elevation (m)

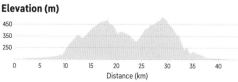

Known for its vineyard-covered hills, hazelnut groves and medieval castles, the Langhe region of Piedmont is excellent cycling terrain, especially if you enjoy matching scenery with world-class wines, truffles and cheese. Starting from Alba, the heart of the Langhe, this loop will take you through the Unesco-listed hills where Barolo is produced and medieval villages dominated by ancient fortifications. The route runs on secondary roads that see little car traffic, but the many ups and downs of this corner of Italy will require some stamina.

Bike Hire

Torto Cicli is your go-to for renting both traditional road bikes and e-bikes to explore the region. The friendly staff will provide you with tips on what to see, drink and do.

Starting Point

Anywhere in the centre of Alba makes a good start. From the train station, ride south along Corso Europa and Corso Barolo until the second roundabout where the loop begins.

01 Nestled in the heart of the Langhe, the hilltop town of Alba embodies the charm of this northern Italian region with its picturesque streets lined with medieval architecture and a gastronomic culture that attracts a steady flow of visitors year-round. Globally known for its highly prized white truffles, Alba might tempt you to reschedule your ride in favour of a hard-to-match restaurant experience – but save it for your return, as the countryside awaits. From Alba's train station take Corso Europa and ride

Best for

FOOD

ESSEVU/SHUTTERSTOCK ©

Alba

southwest until the first round-about, then continue straight on Corso Barolo towards the beautiful hills of Barolo.

02 About 4.5km into the ride, at the end of Corso Barolo, you will encounter another roundabout – take the SP3 in the direction of Gallo. Vineyards will appear on your left, growing on the green hills, and after approximately 1km you will reach the industrial area of Gallo. Keep riding through the warehouses and the urban centre. At around Km 6 you will see a sign on your right pointing straight to Via del Barolo and left to Grinzane Cavour, the hamlet

topped by a 14th-century castle. Stay on the SP3 and keep riding until the end of the town.

03 Shortly after Gallo and Grinzane Cavour the road splits. Take a left towards Castiglione Falletto. Here you start climbing up into the hills, following the low-trafficked secondary asphalt roads that cut through endless vineyards. Many of the vines in the area belong to the Tenuta Montanello winery, whose entrance you'll encounter on your right. Shortly after that, Castiglione Falletto is immediately recognisable; the circular tower of the settlement's castle – origi-nally a defensive fort built by the

powerful Falletti family – peeks out towards the sky.

04 The ascent continues steadily past Castiglione Falletto for another 7km, all the way until Monforte d'Alba, sitting at 480m altitude on the southernmost point of this itin-erary. Once you've completed the climb, it's worth taking some time to explore the charming Monforte d'Alba, one of the best-preserved medieval hamlets in the area. Complementing the town's ancient core is the Horszowski Auditori-um, a natural amphitheatre carved out of the hill, inaugurated in 1986 by famous Polish-American pianist Mieczysław Horszowski. The

☕ Take a Break

The name of this *enoteca* – **Barolo Bar** – in the heart of Monforte d'Alba might not be the most original, but if you're looking for a relaxing spot to break up the journey look no further. With tables and chairs spilling onto the quiet piazza, Barolo Bar is much more than a bar; serving a long list of changing homemade dishes, charcuterie boards and pizzas, it will keep you fed until the next stop.

grassy seats surround the stage that is now home of the Monfort-inJazz Festival, held each year in July and hosting both Italian and international music stars.

05 From Monforte d'Alba the road continues downhill to Barolo for 5.5km. On the way, half a dozen wineries line up one after the other; about halfway you will find yourself in front of a spectacular view of the vineyards that were added to Unesco's World Heritage List in 2014. Nearly all of the vineyards you see here carry Nebbiolo grapes, the only variety that can be used in the famed Barolo wine. As you get closer, the thousand-year-old Barolo Castle will appear dominating the scene. It is worth stopping in Barolo and entering the castle to visit the interactive WiMu, the modern Barolo Wine Museum that is spread across four floors of the building. By touring the 25 rooms that compose this unique museum, you'll get to learn about the history of one of Italy's most revered wines through the historic figures who made it known to the world in the 19th century.

06 Coming all the way to Barolo and not stopping for a wine tasting would be a shame – luckily there isn't a shortage of sipping options around here. Steps away from the Wine Museum, you'll find the historic Marchesi di Barolo winery, an institution of the region established in the early 19th century by a local family. A tour of the winery will take you down to the vaulted brick cellars where the wine rests for years inside large wooden barrels before being bottled. Following a tour of the winery you'll be able to taste the finished product in all of its varieties, best enjoyed alongside a platter of cold cuts or a plate of *agnolotti* pasta.

07 While buying Barolo wine in Barolo might seem like a good idea, it's best to leave souvenir shopping for later as another climb uphill awaits as soon as you leave the town behind. The next destination is the centre of La Morra, 6km north of Barolo, at 513m altitude. As you exit Barolo's historic centre on the SP163 road, take a left when you see the sign pointing to La Morra. A series of sharp bends takes you back to the open countryside dotted by more photogenic castles and farmhouses, such as the Tenuta La Volta and Tenuta Anselma, two of Barolo's historic wine producers.

08 La Morra, a town of 3000 people overlooking the surrounding wine country, is worth a stroll. As you enter the urban centre and reach Piazza Martiri you'll find a tourist office where plenty of detailed information on sights around the area is

M SPIRONETTI ©

Capella del Barolo

Cappella del Barolo

About 20 minutes north of Barolo, on a slight detour from the itinerary covered here, is the most colourful building in all the Langhe, known as the Capella de Barolo (or Cappella delle Brunate). Built in the early 20th century as a shelter for vineyard workers, the abandoned chapel was purchased by the Ceretto family in 1970 together with the surrounding fields. In the 1990s, the owners commissioned artists Sol LeWitt and David Tremlett with the renovation of the little chapel, which transformed it into the contemporary art piece that stands today in the Piedmontese countryside.

Fiera Internazionale del Tartufo Bianco

Each year in October, the city of Alba hosts one of Italy's most prestigious food festivals dedicated to one of the country's most highly prized products: white truffle. Growing in the forests surrounding the city, the precious tuber takes centre stage during the Fiera Internazionale del Tartufo Bianco, an event that sees truffle hunters, traders, chefs and restaurateurs come together to taste and auction the freshest nuggets of Alba's very own truffles. The festival typically lasts for nearly two months, taking place every weekend until early December. Learn more at fieradeltartufo.org.

Procession, Fiera Internazionale del Tartufo Bianco

available. Continue to Piazza Castello to climb the 18th-century bell tower (open on weekends only); from this privileged position you'll get one of the most impressive 360-degree views of the Langhe. The nearby Cantina Comunale offers the opportunity to taste and compare many of the wines produced in the region by both well-established and little-known winemakers – not just Barolo, but also Dolcetto d'Alba, Barbera and other local wine varieties.

09 The ride continues downhill along the SP58 in the direction of Verduno, the next settlement on the way back to Alba. A couple of kilometres before reaching the hilltop town you'll see it in the distance as you emerge from the trees that line the twisting road. Verduno has a sleepy centre with a few restaurants where you can have a late lunch before completing the tour; after the first roundabout you encounter when reaching Verduno, take Via Vittorio Emanuele II to the town centre. If you'd rather continue riding, follow the SP358 provincial road on the right in the direction of Alba.

10 Continue for 5km on the descending road until reaching Roddi. You'll pass by a residential area

TOP TIP:

To tackle the hills of the Barolo region some stamina is required, especially on hot summer days. Make sure to have enough water with you and plan your breaks in towns along the way. If you're unsure whether you're up for climbs, consider touring the region on an e-bike.

with a series of low independent townhouses, and within minutes you should see the highway on your right. A sign indicating 4km to Alba marks a fork in the road. Take a right and soon you'll be back at the roundabout leading into Corso Barolo, the road connecting you to the heart of Alba. Cycle straight towards the town centre and you'll be back at your starting point in no time. Your loop of the Barolo hills is now complete – it's time to reward yourself with some traditional *tajarin* pasta in one of the many local *osterie*, such as the Osteria dell'Arco. Toast to the success of your day with a glass of Barolo.

☕ Take a Break

If you decide to ride through the Barolo, you'll probably want to taste some of the famed wine produced in the region. But with hundreds of labels to choose from, how to know what to drink? At the **Enoteca Regionale del Barolo**, in the centre of Barolo, local experts will guide you through the region's different producers and styles in a tasting session during which you'll be able to compare different varieties of wine. Open Saturday and Sunday only, this regional *enoteca* will deepen your understanding of Barolo one sip at a time.

08

Ciclovia del Toce

DURATION	DIFFICULTY	DISTANCE	START/END
3.5hr	Intermediate	49km	Domodossola/ Fondotoce (Lago Maggiore)

TERRAIN			Mixed

AGF/GETTY IMAGES ©

Chapel, Sacro Monte Calvario

This is a scenic route that follows the course of the Toce river in Piedmont's Lake District, starting at the foot of the Alps in charming Domodossola and ending on the shores of Lago Maggiore, on the border between Piedmont, Lombardy and Switzerland. Spectacular views of the snowcapped Alps will accompany you on the ride through forests and historic towns, with detour options available for those willing to extend the trip further. Visit the Unesco-listed Sacro Monte Calvario in Domodossola then head south towards Lake Mergozzo to immerse yourself in the idyllic nature of northern Italy before arriving in Fondotoce.

Bike Hire

The Bike Motion store, steps away from Domodossola's train station on Corso Colonnello Attilio Moneta, provides rental mountain bikes and e-bikes, plus info on routes and detours.

Starting Point

The track begins very close to Domodossola's city centre, at the end of Via Mizzoccola, which runs next to the train station towards the Toce river.

 01 Begin your journey outside Domodossola's train station. Ride along Via Bonomelli and take the first turn left into Via Mizzoccola, the street leading directly to the banks of the Toce river, where the cycling path begins. Before leaving the city behind, pay a visit to Sacro Monte Calvario, on the southern edge of Domodossola. A Unesco World Heritage Site since 2003 and one of the most important religious sites in northern Italy, the sanc-

Casa della Resistenza

When you reach Fondotoce, stop in at the Casa della Resistenza before the end of your trip. The impressive memorial, designed by architect Cesare Mercandino, pays tribute to the 43 partisans who were executed by Fascist troops in Fondotoce in 1944. Today the space is run by the Istituto Storico della Resistenza, an organisation working to keep the memory of the Italian Resistance movement alive. Exhibitions and events dedicated to the history of WWII are held regularly in the Casa della Resistenza; for further information check the website at casadellaresistenza.it.

Elevation (m)

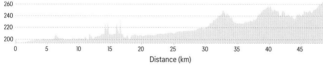

tuary of Sacro Monte Calvario was built over the course of the 17th century amid the greenery of Colle di Mattarella, the hill overlooking Domodossola.

02 The initial stretch crosses a residential neighbourhood and then an industrial area that extends below Domodossola, but it won't be long before you reach Villadossola and its Collina dello Sport, a well-kept green expanse criss-crossed by paths for running and cycling. Follow the cycling path all the way to Villadossola's town centre,

cross the canal over the small bridge, then return to the cycling path on the western bank of the Toce river. Ride across a short un-paved section under the elevated motorway then continue in the direction of Pallanzeno.

03 Continue for 5km past Pallanzeno, and after crossing the Toce river in the vicinity of Pieve Vergonte you will get to the charming town of Vogogna – a place worth a stop. The medieval hamlet of Vogogna has preserved its historic character well, and much of its

architecture still recalls the town's glorious 14th century, the era in which the Visconti family ruled over the area. It was the Visconti that commissioned two of the buildings that Vogogna is most proud of today – the Palazzo Pretorio, the city hall, and the stone-built Castello di Vogogna, a defensive fortress that allowed guards to spot enemies coming from the surrounding valleys.

04 Following some culture is a full immersion into the lush nature of the Ossola Valley – shortly after Vogogna you'll cross the boundaries of the Bosco Tenso WWF Reserve. The protected grounds of this forested section of the itinerary are home to over 40 species of birds, including herons, mountain swallows and kingfishers. In the middle of the park you can find a reed observation cabin where you can hide if you want to try to spot some of the reserve's winged inhabitants.

05 The path continues in the incredible natural landscapes along the Toce to Ornavasso. Here a walking route known as the Strada Cadorna leads to the Forte di Bara, a military fortification built on the mountain's slope to function as a defensive outpost during WWI. The fortifications found in the area remained unused during the war as enemies attacked elsewhere, but much of the military infrastructure still stands to this day and can be explored on foot.

06 Ride south across the large bridge to Candoglia, then continue cycling between the Toce and the Lago di Mergozzo towards Fondotoce,

your final destination. The Fondotoce Nature Reserve expands north of the Toce river, near the area where it merges with Lago Maggiore. As you get closer to the lake, panoramic views of mountains dropping into the flat waters await. The alluvial plain of the Toce river is also renowned for its rich biodiversity; a pair of binoculars might come in handy in this area where birds, reptiles and numerous mammals coexist.

07 Once you've arrived in Fondotoce, you have reached the end of the itinerary, but from here there are many options to continue along the shore of Lake Maggiore, if you wish to do so. Unless you want to cycle back to Domodossola, you can return to your starting point by riding to the Verbania-Pallanza railway station, about 2km west from Fondotoce, and catch a train to Domodossola from there. Book your ticket on trenitalia.com and check for the bicycle symbol to make sure the train has a suitable carriage for your bike.

☕ Take a Break

What better way to break a summer trip in nature than with a refreshing gelato? Steps away from the bridge in Candoglia is **Gelateria Aurora**, a welcoming cafe serving generous portions of homemade gelato on an outdoor terrace. It's very popular among locals during warmer months, but the seemingly endless selection of flavours and combinations make it worth the possible wait. Looking for something more filling than a gelato? Continue riding south to **La Fugascina**, a rustic yet refined restaurant on the shore of Lago di Mergozzo.

ALEMASCHE72/SHUTTERSTOCK ©

Lago di Mergozzo

Lago di Mergozzo

In ancient times Lake Mergozzo, the body of water found north of Fondotoce, was part of Lake Maggiore. Approximately five centuries ago a strip of land formed as a result of continuous inundations, splitting the large lake in two. Thanks to the lack of factories on its shores and the ban on the use of motorboats, Lake Mergozzo is one of the cleanest lakes in northern Italy – both its beaches and the hiking trails that extend from its surroundings are popular destinations during the summer months.

09

Sarre to Fénis

DURATION	DIFFICULTY	DISTANCE	START/END
1.5hr	Easy	19km	Aosta/Fénis
TERRAIN		Paved	

LUCA SANTILLI/SHUTTERSTOCK ©

Aosta

Following the Dora Baltea river, the Sarre–Fénis cycling route is an easy scenic trail that cuts through the green heart of the Aosta Valley, passing castles and natural reserves between the towns of Aosta, Charvensod, Saint-Marcel and Nus. Open only in the warmer months of the year, the path forms an ideal summer escape for cyclists of every fitness level, allowing you to experience the best of Valle d'Aosta's alpine scenery without having to climb up steep mountain slopes.

Bike Hire

La Bicicletteria di Delfo, located right in the heart of Aosta, provides bikes of every kind for hire, from simple city bikes to mountain and e-bikes.

Starting Point

The route is easy to access from a variety of points near Aosta. But to get the most out of the path, enter via the Centro Sportivo Montfleury, 2km southwest from the city centre.

01 The path begins in Sarre, 5km west of Aosta, but the capital city of the Valle d'Aosta region makes for a much better starting point for outsiders. From the heart of Aosta, ride south to the Montfleury sports complex, on the banks of the Dora Baltea river, where you'll find the entrance to the cycling and walking route.

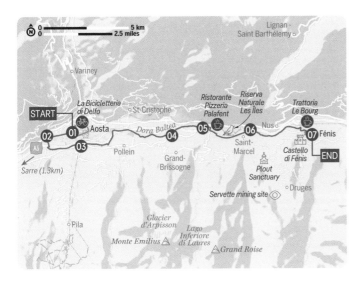

Elevation (m)

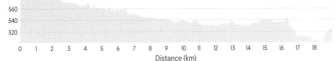

TOP TIP:

While the route actually begins in Sarre, Aosta is easier to access, has multiple bike rental stores and offers more accommodation options.

The Mines of Saint-Marcel

The Servette site in Saint-Marcel comprises some of Italy's highest mines, sitting at 1800m altitude on the slope of the mountains. Dating back as far as Roman times, Saint-Marcel's mines have long been known for their wealth of minerals, which has led to the construction of a large network of tunnels criss-crossing the mountain's interior. In 1957 mining operations stopped and the site was later turned into an open-air museum run by volunteers, which can be visited during the summer. Visit minieresaintmarcel.it for information on tours and opening times.

02 In Montfleury, cross the river into the area of Gressan, where you'll see the track running along the southern bank of the river. In Gressan, the path cuts through a large park loved by locals, with exercising equipment, benches and a cafe open during the summer. As the entire route is shared with pedestrians, it is important to avoid speeding along here – keep it relaxed and continue towards Pont Suaz, 3km ahead.

03 As you pass Pont Suaz, in the municipality of Charvensod, and enter Pollein you will gradually leave the built environment behind and the scenery will turn green. Residential buildings become more scarce and the mountains start dominating your vision. In Pollein, cross the green sports area and continue riding towards Brissogne.

04 In Brissogne you'll be passing next to a golf course and a large outdoor swimming pool before reaching the Palafent facility, a multipurpose space dedicated to the practice of traditional sports. The best known of Valle d'Aosta's traditional sports is *filolet*, a game typically played in spring on a triangular field, where athletes challenge each other by kicking a small ball with a tapered wooden stick to deliver it as far as possible. Tournaments of *filolet* – but also of other heritage sports such as *rebatta* and *palet* – are held in Brissogne during spring and summer.

05 After Brissogne, the path continues into the Riserva Naturale Les Îles, a protected wetland that surrounds two small lakes populated by a long list of migratory birds that travel to the humid shores of the Dora Baltea to nest. Herons and great egrets are just two of over 40 species of animals that have been spotted in the area. If you're into bird-watching, spring offers the highest chances of encountering migratory birds. Inside the reserve you'll find some observation huts, specifically built to watch the rich fauna of the area.

06 The town of Saint-Marcel follows after a short distance, a place known since ancient times for its mineral resources. The cycling path running from Saint-Marcel to Fénis was completed in 2021, allowing cyclists for the first time to complete the whole itinerary without having to take the main road. If you have time, it's worth making a detour in Saint-Marcel to explore the higher-altitude areas – by climbing up the mountain slopes you'll be able to visit the intriguing Plout Sanctuary, a shrine dedicated to the Virgin Mary built in the 1850s on a pilgrimage site believed to have been venerated since the 14th century. Further up you can also visit the Servette mining site, where you'll be able to enter some of the galleries used by miners of the past to extract precious materials from the mountain's belly.

07 Last stop is Fénis, 4km after Saint-Marcel, where you'll be met by the incredible castle marking the town's centre. Erected over the course of a century – between 1320 and 1421 – by members of the powerful Challant family, the Castello di Fénis is unusual in its location at a low altitude. Make sure to take some time to visit the inner courtyard of the castle, where beautiful frescoes adorn the stone-built walls and wooden staircases. If you want to get back to Aosta, return by retracing your steps along the same route that you came from. Alternatively, you can catch the train back from Nus, located on the other side of the river from Fénis.

ALESSANDRO TORTORA/GETTY IMAGES ©

☕ Take a Break

The homey atmosphere of **Ristorante Pizzeria Palafent**, a typically Italian pizzeria near the Les Îles nature reserve, makes for an ideal spot to recharge on the way to Fénis or on your return to Aosta. With a large outdoor seating area and a daily-changing, fixed-price menu for lunch, this restaurant is popular among locals and visitors alike. Another worthy option is the **Trattoria Le Bourg**, located steps away from Fénis' Castle, where you'll be able to taste the local cheeses and seasonal dishes that make up the ever-changing menu.

Arch of Augustus

Roman Aosta

Beside the spectacular scenery that surrounds Aosta, the city is also home to one of the most impressive collections of Roman ruins in northern Italy. Conquered by Emperor Augustus in 25 BCE, the city became a key intersection on the Via delle Gallie connecting Rome to France. Many of the monuments that were built during that epoch still stand in the heart of Aosta, including the imposing Arch of Augustus that welcomed travellers into the city 2000 years ago, the Roman bridge and the Roman theatre. To learn more about the city's ancient history, it's also worth visiting the regional archae-ological museum located in Piazza Roncas.

10

Best for

COASTAL SCENERY

Riviera dei Fiori

DURATION	DIFFICULTY	DISTANCE	START/END
2hr	Easy	24km	San Lorenzo al Mare/ Ospedaletti

TERRAIN	Paved

Santo Stefano al Mare

Stretching for the 24km that separate San Lorenzo al Mare and Ospedaletti, this route allows you to explore the scenic Parco Costiero della Riviera dei Fiori, in the western part of Liguria near the French border. The path is built on the former tracks of the old railway line that once connected Genoa and Ventimiglia, running parallel to the coast and offering some of the region's most spectacular views. Entirely flat and suitable for all abilities, some sections sit so close to the sea that on windy days you might get splashed by the waves.

Bike Hire

There are a few bike rental shops in San Lorenzo al Mare, which all charge around €12 per day for hire. Nolo Bici, in Piazza della Stazione, and Al 10 Nolo Bici, in Piazza Giuseppe Garibaldi, are both reliable.

Starting Point

The cycling path officially begins at the end of Via della Stazione and its first section runs parallel to Via degli Orti, but you can also take it anywhere near San Lorenzo al Mare's main beach.

01 The path connecting San Lorenzo al Mare with Ospedaletti follows the route carved by a 19th-century railway track. This well-kept lane can be joined just steps away from San Lorenzo al Mare's port, near which you'll also find a few bike rental services. After riding for less than a kilometre you'll enter the first tunnel once used by the trains to travel across the seaside cliffs. This first tunnel is well lit but relatively long; running for 1.5km, it stretches all the way to the small municipality of Costarainera.

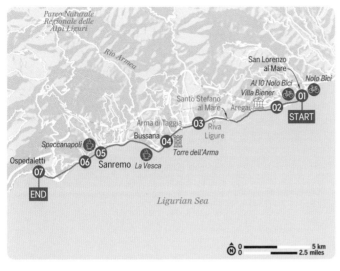

Elevation (m)

02 The track runs parallel to the SS1 road known as Aurelia into the town of Aregai and then Santo Stefano al Mare. From Aregai, a detour inland takes you to the fascinating Villa Biener, a contemporary art space created by artists Judith Török and Carlo Maglitto where an open-air sculpture park populated by otherworldly creatures can be visited. The cycling route then passes via Aregai's marina and then into Santo Stefano al Mare, recognisable by its cream-coloured bell tower standing in the centre of the town.

03 Along the coast between Santo Stefano al Mare and Taggia you should be able to spot some of the defensive towers that were built in the 16th century to protect the fishing communities living in this part of Liguria from pirate attacks. The Torre dell'Arma dominates the promontory in Arma di Taggia near the beach of Bussana, overlooking the Mediterranean from its privileged position. Unfortunately, at the time of writing it was not possible to visit the tower's interior. Besides architecture, Taggia is also worth a stop for its dark olives known as *taggiasche*, a prized and protected fruit grown on the trees dotting the riviera's hilly coastline.

04 The path continues running parallel to the shore to Bussana. The old town of Bussana – known

Festival di Sanremo

The Sanremo Music Festival (pictured) is Italy's most important song contest and the longest-running national singing competition to be televised, running since 1951. It takes place in the city's Teatro Ariston each year in February and sees famous and established artists compete for a week to win the Golden Lion. Next to the award, winners of the competition are given the opportunity to represent Italy at the Eurovision Song Contest, which was inspired by Sanremo. In 2023, the Sanremo Music Festival was watched by over 16 million people across Italy.

as Bussana Vecchia and located 2.5km inland – was abandoned at the end of the 19th century when an earthquake hit the area; it was repopulated by artists and hippies after WWII. Today about 30 permanent residents live in the crumbling Bussana Vecchia, where the old residential structures blend with the vegetation and open-air exhibitions of arts and crafts.

05 The next stop as you continue riding is the city of Sanremo, the best-known centre on the itinerary located 6.5km west of Bussana. On the way you will pass near Villa Nobel, an elegant, eclectic, Moorish-style residence completed in the late 19th century. It was later inhabited by Swedish chemist Alfred Nobel, the founder of the world's most important literary and scientific award, who lived in Sanremo during the final years of his life.

06 Continue riding on the seafront promenade of Corso Imperatrice, past the luxurious boats parked in Sanremo's marina, then by the

city's art nouveau casino, one of the only four legal casinos in Italy, exiting the city centre towards Ospedaletti. The French border is getting closer. As you leave Sanremo behind you'll enter the 1.75km-long Capo Nero tunnel, opened in 2014. On the tunnel's roof hang a series of quotes and images recounting events from the history of the Milano-Sanremo road cycling race (p55), held each year in March since 1907.

07 As you exit the tunnel, you'll find yourself in Ospedaletti where the cycling route comes to an end. Legend has it that Ospedaletti was founded as a result of a shipwreck – travelling on a galley from Palestine to France, a crew of knights found themselves caught up in a storm and managed to survive by swimming to this corner of Ligurian soil. Here they founded a hospital – *ospedale* in Italian – for pilgrims travelling along the coast to the Holy Land. From Ospedaletti, you can return to your starting point by following the cycling route backwards.

Take a Break

There's no shortage of cafes and restaurants on the Riviera dei Fiori, especially during the summer. A safe bet about halfway along the route is **La Vesca**, a seaside cafe positioned between Arma di Taggia and Sanremo, which serves fresh dishes right on the seafront. Enjoy a plate of pasta or a stuffed focaccia with the sound of the waves in the background before continuing onward to Ospedaletti. Less traditional but equally delicious (and carb-heavy) is **Spaccanapoli**, a Neapolitan-style pizzeria in Sanremo.

Infiorata **decorations**

Santo Stefano a Mare's *infiorata*

It's not a coincidence that this part of Liguria's coast is known as the 'Flower Riviera' – the dedication to adorning the streets with pots brimming with colour is evident everywhere on the coastline. It is during Santo Stefano a Mare's *infiorata* (floral display), however, that flowers turn into works of art. Held every two years in May, the event sees artists arriving in Santo Stefano a Mare from all over Italy to use petals for the creation of large-scale illustrations on the town's central streets. Each artist is given 20 sq metres to work with, and after three days a jury declares the winners.

Also Try...

Vernazza, Cinque Terre

Strada Panoramica Cinque Terre

DURATION	DIFFICULTY	DISTANCE
3.5hr	Difficult	41km

Liguria's best-known stretch of coastline is usually explored on foot, but following the panoramic road that runs above the Cinque Terre on a bike guarantees spectacular views of the villages composing this colourful corner of Italy.

Starting from Levanto, the road leads to La Spezia passing above Monterosso, Vernazza, Corniglia, Manarola and Riomaggiore, covering just over 40km. The initial stretch is the most difficult, with a climb that takes you up the hills that overlook the coast, then south along a secondary road with little traffic. Cycling the Strada Panoramica is not for everyone, and if you want to visit the beaches of the Cinque Terre you'll have to double your effort to get to water level and then back up on the ridge.

The Avigliana Lakes

DURATION	DIFFICULTY	DISTANCE
30min	Intermediate	7km

The lakes of Avigliana are a popular weekend destination for many of Turin's residents, offering the chance to leave the big city behind and immerse yourself in the natural scenery surrounding the bodies of water.

The Avigliana Lakes Nature Park, located 30km west of Turin, covers approximately 400 hectares and includes two lakes – the Lago Grande and the Lago Piccolo. The larger of the two lakes, which is also open for swimming, has a cycling path that runs around its shore; it's an easy 30-minute ride of about 7km, which can be extended in multiple directions if you are keen to explore the reserve's surroundings.

VACLAV VOLRAB/SHUTTERSTOCK ©

Gran Paradiso National Park

Via de Sale

DURATION	DIFFICULTY	DISTANCE
4hr	Difficult	40km

One of Piedmont's most fascinating mountain-biking adventures, the Via del Sale starts in the small town of Limone Piemonte and follows the ancient route that salt traders used to travel on to reach the Mediterranean in Liguria.

The itinerary is relatively short – only 40km – but the many steep inclines and high-altitude sections at over 1800m make the trip suitable for experienced mountain bikers only. The route crosses military fortifications and wild forests all the way into western Liguria, until reaching Ventimiglia where the path drops back down to sea level and connects to the paved road.

Cogne Valley

DURATION	DIFFICULTY	DISTANCE
3hr	Difficult	24km

The best-known valley of the Gran Paradiso National Park offers exceptional opportunities for some high-altitude road cycling in the heart of mountainous Valle d'Aosta.

The paved route that runs from Aymavilles to Lillaz might be only 24km long, but with nearly 1000m of elevation gain it will require enough energy to push through the alpine scenery one ascent at a time. If you're up for a summer challenge, tackle the twisting roads of the Cogne Valley amid waterfalls, snowcapped peaks, and alpine chamois balancing on the vertical walls of the majestic mountains. Note, though, that this route is only accessible between June and September, as snow might cover the highest sections of the track during the rest of the year.

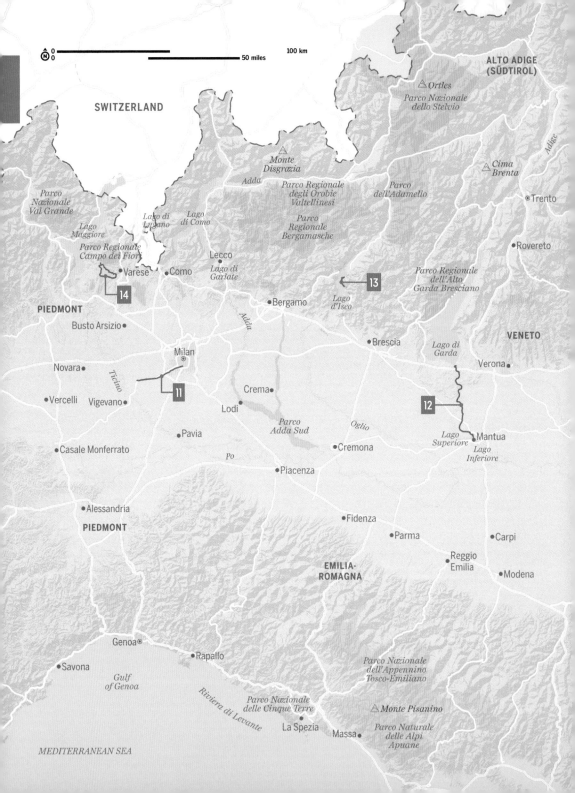

Villas on the Naviglio Grande (p84)

Milan & the Lakes

11 **Naviglio Grande**

Discover Milan's past as a city of canals as you cycle along the Naviglio Grande on a flat path suitable for all riders. **p84**

12 **Pista Ciclabile del Mincio**

Over 40km of pure beauty with the Mincio and the Morainic Hills as a backdrop. **p90**

13 **Ciclabile Vello-Toline**

A short ride along the former lakeside road next to turquoise waters, with stunning views of the snowcapped Orobie Alps. **p94**

14 **Pista Ciclopedonale del Lago di Varese**

Cycle around a lake via quaint villages, bird-filled wetlands and Unesco-listed prehistoric sites. **p98**

Explore

Milan & the Lakes

With its location right in the heart of the Po Valley, Milan is the ideal departure point for a range of no-elevation, straight-as-an-arrow cycle itineraries following the course of its ancient waterways, once part of a network of canals that connected the city to the lakes. And for those who prefer cycling with a view of blue waters surrounded by mountains? Milan is a busy transport hub, and the Italian Lakes are just a short train ride away. But don't limit yourself to the best-known ones – smaller lakes like Iseo and Varese are ideal to discover on two wheels, with interesting itineraries combining nature and history.

Milan

Milan is slowly improving, with new bike lanes and bike-sharing systems being added each year, but it still has a while to go before truly becoming a bike-friendly city. Luckily for local cyclists, there's a network of excellent cycleways running along the towpaths of Milan's Navigli, artificial canals dug centuries ago for the transport of people and goods. The best-known itinerary is the one along Naviglio Grande, the longest waterway connecting Milan to the Ticino river, but it's also worth considering Naviglio Pavese, ending in the city of Pavia, and Naviglio Martesana, a 40km journey to the Adda river through an area rich in birdlife.

The Lakes

The best-known Italian lakes are Lake Como, Maggiore and Garda, three long and narrow lakes of glacial origin all located between one and two hours' drive north of Milan. Despite long-announced cycleways circling all around the lakes, projects are far from being complete – there are only a few kilometres here and there of dedicated cycle paths, such as the 2.5 scenic kilometres in Limone sul Garda, hanging right over the lake waters. Lake Iseo is a better choice for cyclists – besides the 5km cycle path between Vello and Toline, the road along the western side of the lake is very scenic and has little traffic.

WHEN TO GO

Spring and autumn are the best times to visit Milan and the lakes to go cycling. Summers are stiflingly hot and busy, especially around the lakes, while winters can be cold, wet and foggy. Cycle paths along the Navigli are popular with locals on weekends, especially when the weather is nice; consider riding during the week instead.

Mantua & the Mincio

Surrounded by the placid waters of three lakes, the Renaissance city of Mantua rises like a dream with its domes and bell towers between the mist and reeds of the Po Valley. Mantua's lakes were created for defensive purposes by altering the course of the Mincio, a river flowing out of Lake Garda and into the Po. There's a stunning cycleway running for 40km between Lake Garda and Mantua, and the surrounding territory also offers many other bike itineraries, especially around the Morainic Hills just north of the city.

Varese

Home to seven lakes, countless alpine climbs, birthplace of great cyclists and the location of the Tre Valli, one of Lombardy's classic cycle races held for over a century – it comes as no surprise that Varese is strongly committed to cycling, and offers plenty of opportunities and facilities for bike-loving visitors. Those wanting an easy day out on two wheels can ride around Lake Varese and Lake Comabbio, with few climbs and unspoilt nature, while serious cyclists can test themselves on iconic climbs such as Cuvignone and Campo dei Fiori, or even join one of the many Granfondo races happening year-round.

TRANSPORT

The A8 motorway, also known as Autostrada dei Laghi, connects Milan to Lake Como, Maggiore and Varese. To reach Lake Iseo and Lake Garda, take the A4 motorway towards Venice.

It is also easy to reach the lakes by train, departing from Milan Centrale, Cadorna and Porta Garibaldi stations. In Milan, you can take bikes on the *metropolitana* (metro) for free, avoiding peak times and using the last carriage.

WHAT'S ON

Colnago Cycling Festival

A three-day cycling festival held in April in Desenzano on Lake Garda, with bike races, an expo and bike-related events.

Milan Design Week

A week-long design festival in April with a trade fair, events and installations in various locations all over the city.

SioWeekend

Two weekends in November with events and experiences to promote slow tourism in four villages around Lake Como – Bellagio, Menaggio, Tremezzina and Varenna.

Resources

Varese Do You Lake? (varesedoyoulake.it/en) Has information about bike-related events and itineraries in Varese and surrounding areas.

A Ritmo D'Acque (aritmo dacque.it) App and website collecting a series of itineraries for all tastes and skill levels around Milan's waterways.

In Lombardia (in-lom bardia.it/en) Includes information about cycle paths and bike itineraries all over Lombardy.

WHERE TO STAY

There's a shortage of bike-friendly accommodation in Milan, but you can always try calling ahead and asking if there's a place to store your bike. Don't risk leaving your bike out on the street at night. Outside the city and around the lakes you'll find many more hotels and apartments with facilities for cyclists, especially around bike-focused areas such as Varese and northern Lake Garda. Other reliable bike hotels around the lakes are Dolci Colli Bike Hotel in Peschiera del Garda; Hotel Il Perlo Panorama in Bellagio, Lake Como; and Hotel La Pieve on Lake Iseo.

11

Naviglio Grande

DURATION	DIFFICULTY	DISTANCE	START/END
3hr	Intermediate	22km	Milan Darsena/ Abbiategrasso

TERRAIN		Paved

Naviglio Grande, Milan

Discover Milan's past as a city of canals while cycling along the Naviglio Grande, from the ancient port in the heart of the city to Abbiategrasso, a provincial town that was once one of the outposts of the Duchy of Milan. The Naviglio Grande is the longest of the remaining canals, once part of a network of waterways that used to connect Milan to Lake Maggiore, to transport goods and marble blocks for the construction of Milan's Duomo. The itinerary is entirely paved and has no altitude difference, and it is suitable for everyone, including families and beginner cyclists.

Bike Hire

Smile & Bike offers regular and e-bikes for rent, with prices starting from €25 per day, conveniently located along the Naviglio Grande as well as in the vicinity of Centrale station.

Starting Point

The starting point for this bike ride is the Darsena, about 10 minutes by bike from the Duomo and a five-minute walk from Porta Genova metro station.

01 The Naviglio Grande cycle path starts at the Darsena, the artificial basin in the proximity of Piazza XXIV Maggio, built in the 17th century and active until the mid-20th century as Milan's commercial port. After a few decades of neglect, the whole area was revamped for the Milan Expo in 2015, and it's now a pleasant area to walk around, with a market and a few open-air bars. Two of Milan's remaining artificial canals, Naviglio Grande and Naviglio Pavese, both flow into the Darsena. Standing

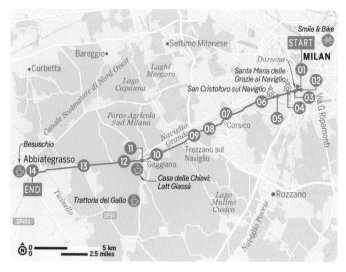

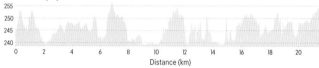

Elevation (m)

255
250
245
240

0   2   4   6   8   10   12   14   16   18   20

Distance (km)

TOP TIP:

The Naviglio Grande can be cycled year-round, but between November and March the canals will have no water due to the *asciutta*, a twice-yearly intervention during which all the water is drained out to maintain the banks, locks and bridges along the canal. This doesn't affect access to the towpath.

Leonardo & the Navigli

The Naviglio Grande was first dug out in the 12th century for defensive purposes, but the network was vastly improved two centuries later, when it was extended to connect Lake Maggiore with Milan, to carry marble for the construction of the Duomo. The lock system to cover the altitude difference between the lake and Milan was developed thanks to the work of Leonardo da Vinci, who was commissioned by the Lord of Milan to devise a system to connect Lake Como to the Milan waterways. Leonardo never actually worked on Naviglio Grande, but his studies and sketches were used by hydraulic engineers in the following centuries.

with your back to the Darsena, the Naviglio Grande is the larger waterway to the right, flowing in a southwest direction.

02 The Naviglio Grande is lined with an *alzaia* (towpath), reserved for bicycles, pedestrians and maintenance vehicles – regular traffic is allowed only in some short sections, but cars are usually few and far between. Pay attention to pedestrians as you ride out of Milan, as there are several art galleries, shops and restaurants along the canal and it's a popular place for a stroll.

03 Start riding on the right-hand side of the canal, proceeding carefully along the cobbled sections. About 200m

from the start, keep your eyes open for the Vicolo dei Lavandai, a tiny waterway topped by a tiled roof supported with wooden beams. Up until the 1950s, this canal is where people from the neighbourhood used to do their laundry – closer to the water's edge, it's possible to see the flat stones used as washing boards. Opposite the Vicolo dei Lavandai, there's a picturesque stone bridge dedicated to Milanese poetess Alda Merini, who lived most of her life along the Naviglio. It's a great photo location, especially in the early morning or at sunset.

04 A few steps after the bridge, you'll find the church of Santa Maria delle Grazie al Naviglio, with an unfinished brick facade. Several

☕ Take a Break

Gaggiano is just after the halfway point of this trip, and has a few dining options close to the canal. **Latt Giassà** is an ice-cream shop, open year-round; it also sells hot chocolate in winter. Right next door you'll find **Casa delle Chiavi**, a cafe run by a local cooperative and focusing on food from local producers. For a larger meal, **Trattoria del Gallo** serves up Lombard specialities including a mean *cotoletta* (cutlet) in a historic building a 3km ride from the Naviglio, along a quiet country road.

churches around Milan and the Po Valley are built out of bricks; marble and stone were reserved for the grandest churches and cathedrals, such as the Duomo.

05 Keep riding, leaving the centre of Milan behind. After 1km from the start, pay attention to trams as you cross Via Valenza. After that, stay on the right-hand side of the canal and ride past a large car park and railway depot, which sometimes houses pop-up markets. About 2km from the start, you'll ride past the church of San Cristoforo sul Naviglio (right).

06 Right after the church there's the clubhouse of Canottieri Olona, a rowing group that you might see practising on the Naviglio. Keep your eyes open for street art – there are some interesting pieces in the vicinity of Canottieri Olona, and others around Ponte delle Milizie a few hundred metres away.

07 After San Cristoforo, the crowds thin out and you should be able to ride more easily. Ride a further 4km until you reach Corsico, the first municipality after Milan. Keep your eyes open for the train station on your right-hand side; once you see it, take the second exit at the roundabout and ride

along the car park, and keep going straight down Via Marconi and Via Nilde Iotti until the T-junction, where you'll turn left down Via Elsa Morante and keep going until you reach the Naviglio again. This short detour is recommended as the stretch of the Naviglio just after Corsico station is one-way only; alternatively, you can stay on the footpath and walk your bike.

08 About 1km after getting back onto the canal, there's a park on your right-hand side with plenty of benches if you need a break. Otherwise, keep riding a further 4km to Trezzano sul Naviglio, the next town along the waterway.

09 Ride under the bridge supporting Milan's *tangenziale* (ring road) for approximately 1km, until you see a sign recommending bicycles to turn right down Via Puccini. If you decide to stay on the Naviglio, dismount from your bike and walk the next section, as it is quite narrow and the cobblestones make it difficult to ride on. There's also a short but steep section leading to Ponte Gobbo, the bridge spanning the canal. Those who prefer to keep riding should turn right down Via Puccini, turn left into Via Croce, carefully cross the roundabout and continue straight, and then second left down Via

San Cristoforo sul Naviglio

San Cristoforo sul Naviglio

The church of San Cristoforo is actually a complex made up of two churches built side by side. The one on the left is the oldest, built in Romanesque style on the site of a previous pagan temple, whereas the church to the right is Gothic and dates back to the 15th century. It's worth going in to admire the exquisite frescoes on the apse, depicting Christ surrounded by angels and the four Evangelists.

The Villas of Robecco

Those wanting to ride further from Abbiategrasso can continue for another 7km to Robecco sul Naviglio, a charming canal-side village that was once a holiday destination for wealthy Milanese families. You can still see some of their lavish villas, such as Palazzo Archinto overlooking the Naviglio, with a castle-like appearance complete with towers and battlements. The *palazzo* houses a museum dedicated to the Naviglio Grande, and it's surrounded by a large public park. Villa Gaia Gandini and Villa Bassana are two other exquisite examples. Keep in mind there is no station in Robecco, so you'll have to either cycle back to Abbiategrasso or continue a further 5km to Magenta.

Palazzo Archinto

Volontari del Sangue to reach the Naviglio again.

10 After leaving Trezzano, the next village is Gaggiano, a further 3km away. Gaggiano is one of the prettiest villages in the surroundings of Milan, with colourful painted houses and a baroque church reflected in the blue waters of the canal.

11 In Gaggiano, the towpath continues along the left side of the canal. To change sides, you have two options: get off your bike and walk it across Ponte Gozzadini, stopping for a picture, or take the car bridge a few hundred metres down, with a sharp left turn after you cross to continue along the waterway.

12 After crossing to the left-hand side of the canal, you'll ride past an ice-cream shop and a cafe, the last that you'll encounter until the end of the itinerary. During the final 7.5km stretch to Abbiategrasso, you'll leave the city and its suburbs behind, cycling through agricultural landscapes, especially beautiful in late spring when the rice fields are flooded. You'll also cycle past a few *cascine*, historic brick farmhouses found in this part of Lombardy. Between Gaggiano and Abbiategrasso there are no further villages and not many places to stop, save for a bench a couple of kilometres after Gaggiano, and another about 5km later.

13 About 5km after Gaggiano, you'll pass a small altar dedicated to the Virgin Mary under the SP30 bridge, and an open-air restaurant just after that. In summer, you can also stop at Agrinaviglio, a small shop right on the edge of the Naviglio selling fresh juices and locally grown fruit.

14 The itinerary ends in Abbiategrasso, a medium-sized town housing a 12th-century castle surrounded by a garden, and a compact historic centre with an award-winning patisserie. You'll ride past a cemetery, under a bridge and along a cobbled road until the Naviglio splits into two branches – one continuing southward, a further 18.5km to Bereguardo, and the other heading north to the Ticino river. To reach Abbiategrasso station, take the left branch when the canal divides, until you reach a triple bridge past the former Mivar factory. Turn right over the bridge, take the underpass to avoid busy SP494 and continue down Via Amerigo Vespucci, then turn right into Via Grossi and left at the roundabout, down Via Mazzini. The station is just at the end of this road, with hourly trains back to Milan.

☕ Take a Break

In the heart of Abbiategrasso's historic centre, it's worth stopping at **Besuschio**, a patisserie open since 1845, predating Italy's independence. There are a few outdoor tables overlooking the main square, perfect to enjoy *pasticcini*, tiny delectable pastries served as an accompaniment to tea and coffee. Besuschio is also famous for its panettone, available year-round, and other cakes including *crakelè*, the patisserie's own invention combining marrons glacés, vanilla and tonka bean.

12

Pista Ciclabile del Mincio

DURATION	DIFFICULTY	DISTANCE	START/END
4hr	Difficult	40km	Peschiera del Garda/Mantua

TERRAIN		Paved

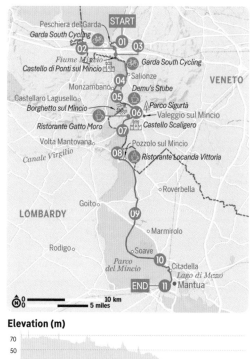

Elevation (m)

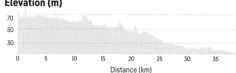

From the shores of Lake Garda to Mantua, the Renaissance gem of Shakespearian memory, the Ciclabile del Mincio stretches over 40km of pure beauty, with the emerald-turquoise waters of the Mincio and the Morainic Hills as a backdrop. The itinerary starts right under the fortified walls of Peschiera del Garda and follows the course of the river, past sleepy villages, reed-fringed wetlands and Borghetto sul Mincio, a medieval hamlet on the riverbank. The route is flat, well-marked and almost entirely paved, perfect for those wanting a full-day outing.

Bike Hire

Garda South Cycling rents a variety of bikes from several locations in Peschiera and along the cycleway. Prices start from €10 for half-day rental. A bike shuttle service from Mantua back to Peschiera is available.

Starting Point

The cycleway starts a short distance from the station of Peschiera del Garda, about an hour and 20 minutes from Milan. Bus 46 from Mantua to Peschiera allows bikes from April to October with an extra charge.

01 Leave Peschiera del Garda station behind and cycle down Viale Stazione, then turn left down Via Venezia until you reach the Mincio river. Continue straight as you cross the bridge over Parco Catullo and then enter the Unesco-listed 14th-century fortified walls into the historic part of the city. If you have time, it's worth looking around the city centre and cycling down Lungolago Mazzini for views over Lake Garda.

A Tortellini Love Story

The best-known speciality of Borghetto sul Mincio is tortellini, stuffed pasta usually cooked in broth and then served with butter and sage. These are different from the traditional Bolognese tortellini – the stuffing is made with a blend of meats with the addition of nutmeg, and the shape is reminiscent of a knot, the reason why they are also known as *nodo d'amore* (love knot). Their origin dates back to a local legend of a military commander who fell in love with a nymph who lived in the waters of the Mincio, and ran away with her leaving behind a handkerchief with two knots to symbolise their love.

02 Ride out of the historic centre and up Via Campo Sportivo, a slight hill. The start of the cycleway will be on your left, marked by a brown sign. Cycle down the unpaved track leading down to the riverbank, paying attention as it's quite steep. If you are with children or on a road bike, it's better to walk down.

03 The cycleway runs along the former Mantua–Garda railway, active until 1967. The first 7km follow the right bank of the river, with slow-moving waters and cypress trees growing along the riverbanks. The path will pass the town of Ponti sul Mincio, known for its Scaliger castle and 18th-century military fort.

04 Just after the Mincio power station, the path moves over to the left side of the Mincio. This section is very scenic, with views over the Morainic Hills to the south of Lake Garda and the town of Monzambano. If you want to ride further, you can head west from Monzambano for approximately 5km to reach Castellaro Lagusello, a fortified village next to a heart-shaped lake.

05 After about 12km, the cycleway moves away from the river and follows a canal, until it arrives in Valeggio sul Mincio, home to a hilltop castle and to Parco Sigurtà, worth visiting in spring for its stunning flower displays. Here you'll find the only unpaved section of the cycleway, so proceed with caution.

06 On the opposite side of the river from Valeggio, don't miss touring the tiny hamlet of Borghetto sul Mincio, known for its alleyways, water mills and unique tortellini – a good option for lunch. The best views over Borghetto can be enjoyed from the Visconti bridge at the entrance of the village. Borghetto is a popular stop and definitely the highlight of this cycleway – it's a good idea to park your bike and look around on foot, especially during the weekends.

07 The next section of the cycleway follows the left bank of the Mincio, with agricultural landscapes all around. Here you can do some bird-watching – storks, egrets, herons, cormorants and other waterfowls are commonly spotted, as are *nutrie* (large rodents similar to beavers).

08 Another good place for a break is Pozzolo sul Mincio, 6km from Borghetto, with a playground with benches and bocce pits right next to the river. After Pozzolo, the cycleway leaves the Mincio river and follows the flood control canal. It's easy to follow, and there are underpasses to avoid crossing busy intersections like the one in Marengo.

09 In Soave, just after two canals flow into one another, the cycleway moves over to the right side of the river once again for about 1km. At

Lotus flowers, Mantua

☕ Take a Break

In Valeggio sul Mincio, **Demu's Stube** has a large *biergarten*-style outdoor space with plenty of seating and a menu that includes pizza, burgers and some local pasta specialities. The place can be busy on weekends. For something a little quieter and secluded, head to **Ristorante Gatto Moro** in Borghetto and order the iconic *nodo d'amore* (tortellini with butter and sage). A few kilometres down the road in Pozzolo sul Mincio, **Ristorante Locanda Vittoria** has outdoor seating and a menu focused on local freshwater fish.

this stage, you'll be approximately 5km from Mantua; keep following the brown signs, as the itinerary runs along tiny country roads to avoid the traffic entering the city.

10 When you reach Cittadella, keep a look out for the cycle path to the left of Canottieri Mincio, and turn there. Keep going until you reach Lago di Mezzo, one of the three lakes created by the lords of Mantua for defensive purposes by altering the

Mantua's Lotus Flowers

In the month of July and August, a unique phenomenon takes place on the placid waters of the Mincio – the blossoming of thousands of lotus flowers of all colours, from powder pink to yellow, orange and red. Lotus flowers are not native to this area; they were introduced in the 1920s by a local woman with the idea of harvesting their roots. A local legend says that the flowers were planted by a heartbroken man, to remember his girlfriend after she left him. The best place to see them is Mantua's Upper Lake, a quick ride away from where the cycleway ends.

course of the Mincio, surrounding the town by water on three sides.

11 Ride along Via dei Mulini to cross the lake and enter Mantua. The cycleway ends at the train station, about 900m down the road. The historic centre is just a 10-minute walk away; depending on how much time you have, you might want to visit Palazzo Ducale to see Mantegna frescoes, or Palazzo Te, a Mannerist masterpiece.

13

Ciclabile Vello- Toline

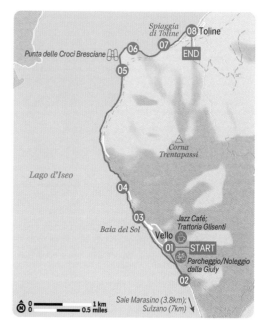

STEFANO EMBER/SHUTTERSTOCK ©

DURATION	DIFFICULTY	DISTANCE	START/END
40min	Easy	5km	Vello/Toline

TERRAIN		Paved

Elevation (m)

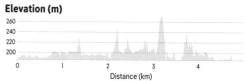

This ride may sound diminutive at only 5km long, but don't let the distance fool you – the views over Lake Iseo and the snowcapped Orobie Alps are so scenic you'll keep stopping to take pictures. The path runs alongside the former lakeside road, hewn from the limestone rock right next to the turquoise lake waters. The course is completely flat and closed to traffic, making it ideal for families and beginners. The path is shared between cyclists and pedestrians, and it gets busy during weekends. Set out in the morning to escape the crowds.

Bike Hire

Parcheggio/Noleggio dalla Giuly in Vello offers both parking and bike rental, at the cost of €4 per hour. It's a good option if you are driving, since there's limited parking space in Vello.

Starting Point

Both Vello and Toline are served by the Brescia-Edolo railway, which also stops at other towns along the eastern shore of Lake Iseo. There are departures every two hours, during the week and at the weekend.

 01 If you have your own bike, exit Vello station and cycle down Via De Gasperi until you reach the lakefront, then turn right and follow the road running along the lake. The start of the cycle path is marked by a red and white gate, blocking car access. Alternatively, hire a bike in Vello; the start of the path is just 100m down the road from the bike shop.

Monte Isola

Lake Iseo may be the smallest of Italy's large lakes, but it contains Monte Isola, the largest lake island in southern Europe. Riding along the Vello-Toline cycle path, you'll be able to see the northern edge of Monte Isola, stretching for 4.5 sq km and including a 600m-high peak – a true mountain in the middle of a lake.

You can reach Monte Isola by ferry from Sale Marasino and Sulzano, and it's possible to cycle the entire circumference of the island along a 9km path, suitable for mountain bikes and including lots of hills and descents.

02 It's worth looking around Vello before starting to ride. There's a pretty lakeside park and a cemetery with a 14th-century church, usually open during the weekend. It is also possible to pick up snacks for the ride or stop for a drink at a cafe.

03 The cycle path was created by reconverting the former lakeside road, with the sheer cliffs of the Corna Trentapassi mountain on one side, and the waters of Lake Iseo on the other. The road soon proved to be too narrow and unstable to support fast-increasing traffic, and was moved further uphill. At the start of the path, pay attention to a plaque with an inscription dedicated to those who worked to restore the cycleway after it was damaged by a landslide in 2015.

04 Cycle through the first tunnels, and under overhanging shelves of rock. The path snakes in a series of scenic turns following the profile of the lake, while limestone rocks tower overhead, occasionally interrupted by the railway that emerges from the mountainside before plunging into another tunnel. On clear days, it is possible to see the villages of Lovere, Castro and Tavernola on the opposite side of the lake.

05 There are several opportunities to stop and sit looking at the lake, with benches and picnic tables surrounded by cypress trees. A good place for a break is Punta delle Croci Bresciane, about 3km from the start, marking the narrowest point of Lake Iseo. With a bit of luck, you can see the promontory on the opposite side of the lake.

06 Ride through another series of scenic tunnels, as the path weaves its way through the mountains. Some tunnels open to the side, framing views of the panoramic road on the opposite shore of the lake. It is also sometimes possible to see Orrido del Bogn, a deep, narrow canyon cutting through the rock along the western shore.

07 The last section of the path runs under arches supporting SP510 above. Street artists have decorated the pillars and arches with lake-inspired graffiti, worth checking out. The cycle path ends just outside the village of Toline, marked again by a red and white gate.

08 This is the end of the mapped itinerary. It is possible to catch the train back, or ride along the path in reverse to admire different views of the lake. This is especially worth doing on summer afternoons, when the path is illuminated by the setting sun. After heading back to Vello, you can eat at an excellent *trattoria* serving creative local specialities.

Those willing to explore further can cycle south of Vello to Sale Marasino (5km) or Sulzano (8km)

MARGHERITA RAGGELLO/LONELY PLANET ®

Lake Iseo

☕ Take a Break

Jazz Café in Vello is steps away from the start of the cycle path; you can pick up snacks or sandwiches to have at the rest stops along the way. For a larger meal, **Trattoria Glisenti** in Vello specialises in dishes made with Lake Iseo fish, served on a scenic terrace overlooking the lake. Make sure to book ahead if visiting on weekends or in summer, as outdoor tables fill up quickly. In Toline, there's a small kiosk on the lakeside.

for views over Monte Isola, the largest lake island in southern Europe. The first section out of Vello is along a dedicated cycle path, then it's necessary to ride along the road, but traffic is not usually a concern. In Sale Marasino, there are the ruins of a brick furnace right along a road, as well as two street food stands

Lake Iseo

Also known as Sebino, Lake Iseo is the smallest of Italy's big lakes, measuring just 25km from north to south. The lake is a popular weekend attraction for locals from Bergamo and Brescia, but sees a fraction of international tourists compared to Lake Como and Lake Garda.

Serious cyclists might consider riding a full loop around the lake – the entire perimeter measures about 65km, a mix of dedicated cycle paths, lakeside promenades and secondary roads. Besides the Vello–Toline cycle path, the most scenic section is between Lovere and Riva di Solto on the western shore of the lake; the road travels right along the lakeside in a scenic succession of loops and bends.

serving fried freshwater fish and chips. Sulzano was made famous by land artist Christo's artwork *The Floating Piers*, realised in 2016, connecting the town to Monte Isola via a saffron-coloured walkway floating on Lake Iseo. Both Sale Marasino and Sulzano are on the train line, if you choose to return by train.

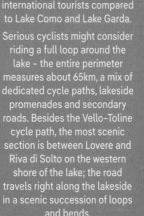

14

Pista Ciclopedonale del Lago di Varese

AGF SRL/ALAMY STOCK PHOTO ©

Lake Varese

DURATION	DIFFICULTY	DISTANCE	START/END
2.5hr	Intermediate	29km	Gavirate

TERRAIN	Paved

Varese is known as the 'town of seven lakes', being located in the vicinity of a variety of glacial lakes, from grand Lake Maggiore to diminutive Lake Ganna, only a few hundred metres across. This itinerary starts and ends in nearby Gavirate, taking you around Varese's namesake lake, a 28km loop path through quaint lakeside villages, decadent fin de siècle villas, wetlands popular with bird-watchers and Unesco-listed prehistoric sites. The route is entirely paved and on dedicated lanes, with minimal ups and downs. The road surface can be rough, though, and there are many bridges, making it unsuitable for bike trolleys.

Bike Hire

E-Bike Travel is a quick walk from Gavirate station and rents a variety of e-bikes from €30 for half-day rental. I Giardini del Lago in Schiranna (useful if driving) has several city bikes for rentals for €5 per hour.

Starting point

Gavirate station is just a short ride from the cycle path. Trains run hourly from Milan Cadorna station and bikes are allowed on board with a €3.50 surcharge. Those driving can use the large car park in Schiranna.

01 Exit Gavirate station and turn right down Via Roma, then continue left down Via Quattro Novembre. Follow the road as it bends right past a car park, then take Via Marconi, the first on the left, and continue straight until you reach the lake shore. The itinerary starts right in front of Golden Beach. Continue left to follow the loop in a clockwise direction.

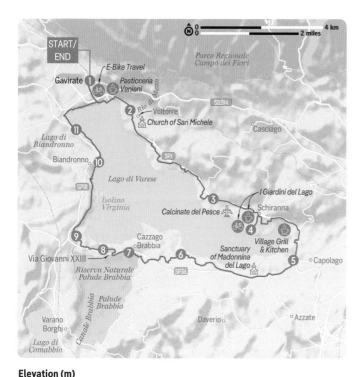

Elevation (m)

Isolino Virginia

Despite the name, Isolino Virginia is not an actual island, but a sedimentary formation resulting from layers of civilisation and millennia of history. Approximately 4m of archaeological deposits have built up over 4000 years, from the early Neolithic era to the Bronze Age, even though the area has been inhabited ever since the paleolithic. The first inhabitants lived on stilt dwellings, built with a dual purpose – escaping predators and being closer to their food source, freshwater fish. The site is one of the most important prehistoric sites in northern Italy and it's Unesco-listed, alongside 111 other alpine pile dwelling sites in Italy, France and Switzerland.

02 The path continues through a forest, moving away from the edge of the lake. Follow the brown signs marked 'Percorso Cicloturistico', as the itinerary often weaves and bends to avoid roads and villages. After leaving Gavirate, you'll cross Voltorre, where it's possible to visit the 12th-century Church of San Michele and its cloister.

03 Shortly afterwards, the itinerary continues past some 17th-century farmhouses arranged around a communal patio, showing a glimpse of the rural past of this part of Lombardy. One of them also houses a restaurant and offers accommodation. Keep riding a further 2km to reach the glider airport of Calcinate del Pesce, right on the edge of the lake.

04 Keep riding to reach Schiranna, the main *lido* (lake beach) of Varese. The itinerary actually bypasses the lakeside at this stage, but if you want to have a break and look at the lake just turn right down Via Macchi and continue past the big car park. There is also a waterpark and open-air swimming pool right by the lake, open in summer.

05 The next part of the itinerary will move away from the lake, crossing areas of great natural beauty. Next up is the hamlet of Capolago, marking the easternmost tip of the lake, then continues to Azzate, past the Sanctuary of Madonnina del Lago. During this part of the itinerary, sections of the path run parallel to the road, but there's always a dedicated lane divided from the cars by a ditch.

06 Continuing along the southern shore of the lake, you'll enter the municipality of Bodio Lomnago, where you can veer from the cycle path to check out the offbeat lake beach and see the remains of a prehistoric stilt village, one of Lombardy's Unesco Heritage Sites.

07 Keep riding to reach Cazzago Brabbia, known for its *ghiacciaie*, 19th-century houses with a cone roof where ice used to refrigerate lake fish was stored year-round. As you proceed along the cycleway, pay attention to the brown signs as there's an underpass to avoid crossing busy Via Giovanni XXIII. Don't attempt riding down as it's extremely steep; get off and walk your bike instead.

08 The itinerary now enters Palude Brabbia, a protected marshland interesting for bird-watchers, as it's both a nesting area for water birds and a rest stop for migratory species making their way from the Alps to the Mediterranean. Over 200 species of birds and mammals have been recorded, including shrews, skunks and rare water birds like grebes and water rails, the symbol of the site.

09 Leaving the protected area behind, you'll notice a turn-off for the 12km cycle path circling nearby Lake Comabbio – the surface is largely unpaved, suitable only for gravel and mountain bikes.

10 Continue along the path surrounded by trees and reeds to reach Biandronno. Between April and October, you can leave your bike and take a ferry to Isolino Virginia, the largest prehistoric stilt site in the area. There's a museum and a nature trail, where visitors can see the replica of a prehistoric stilt house.

11 The last section between Biandronno and Gavirate is the most scenic, running right along the edge of the lake and past some stunning lakeside villas. On a clear day, the Prealps and Monte Rosa are an impressive sight, towering over Lake Varese and nearby villages. Before reaching Gavirate again, you'll ride past Lake Biandronno – a humid bog only fed by rainwater, fast disappearing as rain gets scarcer every year in northern Italy. Cross the wooden bridge carefully, and after a few hundred metres you'll be back in Gavirate, where the tour started.

☕ Take a Break

Before or after your bike ride, make sure you stop to try *brutti ma buoni,* crumbly cookies made with almonds and egg whites and Gavirate's best known export. The recipe was created in 1878 at **Pasticceria Veniani,** still open today. A nice place to pick up a packed lunch or sit for a light meal in a secluded garden is **I Giardini del Lago** in Schiranna, and for a larger meal a good option is **Village Grill & Kitchen,** 2km after Schiranna along the cycle path.

SANTIAGO URQUIJO/GETTY IMAGES ©

Lake Varese

Glide over Lake Varese

Ride along the lake on a sunny day, and you're bound to see gliders riding the winds over the lake, making for the landing strip right on the edge of the lake. Calcinate del Pesce is home to Aero Club Adele Orsi, the largest glider airport in Italy, dedicated to local entrepreneur and gliding pioneer Adele Orsi, who broke many speed records for both single and double gliders. It is possible to arrange gliding lessons and flights over the lake, also offering wonderful views over the Campo dei Fiori and Monte Rosa massifs.

Also Try...

Naviglio Pavese

ALEXANDRE ROTENBERG/SHUTTERSTOCK ©

Naviglio Pavese

DURATION	DIFFICULTY	DISTANCE
3hr	Easy	30km

Linking the Darsena of Milan to the Ticino river in Pavia, the Naviglio Pavese is another of Milan's surviving waterways. It was dug in the 19th century during the rule of Napoleon, with the twin purpose to irrigate the fields south of the city, and connect Milan to the Po.

Similarly to Naviglio Grande, Naviglio Pavese also has a cycleway running along the towpath. Start riding at the Darsena, paying attention along the first 5km when the road is shared with cars. After exiting Milan, you'll find yourself immersed in the agricultural landscapes of southern Lombardy. Eight kilometres before reaching Pavia, stop at the Certosa, a monumental complex in Gothic-Renaissance style including a church and a monastery.

AbbracciaMI

DURATION	DIFFICULTY	DISTANCE
5hr	Difficult	68km

Also known as 'Milan's Circle Line', AbbracciaMI is a ring-shaped itinerary all around the municipality of Milan, linking existing cycle paths to minor roads and paths through the city parks. The itinerary was created during the 2020 lockdown by a group of cycling enthusiasts, since local laws forbade cycling outside of the city limits.

The entire AbbracciaMI loop is 68km long, travelling through lesser-visited neighbourhoods, along rivers and waterways, and across more than 20 parks. Along the way there are also several *metropolitana* and train stations to cut the trip short. The itinerary is marked by red and white signs with a ring-shaped logo. Download a GPX file on at bici.milano.it/abbracciami.

Sanctuary of the Madonna del Ghisallo

Bellagio–Ghisallo

DURATION	DIFFICULTY	DISTANCE
2hr	Difficult	10km

This is one of Lombardy's iconic climbs, taking you to a place that every Italian cyclist has visited at least once in their lifetime – the Sanctuary of the Madonna del Ghisallo, the patron saint of cyclists.

There are several routes to reach Ghisallo, but the 'classic' itinerary starts at Bellagio, and takes approximately 10km to climb 600m, with an average gradient of 6%. Unless you are an experienced road cyclist and a good climber, it's recommended to attempt it with an e-bike. At the top, you'll find the sanctuary with a collection of vintage bikes and jerseys left by cyclists throughout the decades, and the Ghisallo Cycling Museum (open March to November) with exhibits about the history of cycling in Italy.

Lake Comabbio

DURATION	DIFFICULTY	DISTANCE
1hr	Intermediate	12km

Are you looking for a way to extend your ride around Lake Varese? Nearby Lake Comabbio, one of Varese's seven lakes, is ringed by a 12.5km cycle path, connected to the cycle path around Lake Varese by a 4km connection running alongside Palude Brabbia.

Coming from Lake Varese, the connection to Lake Comabbio is well signposted, just after the village of Cazzago Brabbia. The Lake Comabbio cycle path and the connection are mainly unpaved, suitable for gravel and mountain bikes. The itinerary takes you on a journey between the placid waters of this tiny lake and the surrounding forest, with short but frequent ups and downs that deter most visitors – meaning you're likely to have the place to yourself.

IMAGEBROKER/HERBERT BERGER/GETTY IMAGES ©

Lio Piccolo (p122), Venice Lagoon

Northeast Italy

15 **Ciclovia del Sole**

A former rail line takes you across the flatlands of rural Emilia, through scenic villages and country roads. **p108**

16 **Ciclabile del Conca**

Discover the hills and villages of Romagna via a nature oasis, vineyards and farmlands before reaching the Adriatic beaches. **p112**

17 **Ciclopedonale Giordano Cottur**

A hilly journey from the Mediterranean to the Alps, passing scenic tunnels and viaducts. **p116**

18 **Giro Laguna**

A 40km loop path through the Venice Lagoon connects seaside resorts and villages, islets and sandbanks. **p120**

19 **Ciclabile Valsugana**

Cross Valsugana following the course of the Brenta river past orchards, vineyards, historic villages and alpine lakes. **p124**

20 **Ciclabile dell'Adige**

A paved and well-maintained route through the valley created by the Adige river. **p128**

Explore

Northeast Italy

Northeast Italy includes a vast and diverse area, stretching from the windswept border town of Trieste, across the peaks of the Dolomites dividing Italy from Austria and Slovenia, all the way south to Emilia-Romagna, by way of the eastern part of the Po Valley. This diversity translates into a vast array of cycle itineraries – from gravel escapades along the hills of Romagna, to family-friendly cycle paths along alpine valleys, and routes across the remotest islands in the Venice Lagoon, a world away from the tourist-packed city. Commitment to sustainability and good facilities for cyclists make northeast Italy one of the best places in the country for bike-loving visitors.

Trentino-Alto Adige/ South Tyrol

This is Italy's northernmost region, made up of the two cities of Trento and Bolzano, the surrounding valleys and mountains. This is your destination if you're planning to ride among alpine meadows covered in wildflowers, sparkling lakes and the rocky spires of the Dolomites. To make things even better, Trentino-Alto Adige has an excellent network of cycle paths, as well as a system of bike buses, bike trains and even Bicigrill, rest stops for cyclists. It's recommended to plan a cycling trip to this region in summer – some of the best cycle paths are located at higher altitudes and are covered in snow during the winter months.

Trieste

Extending on a narrow strip of land between the Karstic Alps and the Adriatic Sea, Trieste is one of Italy's most fascinating towns, where Italian, Austrian and Balkan influences blend to create an atmosphere that is at once international and deeply unique. There's nowhere else in Italy where sea and mountains are quite so close, and the surrounds of Trieste are crisscrossed with a variety of cycle itineraries connecting the city to forests, vineyards, mountains and Habsburg-era castles. Keep an eye out for the *bora*, the northeasterly wind that often whips the city – but if you are brave enough to go out riding on a windy day, you'll have the path to yourself.

WHEN TO GO

Summer is the best time to travel to Trentino-Alto Adige for bicycle tourists, since high-altitude cycle paths are closed in winter. This is also when the region is at its busiest – visit in May or September to escape Italian holidaying crowds.

It's possible to cycle the rest of northeast Italy year-round, though perhaps avoiding the cold and rain of the winter months.

Venice Lagoon

Escape over-tourism and discover the peculiar ecosystem of the Venice Lagoon, made up of low-lying islands, tidelands and canals. A system of cycle paths and eco-ferries connects different islands within the lagoon, making it a great place to travel around by bike, stopping at historic villages and viewpoints where you can just make out the bell towers and domes of Venice. History buffs will also enjoy riding along the nearby Piave and Sile rivers, the location of decisive battles during the Great War, while families can opt to ride around Jesolo, an Adriatic resort town with excellent facilities.

Emilia-Romagna

Emilia-Romagna is Italy's foodie heartland, where iconic products and recipes such as *tagliatelle alla bolognese* and *parmigiano reggiano* come from. The northern half of the region is covered by the flat vastness of the Po Valley, where locals have used bicycles to get around for the best part of a century, and new cycle paths such as the Ciclovia del Sole make

TRANSPORT

The main motorways in this part of Italy are the A4 connecting Turin and Milan to Venice and Trieste, and the A1 between Milan and Rome via Emilia-Romagna. All the itineraries included in this chapter can be reached by public transport – bicycles are allowed on board regional trains with a surcharge (generally around €3.50), and on Intercity trains with prior booking. On high-speed trains, bikes need to be in bags.

travelling between towns easy and hassle-free. The southern half includes the Apennine foothills and mountains, with bike itineraries snaking through remote valleys, following gravel paths along riverbanks that include stops to appreciate the gastronomic excellences of this region.

 WHAT'S ON

Venice Carnival

Annual festival held in February featuring masked parades through the streets of Venice and exclusive balls in the city's *palazzi*.

Sounds of the Dolomites

Open-air summer concerts in various natural locations that can only be accessed on foot.

Italian Bike Festival

A three-day event in September dedicated to the world of cycling in Misano Adriatico (Romagna), including a Granfondo cycle race.

Resources

Emilia-Romagna Turismo (emiliaromagnaturismo.it/en) Cycling information and routes all over Emilia-Romagna.

Visit Trentino (visittrentino. info/it/guida/sport-estate/ ciclabili) Maps and information about cycle paths in Trentino.

Venezia e Lagune Bike (veneziaelagunebike.it/en/ routes) Maps and itineraries for cycle routes around the Venice Lagoon.

 WHERE TO STAY

Hotels and guesthouses in the region are usually ready to welcome cyclists, but it's worth calling ahead if you are travelling with your own bike. There are also some bike hotels, with excellent facilities for cyclists including bike rooms, workshops and bike-specific information. Two examples are Hotel Germania in Jesolo (Venice Lagoon) and Hotel Dory in Riccione (Romagna). Many hotels in Trentino-Alto Adige and along the Adriatic coast offer half-board and full-board packages at advantageous prices, especially if you are travelling with your family. If you prefer self-catering accommodation, there are apartments for rent all over northeast Italy, though they are usually in short supply during the summer months.

15

Ciclovia del Sole

DURATION	DIFFICULTY	DISTANCE	START/END
4hr	intermediate	40km	Mirandola/ Osteria Nuova

TERRAIN		Paved

Elevation (m)

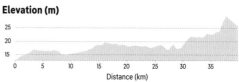

The Ciclovia del Sole between Mirandola and Bologna stretches for 40km along a former rail line, across the flatlands of rural Emilia, a territory that is home to artists, songwriters and food lovers, so iconic it has been called 'Italy in miniature'. The cycleway passes rarely visited local villages, some still bearing the scars of the 2012 earthquake, agricultural landscapes and an interesting nature reserve. The itinerary is flat and almost entirely paved, and includes some short sections along village streets and scenic country roads.

Bike Hire

You can rent bikes (regular and electric) from eXtraBO, a tourist information centre located in Bologna's Piazza del Nettuno. You can also get information and assistance about trains and purchase maps here.

Starting Point

The cycle path starts at Mirandola station, 40 minutes by train from Bologna Centrale, and ends at Osteria Nuova train station, 15 minutes from Bologna. Bikes are allowed on trains with a €3.50 supplement.

01 The Ciclovia del Sole was created thanks to the conversion of the former Bologna–Verona railway, which now travels a short distance away. It includes long, straight-as-an-arrow sections running parallel to the railway, and sections alongside existing cycle paths when it crosses towns and villages. The start of the cycleway is at the end of an alleyway to the right of Mirandola train station. The motto of the Ciclovia del Sole is 'Follow the Sun' – you'll notice a big yellow sun painted on the cycle

Eurovelo 7

The Ciclovia del Sole is part of the Eurovelo 7, a trans-Europe cycle route connecting Norway's Nordkapp to Malta. The entire route is 7400km long and travels through nine different countries; the itinerary includes a mixture of cycle paths and secondary roads, but work is currently under-way to open more dedicated sections. In Italy you can cycle along dedicated paths along three stretches of the Eurovelo 7 – from the Brenner Pass to Verona along the Adige river; from Peschiera del Garda to Mantua (p90); and along the Ciclovia del Sole.

path, used to mark the way along the whole route. The historic centre of Mirandola is quite far from the station; to visit, cycle west for 5km from the station along Via Gramsci until you reach Castle of the Pico, once home to a famous Renaissance philosopher.

02 Just before entering the San Felice sul Panaro, follow the signs pointing right then left along Via Canalino, then cycle following the railway again until you reach an underpass. Cross over to the other side to enter San Felice. On Friday, the market is on – perfect for picking up some packed lunch.

03 In front of San Felice sul Panaro station, turn left following the Ciclovia del Sole signs; keep following the suns painted on the road until you reach the dedicated cycleway again. Then it's a long 4.5km stretch to the next village.

04 Street-art lovers should set some time aside to visit Camposanto, home to 30 large-scale murals painted by local artists during the Quadricromie art festival. You'll see some around the pillars supporting the station, including one dedicated to 'Santo Pedaleone' and 'Santa Pedaleona', protectors of cyclists.

05 After Camposanto, follow the cycleway up the riverbanks of the Panaro – it's the only uphill section along the entire way, but it's very brief. Ride down and continue along another long, straight section. Along the Ciclovia del Sole, former stations have been converted into 'bike stops', with racks, picnic tables, water fountain and a bike stand complete with tools. One of the nicest is in Bolognina, about 3km from Camposanto.

06 Shortly after Bolognina, the itinerary abandons the railway and continues left along an unpaved section about 1km long. When it ends, turn right onto Via del Papa and ride along the cycle path on the left-hand side until you reach Crevalcore. Make sure you stop to visit the tiny Leo Preti Museum, the smallest in Italy, with a collection of puppets and puppet theatres.

07 Ride with caution around Crevalcore following the yellow sun until you leave town, cross another underpass and start cycling along the railway once again. The next section of the path runs between the railway and a canal for about 7km, until a left turn just opposite a 'bike stop'.

08 The Ciclovia del Sole bypasses the centre of San Giovanni in Persiceto, one of the prettiest towns along the route. It's worth parking your bike at the train station and going for a walk around. Make sure you stop in Piazzetta Betlemme, completely covered in cinema-inspired murals by Gino Pellegrini, a San Giovanni native who worked in Hollywood as a set designer.

MICHELE D'AMICO SUPERSKY77/GETTY IMAGES ©

Spoonbill, La Bora Nature Reserve

☕ Take a Break

Antica Osteria Mirasole in the centre of San Giovanni in Persiceto was awarded the title of best trattoria in Italy in 2020 and 2021. It serves traditional Bolognese cuisine, and is especially known for its homemade pasta and local charcuterie. Another good option in summer is **Azienda Agricola Valle Torretta**, a farm-to-table restaurant with creative vegetarian dishes. It's located 3.5km east of Crevalcore, and is also home to an artist collective. Along the cycleway, there are rest stops with benches, picnic tables and water fountains.

09 After San Giovanni, the cycleway winds down minor country roads and paths, always marked by the big yellow sun. This is where you'll find the entrance to La Bora, a rescue centre rehabilitating native turtles. Shortly afterwards the path joins the railway again for the last 4km stretch to Osteria Nuova, including a scenic covered bridge.

La Bora Nature Reserve

On the outskirts of San Giovanni in Persiceto, the Ciclovia del Sole passes by the entrance of La Bora, a nature reserve dedicated to the protection of the Po Valley ecosystem and its native fauna. There is a small visitor centre, and it is possible to walk around a nature trail that offers views over two lakes, and a small patch of lowland forest, almost entirely wiped out during the industrialisation of the Po Valley. There is also a rehabilitation project to repopulate swamp turtles, a native species almost entirely wiped out by other turtle species.

10 The dedicated cycleway ends at Osteria Nuova train station, from where there are twice-hourly trains back to Bologna. Those who want to ride longer can continue following the signs another 10km all the way to the centre of Bologna, but there are some sections along busy state roads. The conversion of the final stretch of railway is currently ongoing, due to be completed in 2026.

16

Ciclabile del Conca

DURATION	DIFFICULTY	DISTANCE	START/END
3hr	Intermediate	25km	Cattolica/ Misano Adriatico

TERRAIN		Gravel

LUKASZ SZWAJ/SHUTTERSTOCK ©

Sangiovese grapes

This 25km unpaved scenic ride is ideal for first-time gravel riders, and for those wanting to leave the bustle of the riviera behind to discover the hills and villages of Romagna. The Conca cycle path develops around the banks of the river of the same name, on the border between the municipalities of Misano Adriatico and Cattolica, stretching as far as the offbeat village of Morciano di Romagna. The cycle path crosses a nature oasis with excellent bird-watching, vineyards and farmlands, before reaching the golden Adriatic beaches.

Bike Hire

Via Panoramica in Gabicce Monte has an excellent selection of bikes, perfect to tackle this itinerary. Gabicce Monte is 5km from Cattolica but can deliver bikes to the start of the cycle path upon request.

Starting Point

Cattolica, the starting point of this cycle path, is 3km from the Cattolica-San Giovanni-Gabicce station, and 2km from the Misano Adriatico station, both on the Bologna–Ancona railway line.

01 The Ciclabile del Conca runs along the banks of the Conca river, from its mouth on the Adriatic Sea to the hills of Romagna. This itinerary starts in Cattolica, and follows the left bank of the river, cycling towards the hills with the river on your right-hand side. (You can also cycle in the opposite direction if you prefer, starting in Misano Adriatico.)

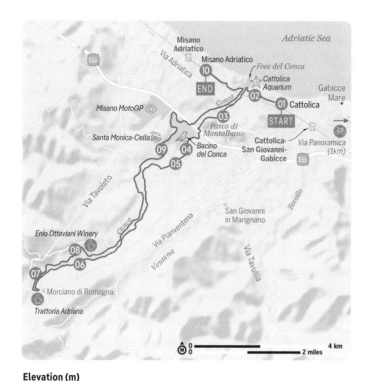

Romagna & Sangiovese

This cycleway is probably at its best in late summer, when the days are still warm. September is a really good month, as it's harvest time for the vineyards surrounding the path. Most of the grapes you'll see are Sangiovese, one of the most popular grape varieties in Italy, and the main ingredient in the blend used to make Chianti. Romagna is the region where Sangiovese is most commonly enjoyed as a single-variety wine. Thanks to its acidity and medium body, it's the perfect accompaniment to *piadina*, a flatbread found everywhere in Romagna, as well as fresh pasta, grilled meats and other specialities.

Elevation (m)

02 Cycle down Corso Italia until you reach the Cattolica Aquarium. The path starts in the Foce del Conca park – from here, ride down to the riverbank and turn left. The first part of the trail is quite muddy, but after a few hundred metres there's the option to ride up to an embankment, with a flat gravel trail running on top.

03 After about a kilometre, the cycle path leaves the embankment and loops away from the river, climbing a little. There's a spot to sit down, overlooking the Parco di Montalbano, to catch your breath if you're not used to hills. Next take the left fork and continue cycling along a good gravel path, until you reach the Conca dam. Ride through the underpass and turn right into Via Frassineto – cycle for a few hundred metres past the water processing plant, then follow the signs and take a right turn to join the cycle path again.

04 You'll now be cycling past the Bacino del Conca (Conca basin), an excellent bird-watching spot. There's a small hide set up for birding enthusiasts; visiting species include black stork, great white heron, pelican and even flamingos sometimes.

05 Keep riding along the basin until the path leaves the riverbank for a short while to avoid a golf club. Follow the signs to rejoin the cycle path, riding along an excellent shaded gravel path. After a couple of kilometres there's another option for a break, where there's a little playground and kiosk open in summer.

06 Ride another 3km following the riverbank fringed by reeds, with the river waters progressively turning paler and faster, a sign that you're heading towards the hills. You'll arrive in Morciano di Romagna, a historic *borgo* worth visiting for its futuristic-style square and cobbled streets lined with colourful painted houses. Morciano is the turning point for this itinerary – from here, you will start your return journey along the other side of the Conca river.

07 Follow Via Matteotti in Morciano to cross the bridge running over the Conca – make sure you stay in the right-hand lane reserved for cyclists and pedestrians, as traffic can be intense. On the opposite side, follow the path leading down to the riverside, proceeding with caution along the steep descent.

08 The first part of the path on this side of the Conca can be quite muddy, and it may be necessary to push your bike to avoid getting bogged. After 3.5km from the start, keep your eyes open for the signs pointing to the Enio Ottaviani Winery, inviting tired cyclists to stop for a glass of wine. Try to resist the temptation of having too many glasses of Sangiovese, as there are still about 9km to go!

09 The path on this side is in much better conditions and easier to follow, but be sure to keep an eye open as this area is very popular with Nordic walkers, especially during the weekend. Before reaching the Conca dam, you'll pass a sport fishing club and the village of Santa Monica-Cella, very close to the Misano MotoGP race track, dedicated to the late MotoGP racer Marco Simoncelli. Yes, those strange sounds you might hear are the rumblings of motorbikes.

10 The cycle path ends right opposite where it started, at the mouth of the Conca river. Before heading back, have a look around Portoverde, an upscale scenic marina and residential area, where you can enjoy a spritz as a reward after riding from the Adriatic to the Romagna hills and back.

☕ Take a Break

The turning point for this ride is Morciano di Romagna, where there are a few options for a good local meal featuring fresh pasta like *cappelletti in brodo* with cheese filling, a Romagna speciality. **Trattoria Adriana** comes highly recommended, but during the off season it's often closed on the weekend. Another option is the **Enio Ottaviani Winery**, where you can stop for a quick glass of organic wine or enjoy a complete wine-tasting experience, including a selection of cured meats and cheeses from local producers.

DOCTOR_J/SHUTTERSTOCK ©

Morciano

Morciano, Birthplace of Artists

It's hard to believe that sleepy Morciano is the birthplace of not one but two of Italy's great sculptors. One of them is Umberto Boccioni (1882–1916), creator of the iconic Futurist sculpture *Unique Forms of Continuity in Space*, found on the back of the Italian 20¢ coin and housed at the Metropolitan Museum in New York. The other is Arnaldo Pomodoro (b 1926), a postmodern sculptor known for his artworks made with metal spheres. In the main square of Morciano you can see *Colpo d'Ala*, a bronze sculpture rem- iniscent of a bird taking flight, actually dedicated to Boccioni by Arnaldo Pomodoro himself.

17

SOPOTNICKI/SHUTTERSTOCK ©

Trieste

Ciclopedonale Giordano Cottur

DURATION	DIFFICULTY	DISTANCE	START/END
2hr	Difficult	13km	Trieste/Mihele (Slovenia)

TERRAIN	Mostly unpaved, some sections paved

From the heart of Trieste to the wilderness of the Slovenian Karst, the Ciclopedonale Giordano Cottur (also known as Ciclabile Val Rosandra) is a journey from the Mediterranean to the Alps in just over 13km, following the route of a former Austro-Hungarian railway, passing scenic tunnels and viaducts. The cycle path was restored and dedicated to Trieste cyclist Giordano Cottur in 2010; it's paved for the first 4.5km from Trieste, and unpaved for the rest of the way. This route is uphill – mountain bikes are preferred over gravel bikes, since there are sections with loose rocks.

Bike Hire

Trieste Green Tour hires mountain bikes, regular and electric, from €30 per day. Some hotels in Trieste have city bikes for rent, but these are only suitable for the initial paved section.

Starting Point

The cycle path starts from the car park in Via Gramsci, 2km from the centre of Trieste. The section along Via del Molino a Vento is quite steep and you may have to push your bike up.

01 The path follows the course of a former railway, built in Austro-Hungarian times to connect the Adriatic coast to the existing rail line between Istria and the heart of the empire. Due to the karstic nature of the territory, which will become visible as you make your way towards the Slovenian border, the rail line never operated at full capacity and ceased operations in 1959. The Ciclopedonale Giordano Cottur starts at the car park in Via Gramsci, in Rione San Giacomo. Away from the glitzy

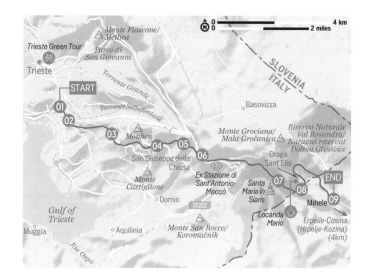

TOP TIP:

When you're riding through the tunnels on this route, be aware that while the longest tunnels are illuminated, several shorter ones are dark, so be sure to proceed with caution even if you have headlights.

downtown cafes, San Giacomo is very much a 'local' neighbourhood, where family-owned shops outnumber supermarkets. Leave San Giacomo church behind and ride two blocks, until you see a car park on your right-hand side. Cycle down the hill to get to the start of the itinerary.

02 The path is entirely uphill, rising slowly but steadily and gaining approximately 400m altitude difference over 14km. You'll start climbing as soon as you pass the abandoned checkpoint right at the start. Make sure you get into an easy gear that will allow you to pedal without exerting yourself too much. The first 4.5km of the cycleway are paved, rising steadily and crossing residential districts

in the outskirts of Trieste. The path may be shared with runners, families and people walking their dogs, so proceed with caution. The itinerary also crosses a few bridges, where you'll get scenic views over Istria and the waters of the Adriatic.

03 About 3km into the ride, you'll pass a sign pointing to a bike shop, useful in case of need. Ride on to cross a bridge with a spectacular view, with the Port of Trieste on one side and the Karst with vegetable gardens on the mountainside on the other.

04 You'll finally have the feeling of leaving Trieste and the Mediterranean behind once you cycle under the

Bora

You can't talk about Trieste without mentioning the *bora*, a northeasterly wind that is most common in the winter, blowing in gusts that regularly exceed 120km/h. According to legend, Bora was the most beautiful of Aeolus' daughters. She fell in love with the warrior Tergesteo, who was then killed by her jealous father. Moved by her sorrow, Aeolus allowed the two lovers to be reunited for a few days each year – on those days, the *bora* blows. The *bora* has inspired generations of Triestine writers, poets and artists – there's even a museum dedicated to the *bora*, the Museo della Bora, which hosts workshops and child-friendly activities.

motorway, and the path turns into gravel. Ride down to join the path running through Val Rosandra, lined with secular trees, slowly revealing its wild, pristine beauty.

05 It's impossible to get lost – the gravel path is wide and very easy to follow. Less than a kilometre from when the paved path stops, ride through the first tunnel, which was dug almost 200 years ago in record time, followed by a scenic curved viaduct supported by limestone, also dating back to Austro-Hungarian times. The cycleway is an excellent way to explore the karstic characteristics of this territory. You'll ride through canyons and caves, under overhanging shelves of rock and across tunnels where you might be greeted with a gust of *bora*.

06 After the viaduct, the cycle path passes by the village of San Giuseppe della Chiusa, and 1km later you'll reach the abandoned station of Sant'Antonio Moccò, with tables and chairs perfect for a break.

07 A further 2km down the road, keep your eyes peeled for the tiny church of Santa Maria in Siaris, a diminutive stone construction surrounded by rocks and forest, which can only be reached on foot. The church has stood ever since the 14th century, and it is still visited yearly by pilgrims in May and August.

08 Shortly after that, you'll notice a sign marking the Italy–Slovenia border. The path crosses into Slovenia for a few hundred metres, then loops back into Italy heading towards the border village of Draga Sant'Elia, once a busy Austro-Hungarian border post and now a base to explore hiking paths heading to the heart of Val Rosandra.

09 The cycleway crosses into Slovenia again about 2km after Draga Sant'Elia. The official end of the itinerary is Erpelle-Cosina (Hrpelje-Kozina), about 5km beyond the Slovenian border, where the rail line used to have its terminus. However, the dedicated cycle path ends at the hamlet of Mihele. To return to Trieste, turn your bike and roll downhill all the way, paying attention to the loose rocks along the way.

☕ Take a Break

Locanda Mario in Draga Sant'Elia, the last village before the Slovenian border, is a no-frills eatery offering local specialities including *ljubljanska* (schnitzel stuffed with ham and cheese), fried frogs legs and venison gnocchi, washed down with wines from the Karst. There are also a couple of places to eat in Mihele, the Slovenian village at the end of the cycle path.

Alternatively, head to one of Trieste's **buffet restaurants** and get a sandwich with home-cooked, hand-cut ham to take away and enjoy it at the tables opposite the abandoned Sant'Antonio Moccò station.

Karst tunnel near Triests

Giordano Cottur

This cycle path is named after Giordano Cottur (1914–2006), a road cyclist and sport director from Trieste. He was especially active in the 1940s, placing third three times at the Giro d'Italia behind the great Coppi and Bartali. Cottur is especially known for the victory in his native Trieste in 1946, when the city was still contested between Italy and Yugoslavia in the WWII aftermath. A group of Yugoslavian protesters threw rocks at the peloton, and most cyclists retired from the race – save for a group including Cottur, who went on to win. After retiring from cycling, he opened Cicli Cottur, a bicycle store in Trieste still active today.

18

Best for

WILDLIFE

Giro Laguna

DURATION	DIFFICULTY	DISTANCE	START/END
4hr	Intermediate	40km	Lido di Jesolo

TERRAIN	Mostly paved, some unpaved sections

TANJA VIGANO/SHUTTERSTOCK ©

White heron, Venice Lagoon

Leave the crowded *calli* of Venice behind and head to the wilderness and unique ecosystem of the Venice Lagoon on this 40km loop path connecting the seaside resort of Lido di Jesolo to the villages of Cavallino and Treporti, and then to Lio Piccolo and Lio Maggiore, a collection of islets and sandbanks shaped by the tides and the currents of the Adriatic. You can ride the complete loop between April and October, when the eco-ferries operate – otherwise ride 27km until Lio Piccolo, then ride back or have a bike shuttle pick you up.

Bike Hire

Hotel Germania in Jesolo is the best organised bike hotel in the area, open February to November, with a bike room and facilities for cyclists. It offers bike shuttle and rental services, with a selection of mountain bikes, regular and electric.

Starting Point

This route starts in Lido di Jesolo, where you'll find most accommodation options. If you are staying in Venice, it is possible to catch a ferry to Punta Sabbioni, just 3km from the beginning of the route.

01 Ride west down Via Dante Alighieri and Via Bafile, lined with shops and restaurants, with a comfortable cycle path on the left-hand side of the road. Keep going straight until the road changes name, becoming Via Giuseppe Verdi. Turn left into Via Pigafetta and keep riding until you reach a T-junction at Viale Padania, where you'll be turning left. Soon you will leave the bustle of Lido di Jesolo behind and enter the Venice Lagoon, a liminal space where the boundary between land and water is not always clear.

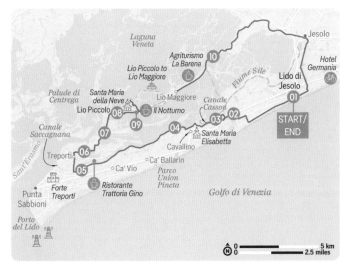

LUANA77/SHUTTERSTOCK ©

Elevation (m)

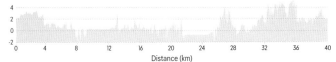

Distance (km)

02 Follow the cycle path over the bridge that crosses the Sile river, where it's worth stopping for pictures of Jesolo port with the iconic *bilance*, old fishing machines connected to stilt houses. Take a sharp left and ride under the bridge to join the cycle path along the Canale Casson.

03 The Canale Casson was dug in the 17th century by the Venice Republic, to connect the lagoon to the Sile river, which could be sailed all the way to the city of Treviso. You'll be riding along the canal for about 2km, watching egrets and herons swoop down between the reeds and the emerald-coloured water. The canal cycle path ends in Cavallino, where you can have a break and visit the tiny church dedicated to Santa Maria Elisabetta.

04 Next follow the edge of the lagoon down Via Pordelio and Via della Marinona for about 6km. There's a new dedicated cycle path hanging over the lagoon continuing all the way to Treporti, but at the time of writing two sections were closed for maintenance and it was necessary to proceed along the road. This section is especially scenic at sunset, when the golden light illuminates the still waters turning them into a giant mirror.

Sant'Erasmo

Have you ever wondered where all the fruit and vegetables served in Venice's restaurants come from? The answer will be right in front of you as you stand on Punta Sabbioni – they come from Sant'Erasmo, a lagoon island also known as 'Venice's garden' ever since the time of the Serenissima Republic. Sant'Erasmo is especially known for its artichokes (pictured above) and asparagus, as well as its serene atmosphere away from the bustle of the city. Ferries to Sant'Erasmo depart hourly from Punta Sabbioni, and it's possible to ride around the island on a 9km loop.

05 When you reach the bridge over the Canale Saccagnana in Treporti, you have the option of taking a short detour. To do so, cycle down to Punta Sabbioni, where you can see the San Marco bell tower in the distance, and then continue all the way down to the lighthouse, marking the entrance to the Port of Venice. Then loop back towards Via degli Armeni, riding past Forte Treporti, a 19th-century military fortress. This will add approximately 6km to your itinerary.

06 Cross Canale Saccagnana and continue straight. Turn right in Via Saccagnana past the tiny cemetery, and keep going following the signs pointing towards Lio Piccolo. You're now in the heart of the Venetian Lagoon, riding on a sequence of islets separated by reeds, canals and vegetable gardens that supply many of Venice's upscale restaurants.

07 There's a small viewpoint on the left-hand side, about 3km before reaching Lio Piccolo. On the left, you can see the brightly painted houses of Burano, the Byzantine bell tower of Torcello and the gardens of Sant'Erasmo; on your right there's Lio Piccolo, surrounded by an endless expanse of reeds and water.

08 Lio Piccolo is now a sleepy hamlet with only 22 inhabitants, but it was a busy harbour in Roman times – remains of mosaics dating back to Imperial Rome have been found underwater. Nowadays, there are about 10 houses overlooking an unpaved square, with elegant Palazzo Boldù dating back to the 18th century, the church of Santa Maria della Neve and the bell tower, open during the weekends.

09 Keep riding, leaving Lio Piccolo behind, until you reach Il Notturno, a restaurant serving specialities made with local fish. This is where the paved road ends; if you have booked a ferry to take you across to Lio Maggiore, this is also where the boat will meet you.

10 To close the loop, ride along Via Lio Maggiore for about 8km until you reach Jesolo, from where you can then head back to Lido di Jesolo following the cycle path along Via Roma Destra.

☕ Take a Break

Between April and October, a great place for lunch is **Agriturismo La Barena** in Lio Maggiore, serving dishes made with locally grown vegetables and fish from the lagoon on a terrace overlooking a canal. Another popular option is **Il Notturno** in Lio Piccolo, run by a charismatic restaurateur and specialising in eels and other grilled fish. During the off season, there are fewer options; your best bet will be taking a packed lunch, or stopping at **Ristorante Trattoria Gino**, right on the edge of the Pordelio Canal in Cavallino-Treporti.

CHICCODODIFC/GETTY IMAGES ©

Lio Piccolo

Lio Maggiore & Lio Piccolo

Lio Maggiore and Lio Piccolo are not single islands, but archipelagos made up of lagoon islets separated by canals and covered with vegetable gardens, trees and shrubs. Lio Piccolo is the oldest settlement in the Venice Lagoon, and it is surrounded by tidelands and *valli di pesca*, lagoon areas where fish have been farmed since the Middle Ages. The channel between Lio Maggiore and Lio Piccolo has no bridges, so to travel between the two to complete the lagoon loop it is necessary to hop on the Blue Dream eco-ferry, active from April to October, from Wednesday to Sunday. Find more information at bluedreamcavallino.com.

19

Ciclabile Valsugana

DURATION	DIFFICULTY	DISTANCE	START/END
3hr	Intermediate	40km	San Cristo-foro/Grigno

TERRAIN		Paved

Mòcheni Valley

Cross Valsugana following the course of the Brenta river, from the deep-blue waters of Lake Caldonazzo to Grigno, the last town in Trentino before Veneto. Most of the itinerary is slightly downhill, so let your bike roll as you admire the beauty around you – apple orchards and vineyards, historic villages and alpine lakes, with the peaks of the Dolomites towering above. The itinerary is entirely paved, mostly on dedicated cycle lanes, and it runs very close to the Valsugana railway connecting Trento to Bassano del Grappa, offering several opportunities to cut the trip short if necessary.

Bike Hire

Valsugana Rent Bike offers bike rental from seven locations along the Ciclabile Valsugana, making it easy to pick up a bike in one place and drop it off elsewhere.

Starting Point

Start at San Cristoforo al Lago station on the Valsugana railway, about 30 minutes from Trento. Bikes are allowed on board trains, but there's limited space outside of high season.

01 The Ciclabile Valsugana starts in Valcanover, not far from the San Cristoforo al Lago train station. Get off the train and you'll see the cycle path right in front of you, on the other side of the tracks. Cross carefully, get on your bike and turn left, following the cycle/pedestrian path signs.

02 A few hundred metres down the road you'll notice the first highlight of the trip, Lake Caldonazzo, surrounded by the peaks of the

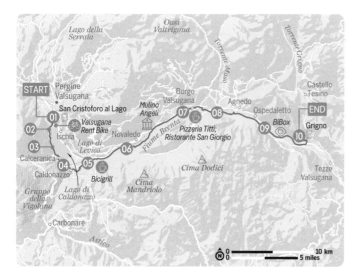

TOP TIP:

Bicigrill rest stops (p129) on this route have a useful table for small bike repairs and bike-specific information.

Elevation (m)

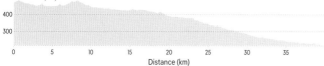

The Mòchena Language

The Mòcheni Valley is located just north of Lake Caldonazzo, and besides being an area of great natural beauty, it is also home to a tiny language minority – the *mòcheni*. The language is derived from High German, and was brought to the area by Bavarian migrants who settled in this remote valley in the 12th century. The language survived barely unchanged for centuries, and it is still spoken by approximately 1400 people in the valley and the town of Pergine Valsugana. The language was banned during Fascist times and almost disappeared, but it is now experiencing a sort of renaissance, thanks to local municipalities and culture groups organising free courses for residents.

Lagorai massif. The cycle path continues along a short section along a wooden bridge, suspended over the waters of the lake. It's the ideal place to stop and admire its blue waters, the lakeside villages of Ischia and Calceranica, and the Dolomites towering behind.

03 Keep following the profile of Lake Caldonazzo until you reach Calceranica. Leave the lake behind and follow the cycle path uphill through an underpass with bike-themed street art, until you reach the village. The dedicated path ends right before a roundabout; follow the bike markings on the road or the brown bike signs through the village. Just past the bridge over the Rio Mandola, in summer it's possible to visit the old Calceranica pyrite mine.

04 Keep following the itinerary towards Caldonazzo, just 2km south. The cycleway is on a separate lane running alongside SP1 – ride until you reach the San Sisto Church and Castel Trapp, a medieval manor turned riding school, and turn left down Via del Capitel, a tiny country road surrounded by apple orchards.

05 Turn left down Via Zaffo and continue down the first road on the right until you reach the Brenta river. From now on, the cycle path will run along the riverbank, frequently switching between the two sides. Here you also have the option of riding a further kilometre to visit Levico, known for its lake and thermal waters.

06 Riding along the Brenta, you'll pass the village of Novaledo followed by Marter, where in summer it's possible to visit the unique Museo degli Spaventapasseri (scarecrow museum), housed in Mulino Angeli, a former mill that once produced flour for the whole of Valsugana.

07 Keep cycling following the course of the Brenta to reach Borgo Valsugana, the prettiest *borgo* you'll encounter on this itinerary. In Borgo Valsugana, it's worth parking your bike to visit the historic centre – the *borgo vecio* on the left side of the river wasn't damaged in WWI, whereas the other half of the village was rebuilt after the war. The two parts of town are connected by the Ponte Veneziano (Venetian Bridge), dating back to the 15th century. If you have time, there's an interesting permanent exhibition about the Great War, when this area was along the border between Italy and the Austro-Hungarian Empire. The cycle path continues along the Brenta, and as you leave the village behind there's the option of continuing a further 10km uphill to Arte Sella, a land art exhibition open in summer.

08 After Borgo Valsugana, the itinerary continues for about 4km along the right bank of the Brenta, and it can be in the shade in the winter or early spring. After Castelnuovo, the cycle path moves to the left side of the river again. The last part of the ride is where the valley is at its narrowest, so be sure to pay close attention as some ice may last well into spring. Continue past the villages of Agnedo and Ospedaletto – the path is slightly downhill and it's very easy to pick up speed.

09 Five kilometres later, in Tollo di Grigno, you can rest and read information about Valsugana at BiBox, two wooden boxes with seats to get respite from the rain and the summer heat.

10 The itinerary ends at Grigno station. From the cycle path, turn left following the signs for Grigno, about 4km from the BiBox. Ride down the underpass and through a roundabout, then cycle left down Via Trento and Via Stazione. There are hourly departures to both Trento and Bassano del Grappa.

☕ Take a Break

From 1 April to 30 October, it's possible to stop at **Bicigrill**, rest stops with food and drink, often showcasing local specialities. The two most popular Bicigrill along this route are **Big Fish** in Levico, focusing on freshwater fish, and the **Bicigrill Castelnuovo**, known for its delicious sandwiches.

Outside of spring and summer, your best bet will be stopping at Borgo Valsugana where **Pizzeria Titti** and **Ristorante San Giorgio** are two reliable choices.

FLORIAN AUGUSTIN/SHUTTERSTOCK ©

Lake Caldonazzo

Lake Caldonazzo

Lake Caldonazzo is the largest lake entirely located within Trentino, with a surface area of just over 5 sq km. It's at an altitude of 450m above sea level, higher than Trento and the other main cities along the Adige valley; for this reason, it's a popular destination in summer, to escape the heat of the cities. The lake was awarded the Blue Flag for the excellent quality of its waters and for the commitment of its municipalities to sustainability. Lake Caldonazzo is the ideal destination for lovers of water sports – it's the only lake in Trentino where water-skiing is allowed, and other activities including sailing, kayaking and stnad-up paddleboarding are also available.

20

Ciclabile dell'Adige

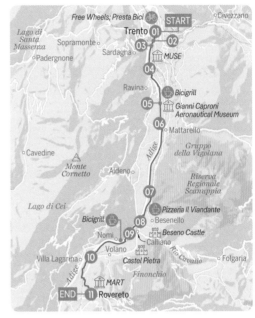

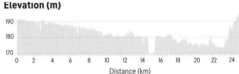

Elevation (m)

DURATION	DIFFICULTY	DISTANCE	START/END
2hr	Easy	25km	Trento/ Rovereto

TERRAIN	Paved

The Ciclabile dell'Adige follows the valley created by the Adige river, from the Austrian border at Reschensee all the way to Verona. The route is paved and well maintained, and can be broken up into several stages – this itinerary focuses on the Trento–Rovereto stretch, ending at MART, one of Italy's most important contemporary art galleries. Together with the Ciclabile del Mincio (p90) and the Ciclovia del Sole (p108), the Ciclabile dell'Adige forms part of the Eurovelo 7, a trans-Europe cycle route connecting Norway's North Cape to Malta.

Bike Hire

There are several shops renting out bikes in Trento. Two reliable options are Presta Bici, with different models from simple city bikes to road bikes, and Free Wheels with excellent eMTB available.

Starting Point

The cycle path is a short distance away from Trento station and from the historic centre. Frequent trains connect Trento and Rovereto, and travel time is approximately 20 minutes.

01 This itinerary starts in Piazza Duomo, the heart of Trento. Leave the elegant square behind and cycle down Via Verdi until you reach the Adige river. The cycle path is on the left bank of the river, the same side you are coming from.

02 If you're coming from the station, turn right as you exit and ride down Piazza Dante, turn right again after the bus station and cross the overpass bypassing the railway tracks. The

Bicigrill

Cycling around Trentino, you're bound to see signs pointing to 'Bicigrill', rest stops for cyclists with food and drinks, as well as small workshops and tools to make small repairs. The name was inspired by Autogrill, the rest stops found along motorways all over Italy. However, unlike Autogrill, which are all owned by the same company and offer similar products, Bicigrill are all independent, and showcase the personality of the owner and products of the surrounding area. The 'original' Bicigrill is the one in Nomi, open since 2003, and one of the few in the region to open year-round.

Ciclabile dell'Adige will be just on the other side of the roundabout, next to the Bar Funivia 2.0.

03 Keep riding south to slowly leave Trento behind. On your right, you'll see the cable car heading to Sardagna, a village that's part of the Trento municipality. After that, the path travels past Palazzo delle Albere, a 16th-century building once owned by Trento's bishop princes, now turned into an exhibition space shared between the MUSE (Trento Science Museum) and MART (Museum of Modern and Contemporary Art of Trento and Rovereto). Right next to it you'll also notice the glass and steel frame of MUSE, with a large public park in front of it that's popular with locals for a picnic.

04 Keep riding up the embankment until you reach the Ravina bridge, then cross over to the right side of the Adige. By this stage, Trento will be behind you, and you'll have entered a landscape of vineyards and apple orchards, especially beautiful in spring and summer.

05 The path crosses back over to the left-hand side when you reach a roundabout with three pyramids, an installation dedicated to the city of Trento by contemporary artist Stefano Cagol. Shortly after crossing, ride past Avio Club Trento, a small airstrip also housing the Gianni Caproni Aeronautical Museum.

06 In case you missed the previous turn-off, you have the opportunity to cross the Adige again in Mattarello, a hamlet in front of the Vigolana massif. When the cycle path is on the left of the river, it travels parallel to the state road connecting villages of the Adige valley. The Verona–Brennero rail line is also a short distance away.

07 Shortly before entering Besenello, the cycle path crosses to the right side of the Adige once again, running alongside the busy Brennero motorway. Above Besenello, you might notice the medieval silhouette of Beseno Castle, dating back to the 12th century.

08 The castle is open and can be visited – you can leave the cycleway at Besenello and climb 1.5km to the entrance. If you'd rather see a castle that doesn't require climbing, make your way to Castel Pietra, a medieval fortress that stood on the border between Tyrol and the Venetian Republic, conquered only once throughout history by none other than Napoleon himself. It's just 1.5km from the cycle path, in the village of Calliano.

09 Shortly afterwards, you'll reach the village of Nomi, easy to recognise thanks to the futuristic bridge spanning the Adige. Cross the bridge to continue to Rovereto riding along the left of the Adige, or stay on the right side if you are hungry, as

☕ Take a Break

This stretch of the Adige Valley Cycle Path includes two **Bicigrill** – one just south of Trento, known for its homemade burgers (vegetarian options are also available), and one in Nomi, with a Viking theme and Bavarian specialities. The Nomi Bicigrill is open year-round, whereas the one in Trento closes between October and April. In autumn and winter, your best bet will be stopping in Besenello, the halfway point of this ride – **Pizzeria Il Viandante** has good deals on set lunch menus and good pizzas, and also offers outside seating.

Trento vineyards

there's a Bicigrill a few hundred metres down the road.

10 The next villages will be Volano and Villa Lagarina, where the cycle path briefly leaves the banks of the Adige and travels among the vineyards. Soon, houses and industrial buildings reveal that you are about to enter Rovereto, the second-largest town in Trentino.

Trentodoc

Everyone has heard about prosecco, but what about Trentodoc? Many of the wineries you'll see while cycling around Trentino specialise in this sparkling wine, available in both white and rosé versions and only made with grapes from a specific area in the Trento province. Trentodoc is the second-oldest sparkling wine appellation after Champagne, and labels sporting the Trentodoc badge are produced according to rigorous regulations. Grapes are grown on special pergolas and hand-harvested, and only four varieties are allowed – pinot blanc, pinot noir, pinot meunier and chardonnay. A good place for a Trentodoc tasting is Pedrotti Spumanti, conveniently located near the cycle path.

11 To get to MART, turn left at the roundabout in Via Valdiriva, following signs for the stadium. Ride around the stadium on Via Magazol until you reach Viale Trento, and continue until you get to the entrance of the art gallery. You can lock your bike at the rack near the entrance or in the large car park next door. To get back to the train station after your visit, turn left down Corso Bettini and then right into Corso Rosmini.

Also Try...

Lake Garda

Strada del Ponale

DURATION	DIFFICULTY	DISTANCE
2hr	Intermediate	10km

The Strada del Ponale was built in the mid-19th
century to connect Riva del Garda to the Ledro
Valley, isolated from the rest of the region
up until that point. The road was dug into the
mountainside to cover the 10km distance and
600m elevation difference separating Lake Garda
to Ledro, via a series of spectacular switchbacks.

The road was operational until 2004, then the
asphalt was removed and the Ponale was turned into
a hiking and cycling path. The first 5km are the most
scenic and suitable for all riders, as the route climbs
gradually, but you'll need a mountain or gravel bike
as the surface is unpaved. The final stretch to Ledro
is a little steeper – consider renting an e-bike.

Pista Ciclabile dell'Oltradige

DURATION	DIFFICULTY	DISTANCE
2hr	Intermediate	22km

This cycle path connects the city of Bolzano
to Lake Caldaro, an alpine lake at the centre of
South Tyrol's prime wine region. It's entirely paved
and travels through forests, vineyards and apple
orchards, including a couple of well-lit tunnels.

The itinerary starts from Piazza Walther in the
centre of Bolzano and travels alongside the Isarco
river, then joins the Ciclabile dell'Adige until Castel
Fimiano, home to the Messner Mountain Museum.
The route then follows the former Oltradige railway,
climbing slowly but steadily, before descending to
Lake Caldaro, where you'll end at Campi al Lago. For
local wines, stop at Cantina Produttori San Michele
Appiano, a social winery collecting several local
producers, located close to the halfway point.

Fiemme valley

Ciclabile del Navile

DURATION	DIFFICULTY	DISTANCE
1hr	Easy	9km

The Navile Cycle Path takes you on a 9km journey from the centre of Bologna along the canal of the same name, once part of an intricate system of waterways and canals that connected the city to Venice and the Adriatic Sea.

The itinerary starts from Porta Lame, southwest of the train station, and joins the Navile canal in the proximity of Sostegno della Bova, the first of a series of locks used to regulate the water level and allow boats to pass through. After cycling through Villa Angeletti Park, the cycle path runs past the Industrial Heritage Museum, presenting exhibits about Bologna's industrial history. The cycleway continues past several more *sostegni* (locks) dating back to the 15th and 16th centuries, until its end in Castelmaggiore.

Ciclabile Fiemme-Fassa

DURATION	DIFFICULTY	DISTANCE
4hr	Difficult	42km

Trentino has no shortage of spectacular scenery, but it's hard to beat the Fiemme and Fassa valleys for natural beauty. The Ciclabile Fiemme-Fassa connects the two valleys through historic villages, mountain streams and alpine meadows, overlooked by the rocky peaks of the Dolomites.

The itinerary runs between Canazei and Molina di Fiemme, with 700m altitude difference. It can be covered in either direction, but it's recommended to start in Canazei and ride downhill. The entire cycle path is paved, well signposted and has kilometre markers, as well as water fountains and Bicigrill. In summer a shuttle bus that accepts bikes allows you to return to the starting point. The Fiemme-Fassa Cycle Path is open between April and October.

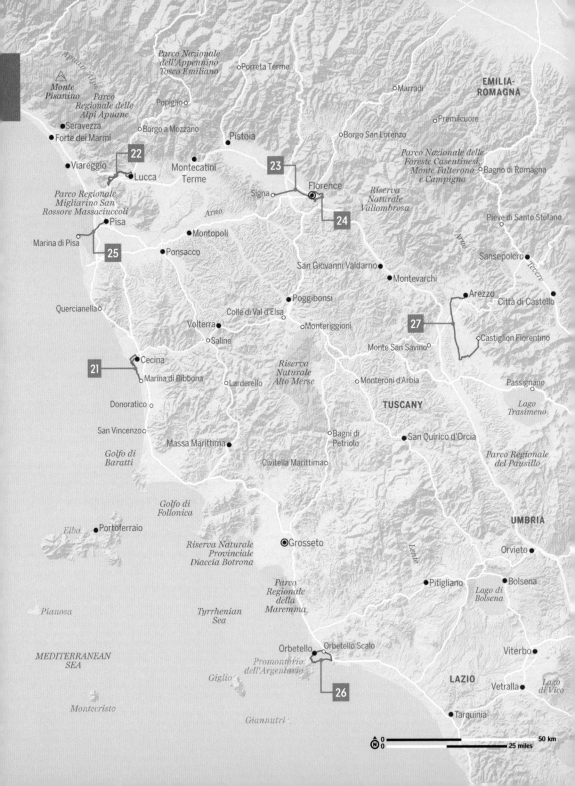

Monte
Pisanino
Apuan Alps

*Parco Nazionale
dell'Appennino
Tosco Emiliano*

Porreta Terme

Marradi

**EMILIA-
ROMAGNA**

*Parco
Regionale delle
Alpi Apuane*

Popiglio

Premilcuore

Bagno di Romagna

Seravezza

Borgo a Mozzano

Pistoia

Forte dei Marmi

Borgo San Lorenzo

*Parco Nazionale delle
Foreste Casentinesi,
Monte Falterona
e Campigna*

Viareggio

22

Montecatini
Terme

23

Pieve di Santo Stefano

Lucca

Signa

Florence

*Riserva
Naturale
Vallombrosa*

*Parco Regionale
Migliarino San
Rossore Massaciuccoli*

Pisa

24

Sansepolcro

Arno

Montopoli

San Giovanni Valdarno

Città di Castello

Marina di Pisa

25

Ponsacco

Montevarchi

Arezzo

Quercianella

Volterra

Colle di Val d'Elsa

Poggibonsi

Monteriggioni

27

Castiglion Fiorentino

Saline

Monte San Savino

Cecina

21

Marina di Bibbona

*Riserva
Naturale
Alto Merse*

Monteroni d'Arbia

Passignano

*Lago
Trasimeno*

Larderello

TUSCANY

Donoratico

San Vincenzo

Massa Marittima

*Golfo di
Baratti*

Bagni di
Petriolo

San Quirico d'Orcia

*Parco Regionale
del Pausillo*

Civitella Marittima

*Golfo di
Follonica*

UMBRIA

Elba

Portoferraio

*Riserva Naturale
Provinciale
Diaccia Botrona*

Grosseto

Orvieto

Pianosa

*Parco
Regionale
della
Maremma*

Pitigliano

*Lago di
Bolsena*

Bolsena

*Tyrrhenian
Sea*

**MEDITERRANEAN
SEA**

Orbetello

Orbetello Scalo

Viterbo

Giglio

*Promontorio
dell'Argentario*

26

LAZIO

Vetralla

*Lago
di Vico*

Montecristo

Giannutri

Tarquinia

0 ___ 50 km
0 ___ 25 miles

STEPNIAK/SHUTTERSTOCK ©

Dumo di San Martino (p142), Lucca

Florence & Tuscany

Explore

Florence & Tuscany

Locals joke that a Tuscan can ride a bicycle before they can walk. It might be a cliché, but of all Italy's regions, Tuscany is possibly the most immersed in its enthusiasm for cycling, with itineraries suitable for all ages and abilities. Florence has an excellent network of cycle lanes, as does Pisa, and throughout the region more is being done to promote cycle tourism. From the north to the south of the region, from coastal areas to its mountainous heart, old railways and ancient paths are being converted into walking and cycleways, linked to a network of official on-road cycle routes.

Florence & Pisa

Two of the most popular destinations in Tuscany, Florence and Pisa are both destinations set up with comfortable cycling infrastructure. The cities are crisscrossed with cycle lanes, mostly used by residents commuting to and from places, and have dedicated cycleways leading out of the city centre. Visitors can see the city sights on two wheels and explore the surrounding area on a great day out. While the cities have plenty of bike rental shops to choose from, each also has their own shared bike schemes for the casual cyclists who simply wants to get from their hotel to a museum or a piazza to meet a friend.

Lucca

Lucca is celebrated as the hometown of Italy's renowned composer Giacomo Puccini, whose presence is everywhere in this walled city, including the recently established cycleway, the Ciclopedonale Puccini. Cycling is very much embedded in the soul of Lucca, which is home to many professional cyclists who come here to train among the surrounding hills. This paves the way for friendly traffic for leisure cyclists, who wish to see beyond the ancient walls, take a ride along the river or check out the beautiful villas that once belonged to the rich and influential merchant families of the area.

WHEN TO GO

Spring and autumn are the best times to plan a cycling trip to Tuscany when roads are quieter and there are lively cultural festivals to experience. In spring, routes are alive with birdsong and the crisp sprouts of green, while in autumn, the landscape turns shades of yellow and red. Summer will guarantee fine weather, and could make coastal riding attractive when combined with a swim in the sea. Set out early and pack plenty of water to avoid heat exhaustion.

The Coast of Tuscany

While Tuscany is famous for its rolling hills with country roadsides punctuated by cypress trees, the coastal areas of Tuscany are also strikingly beautiful. Along the 230km of coastline, many towns have established cycle paths that stretch along the wild, sandy beaches. The Etruscan Coast in particular is known for its pre-Roman history and its wild dunes and pine forest. From resort towns to protected coastal forests and wildlife sanctuaries, there's a bike ride for every ability and interest.

Southern Tuscany

The further south you travel in Tuscany, the harsher and wilder the landscape becomes. From reclaimed lands between Arezzo and Chiusi to the sulphur spring areas around mountains further south, this is the unexpected backdrop of the usual picture-postcard Tuscany. The excellent Sentiero della Bonifica (Reclamation Way) is featured as a traffic-free, long-distance leisure bike trail that is suitable for all, and the areas around Mt Amiata are frequented by seasoned mountain bikers.

TRANSPORT

A good network of trains links the cities and towns of Tuscany, and is the best way to get around if you're travelling with a bike. When purchasing train tickets you need to declare that you are travelling with a bicycle, and you'll only be allowed to travel on regional services.

 WHAT'S ON

Tuscany hosts a number of cycling-related events throughout the year, including the iconic **Strada Bianche**, a professional race on the white gravel roads around Siena, held in March, and **L'Eroica** in September/October, an amateur event race on vintage bikes. Interest in bikepacking is on the rise and the annual **Tuscany Trail** is the world's largest bikepacking event attended by 3000 participants from all over the world – it's so popular it's often sold out.

Resources

Visit Tuscany (visittuscany.com/en/theme/cycling) The official tourism website has comprehensive coverage of cycle routes in the region, from short day rides to epic multiday itineraries.

Luxury Bike Hotels (luxurybikehotels.com) Itinerary suggestions along with cyclist-friendly accommodation.

Italy Bike Hotels (italybikehotels.com) More itinerary and accommodation inspiration.

 WHERE TO STAY

There's no shortage of hotels in Tuscany, whether you plan to stay in a city centre or a rural location. For a bit of privacy and to experience the serenity of the Tuscan landscape, consider staying in a villa away from the bustling cities. For those interested in slow food and great cuisines, a range of *agriturismi* (farm-stay accommodation) offer stays with wine- and food-tasting experiences with a focus on local, seasonal produce. These off-the-beaten-track locations will also make perfect bike-riding bases among the celebrated Tuscan hills.

21

Costa degli Etruschi

DURATION	DIFFICULTY	DISTANCE	START/END
2hr	Easy	25km	Cecina train station

TERRAIN	Paved bike path, forest track, shared road

Elevation (m)

An easy introduction to Tuscany's coast, this is a family-friendly ride around Cecina, a summer resort bustling with seafront cafes and restaurants, as well as along inviting forest paths smelling of fresh earth. The town's excellent cycle paths, running along the main roads and the river, make exploring by bike a pleasure. The forest reserve is just the place to cool down should you be visiting on a hot summer's day.

Bike Hire

SDBike, an independent bike store on the main waterfront in Cecina, has various tourist bikes starting from €2 an hour.

Starting Point

Cecina train station is on the Pisa–Livorno–Grosetto line. Train fare from Pisa Central to Cecina costs from €6.60 one way, or from Livorno from €4.80 one way.

01 Leaving the forecourt of Cecina train station, head straight up the one-way street Piazza Antonio Gransci to have a look around Cecina's main square, Piazza Francesco Domenico Guerrazzi, where you'll find a lovely fountain and the Duomo. Turn left at the square and you'll see the road heading straight towards Cecina river. Go straight, but take care when the road becomes a one-way street as you will be riding against traffic. Keep to the side and continue.

The Etruscan Civilisation

The Etruscan Coast is named after the Etruscan civilisation that inhabited this area from the start of the 9th century BCE. Known to be the original superpower of the Western Mediterranean, ruling over most of modern-day Italy, the Etruscan civilisation had a deep knowledge of art, farming and metallurgy, and was much more advanced than other Iron Age societies. Their works of art and metal sculptures greatly influenced the Greek and Roman cultures that followed. During your ride, stop in at Cecina's Archaeology Museum to learn more about the Etruscans.

02 Cross the bridge over the river and follow the cycle lane straight ahead and then as it turns left onto Via Francesco Domenico Guerrazzi at the roundabout; keep the plot of crops to your left-hand side. About 500m after turning left at the roundabout, you'll come to an iron gate immediately in front of you, where the cycle lane veers to the left. Feel free to push through this gate with your bike. This is a small museum complex housing Cecina's Archaeology Museum and the Museum of Work & Life of Northern Maremma. It's worth a visit if you're interested in regional history and culture.

03 You could return to the iron gate to join the cycle lane, or exit the museum through the opposite gate where a small car park on your left also has an unofficial entry point onto the same bike path. Once again, you'll be flanked by farms on each side of the road; at the next roundabout, turn left.

04 Continue straight ahead towards the bridge back over the river. The cycle lane ends at the bridge so take care crossing to the correct side of the road to cycle over it. At the end of the bridge, turn right onto a cycle lane that runs parallel to the river. As it ends, turn left.

05 Take necessary precautions as you will share this road with traffic. Turn right at the end of this gravel driveway, then follow the natural left turn of the road until you see the sea. Turn right again on Via della Fortezza. You'll find a small pier reaching out over the sea at the end of this road. Feel free to cycle up the pier for a look at the beach.

06 Back onto Viale della Vittoria, the beachfront boulevard, you'll follow this bustling road shared with cars and pedestrians to the end. There are plenty of restaurants, cafes and trinket stores if you feel like a bit of a browse. Otherwise, continue on, being careful of cars.

07 At the end of this busy high street is a car park and you'll notice a change in the landscape. In front of you is the protected pine forest of Cecina, Riserva Naturale Tomboli di Cecina, a nature reserve that you'll explore on bike. Look for a wooden entrance gate across the car park and enter.

08 In the forest you're free to cycle on the wide dirt tracks, but avoid the narrower ones that are for walkers only. Stretching 15km in total, this beachside Mediterranean pine forest is considered the green lung of the area. Where the forest meets the sea are wild sand dunes shaped by the wind and crashing waves. Enjoy the view and the serenity before you continue in the direction of Marina di Bibbona.

SILVIA.COZZI/SHUTTERSTOCK ©

☕ Take a Break

You could take it easy and stop in one of the cafes and restaurants along the Cecina waterfront, or you could wait until you reach the route's approximate half-way point in Marina di Bibbona, after passing through the forest. Next to a car park with bicycle parking, **Pasticceria Gelateria Il Ghiottone** has a tempting range of gelato flavours, delicious pastries and cakes, as well as a lovely outdoor seating area so you can keep an eye on your bike while you enjoy a coffee break.

Forest, Marina di Bibbona

09 Emerging out of the forest is Marina di Bibbona. Have a rest here with a meal or a gelato before you turn around and retrace the path back through the forest into Cecina. The mapped route will take you through town; however, feel free to backtrack onto the beachfront high street until the cycle lane along the river.

Riserva Naturale Tomboli di Cecina

The protected pine forest that beautifully lines the Etruscan Coast is, in fact, the result of town planning. In 1839 Grand Duke of Tuscany Leopoldo wanted to protect local crops from the salty wind coming from the sea, and introduced an agricultural policy of lining the coast with pine forests, which you'll notice in parts along the Tuscan coast. The Riserva Naturale Tomboli di Cecina is home to wild birds and animals, as well as the native shrub *limonium etruscum* (Estruschi caspia) that can only be found in this part of Tuscany. The sand dunes that form part of the nature reserve are home to lilies and sea poppies.

10 While you follow the cycle lane along the river, you'll notice that the bank begins to rise, forming a barrier between the river and the town. You are now cycling on Cecina's flood defence. Enjoy this quiet ride to the first bridge that you crossed at the start of the route before winding your way back to the station.

22

CICLOPEDONALE PUCCINI

Best for

ART & CULTURE

STEVE LOVEGROVE/SHUTTERSTOCK ©

Ciclopedonale Puccini

DURATION	DIFFICULTY	DISTANCE	START/END
2.5hr	Easy	30km	Lucca

TERRAIN	Paved bike lane, shared roads, gravel path

Duomo di San Martino

The popular Ciclopedonale Puccini cycle route follows the bank of the Serchio river for about 40km before diverting to reach Lake Massaciuccoli. On this particular leg of the cycle route, you will journey in the name of Lucca's most famous son – opera composer Giacomo Puccini – first on the cycleway, then via country roads and nearby villages before returning to Lucca to cycle on the circular path along the city wall for a different view of this beautiful yet unassuming city. Mostly traffic free, this route is perfect for families.

Bike Hire

There are a number of bike hire options in Lucca. The centrally located Ciclismoplus has well-serviced road bikes and e-bikes for rent, starting at €40 per day. Book early as cycling is very popular here.

Starting Point

Start your ride at the base of San Martin Cathedral, one of Lucca's major landmarks located on a quieter corner of the old city. It's easily pinpointed by the 13th-century clock tower.

01 From Lucca's Duomo di San Martino, take the small street next to the cathedral southwards until you meet Corso Garibaldi. Turn right onto this magnolia-lined street shared with car traffic.

02 Follow the Corso until the junction with Via V Veneto. Turn left here. Take this road until you come to an end, then take a path up to the top of the city's wall. Turn left on the wall path

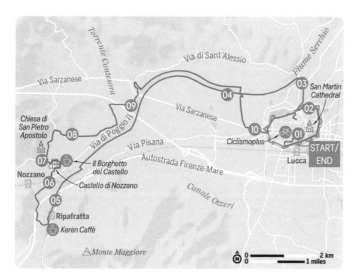

ELEPHOTOS/SHUTTERSTOCK ©

Elevation (m)

Distance (km)

and follow it in the anticlockwise direction for around 2km until you reach Porta Santa Maria. Take the path next to the gate and descend onto the road below. Join the traffic to exit through the narrow gates. Turn right onto the cycle path immediately after the gate. Follow the cycle path and curve to the right of the big roundabout.

03 Just before the next roundabout, walk your bike across the zebra crossing, then join the cycle path along Via Matteo Civitali (SS12). The bike lane ends at the intersection with Via del Brennero. Cross the road to continue on Via Matteo Civitali (no longer SS12) until its end, turn left, then

carefully follow the traffic turning right, and left again onto a path leading to the river.

04 This small road soon turns left. Follow it. It will feel like it's a cycle lane but this is still a section of the route shared with occasional traffic for about 2km until the cycle and pedestrian bridge, where it becomes a traffic-free gravel path. For the next 6km, you will be cycling on a gravel path shared with pedestrians, except for a road crossing you need to make at Via Sarzanese.

05 Continue to follow the gravel until the village of Ripafratta, where the bike path ends at a small car park.

Giacomo Puccini

Giacomo Puccini (1858–1924) was an Italian composer well known for his operas. Born in the north of Lucca (pictured above), he lived most of his life in and around the city and today Lucca is particularly fond of its most famous son. Opera fans should coincide their visit with the annual Puccini Festival around July/August; small concerts are held in the historic city and major performances take place at the open-air theatre, the Teatro dei Quattromila at Torre del Lago, against the beautiful backdrop of Lake Massaciuccoli. At other times, consider a visit to Villa Puccini (unfortunately not part of this bike ride), where the composer lived and worked until pollution from the lake forced him to move to the coast.

There is a bridge immediately to your right. Cross the bridge, then turn left to cross a subsequent bridge over the river. At the end of the road, turn right.

06 You'll come to the end of Via di Filettole at the bottom of the hill where the village of Nozzano begins and the Castello di Nozzano perches above; turn right here onto Via di Nozzano. Follow Via di Nozzano as it circles Nozzano, eventually turning right onto Via di Balbano and heading away from the village. From now on, you will be cycling on a road with traffic.

07 As you approach the Chiesa di San Pietro Apostolo on the left, pull over onto the grass and look back for a particularly scenic view towards Nozzano village. Continue with the flow of traffic on Via del Bordogna.

08 Turn right at a junction onto Via Vecchia di Nozzano. Initially lined with farms, it changes name to Via dei Bollori at the start of the residential houses. Ride on until a junction with Via Panchina, a paved pedestrian and cycleway

along the Contesora canal. Turn left onto this path and follow it until the end, then turn right onto Via della Chiesa XXIV.

09 At the T-junction with Via di Poggio Seconda, turn left. The street becomes one way after an intersection and ends at Via di Sant'Alessio. Turn right on this sharp corner. After 30m turn right onto a nature path. This path takes you to the opposite side of the river from the cycle path you will have taken earlier in the day. Keeping the river to your right, follow it for 3km until you come to the bike and pedestrian bridge you saw earlier. Take the bridge across, then follow the road in the same direction until it meets Via G Puccini. Turn left.

10 The cycle path will take you to Porta Sant'Anna. Go through the gate, up the ramp onto the wall and, this time, follow the path in a clockwise direction. Just after a sculpture of Bruno Catalano, take the ramp down and zigzag through the medieval streets to Piazza dell'Anfiteatro, when it'll be time for an *aperitivo*!

☕ Take a Break

Keren Caffè is a perfect little espresso stop on the roadside in Ripafratta, at around the halfway point just before you turn right towards Nozzano. Depending on the time of day, the cafe also serves a selection of pasta dishes for what Italians call 'little hungers'.

Otherwise, wait until you get to Nozzano. The restaurant **Il Borghetto del Castello** has a menu of pizza, pasta and seafood dishes, and there's outdoor seating where you can keep an eye on your bike and the view towards the hilltop castle.

MARCO ROSARIO VENTURINI AUTIERI/GETTY IMAGES ©

Castello di Nozzano

Castello di Nozzano

The Nozzano Castle dates back to the 12th century as an outpost fortification to defend the town of Nozzano below. The position of the castle was strategic, placed on the heavily fought-for border between Pisa and Lucca. Inside, the castle contains a small historic hamlet, where, once a year in September, a festival dedicated to re-enacting life in the Middle Ages is held. If you happen to be cycling through around the same time, expect processions of locals in historic costumes, traditional food and medieval craft markets – remember to convert your euros for the official medieval currency at the door!

23

PETR POHUDKA/SHUTTERSTOCK ©

Ponte Vecchio

Ciclopista dell'Arno

DURATION	DIFFICULTY	DISTANCE	START/END
1hr	Easy	15km	Central Florence/Signa

TERRAIN	Mostly gravel cycle path

The Arno river flows from its source near Mt Falterona for 241km into the sea near Pisa. From Florence, a ride on the cycle path along the banks of this serene river is the perfect getaway from the bustling city. The established cycle path is completely traffic free and flat, and will form a small part of a larger project to develop the rest of the Ciclopista dell'Arno (Arno Bike Path) through Tuscany. Take a leisurely ride on this scenic path until Signa, where you can take a train to Florence or cycle back the same way.

Bike Hire

Florence by Bike (florencebybike.it) has bike rentals for both adults and children, ranging from city bikes to race bikes and e-bikes. Prices start from €15 per day.

Starting Point

You can join the Arno Bike Path almost anywhere along the riverbank in Florence. For this itinerary, however, you'll make a symbolic start on the north bank of the famous Ponte Vecchio.

01 From Ponte Vecchio, Florence's beloved medieval merchant bridge, head west along the riverside and cycle with traffic on Lungarno degli Acciaiuoli, picking up the cycle lane after a short distance at Ponte Santa Trinita. Go straight, passing two bridges – Ponte alla Carraia and Ponte Amerigo Vespucci – on your left, until you approach Ponte alla Vittoria where the cycle lane turns right. Follow the cycle lane to the right, then turn left into a square with the monument of Vittorio Emanuele II. Veer left again towards the river and pick up

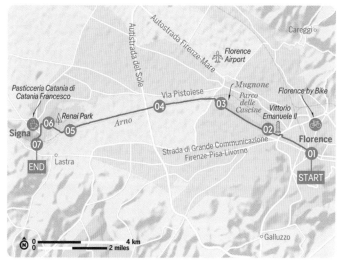

BRUNO BOTTICELLI ©

Elevation (m)

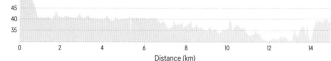

Distance (km)

the cycle lane again to continue along the river.

02 With the river on your left and the vast green space of Parco delle Cascine, the monumental and historic green lung of Florence on your right, this is a particularly pleasant section of the city for a bike ride. As a variation, you could go into the park and follow the many paths in the same direction; here you'll find fountains, monuments and an amphitheatre to visit. Alternatively you can cycle across the pedestrian- and cycle-only Passerella dell'Isolotto bridge at Piazza JF Kennedy and try the opposite bank of the river for a change in perspective. If you do

this, you'll need to cross over at the next bridge to continue.

03 Whichever variation of the route you followed, you will eventually reach the end of Parco delle Cascine. Cross a small bridge near the monument of an Indian prince and behind a cafe at the confluence of the Arno and the Mugnone rivers. At the end of the bridge, turn left, keeping an upmarket restaurant to your right.

04 Follow this road, now shared with light traffic as it ducks under the highway. Shortly after this, you will enjoy a traffic-free gravel path wedged between the railway line and the river for the next

The Indian Prince

At the end of Parco delle Cascine is a curious monument (pictured above) to an Indian prince. The prince in question is Prince Rajaram Chhatrapati, Maharaja of Kolhapur, who died in Florence in 1870 after contracting an illness. His death caused a diplomatic dilemma in the newly formed Kingdom of Italy. The importance of having a funeral fit for royalty was discussed; however, his servants insisted that he be given a traditional Hindu funeral with riverside cremation. Despite this practice contradicting the Catholic faith and the city of Florence not allowing cremation, the prince was given his final wish. The monument marks the location where the cremation took place.

8km of the route. Other than the noise from passing trains, this is the quietest and greenest section of the ride and is the main feature of the Arno Bike Path.

05 There's a small tributary as you approach Signa, a town that is part of greater Florence, where the path will turn right away from the river, crossing under the railway lines to meet a road. The large green space of Renai Park is on your right, with lakes suitable for a swim in the summer and plenty of bike paths for you to explore should you have additional energy and time. Take the gravel cycle path that runs along this road until just after the entrance to the leisure park called 'Happy Park', then turn left onto a bridge with the road name Via dei Renai that crosses the Bisenzio river.

06 After the bridge, walk your bike across the zebra crossing and take the narrow path (still Via dei Renai) on the opposite side. Cycle along until the T-junction with Via Roma. If you miss the small side path near the zebra crossing, you could follow the main road southwards, which will eventually lead to Via Roma after a natural right bend on the road. Turn left on Via Roma.

07 You are now in the centre of Signa, a typical commuter town with an unassuming church and sun-faded houses. Take Via Roma until you come to a Y-junction, where you should take the left fork onto Via della Stazione, leading you to the station for your train home. At this point, you could also choose to ride back the same way you came. Or, if you're feeling adventurous, cross the river via the bridge on the other side of the station, and ride back to Florence along the opposite bank, detouring to visit the beautiful garden of Villa Caruso nearby. Note, though, that this is not part of the mapped itinerary.

 **Take a Break**

There aren't any shops along the way, but you could make a detour when you come to the train stations of Le Piagge, where there's a snack bar just outside the station, or S Donnino, where there's a restaurant. Alternatively, pack a few snacks and enjoy them on the train ride back after the ride. In Signa, while waiting for your train, stop by **Pasticceria Catania di Catania Francesco** for a coffee and pastry.

PEL_197/GETTY IMAGES ©

Cycle path along the Arno river

The Arno & Florence

At 241km long and covering 8228 sq km, the Arno is the most important river in central Italy after the Tiber and has a strong link to the history of Florence. The river served as an important transport route between the sea and the Apennines ranges, with Florence a key transit point. This provided a lot of trade and work for the local inhabitants, until 1333 when the river stopped being navigable due to lack of flow. Nevertheless, the Arno has flooded the city many times, with the 1966 flood being one of the worst in history. Along the riverbank in Florence you'll notice plates marking the 1966 flood level.

24

Best for

ART & CULTURE

Florence: Parks, Michelangelo & Football

DURATION	DIFFICULTY	DISTANCE	START/END
1.5hr	Easy	16km	Piazza di Santa Maria Novella

TERRAIN	Shared roads, pedestrian streets, on-road bike paths

Piazza della Repubblica

Florence is considered the birthplace of the Renaissance and where the great Italian artist Michelangelo's presence is most prominent. Cycle from one Renaissance highlight to another, past the Accademia Gallery where the statue of David can be admired, then, for something a little different, learn about the Italian passion for football at the National Football Museum. This is a bike tour of Florence like no other. Utilising the city's excellent cycle path network, with most of the route on dedicated cycle lanes, it's a ride that will reveal parts of Florence you won't necessarily get to explore on foot.

Bike Hire

Bike rentals with a range of options include Florence by Bike and Tuscany Cycle. Alternatively, the Mobike scheme gives you the freedom of hourly rates.

Starting Point

Piazza di Santa Maria Novella is a popular meeting point near Santa Maria Novella train terminal. Start the ride on the south side of the square, near the taxi stand.

 01 Leave Piazza di Santa Maria Novella by Via del Sole, following the one-way system that merges onto Via degli Strozzi, passing two former palaces now used as hotels and art galleries. Keeping to your right to allow cars to pass along these narrow streets, you will eventually emerge onto Piazza della Repubblica through the arch (Arch of Triumph).

 02 Explore Piazza della Repubblica, considered the centre of Florence since the time of the Romans and the site of bustling markets in

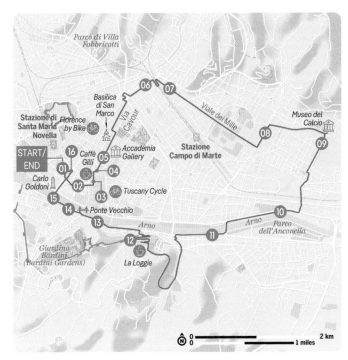

Elevation (m)

100
80
60

0   2   4   6   8   10   12   14

Distance (km)

original *David* by Michelangelo is on exhibit. Just beyond that is Piazza San Marco.

05 Turn left and cycle through Piazza San Marco, then turn right towards Basilica di San Marco and onto the cycle lane on Via Camillo Cavour. Follow this all the way, taking care at street junctions and looking out for crossing cars. This will take you to the Piazza della Libertà, featuring the 18th-century Arc de Triomphe and the 13th-century Porta San Gallo. Cycle through, following the turns of the cycle lane onto Viale Don Giovanni Minzoni.

06 Follow the cycle lane along this main road to the end where you'll come to the railway lines. There is an underpass filled with graffiti that you can take to cross to the other side. Known as 'the Cure' locally, it is shared with pedestrians and you will be required to walk your bike, giving you a chance to browse the graffiti gallery.

07 Coming out of the subway, cross the road and take the cycle lane on Viale dei Mille. You'll follow this through a suburban area of Florence towards the city's sporting complex, including a stadium and various outdoor courts. While the team in Florence isn't in a major league, football is still a big deal here and it can get rowdy around these parts on match days. Cycle around the stadium if you like, or continue down the cycle lane to the end of the road, then turn left onto the tree-lined cycle lane wedged between two streets, taking care crossing at U-turn points for cars.

the medieval times. The Column of Abundance marks the spot where a Roman forum once stood. Today street artists and buskers keep the square busy and vibrant, and the historic cafes are particularly lively after sunset. Leave the square by Via degli Speziali, the street directly opposite the Arch of Triumph.

03 Find yourself on Via dei Calzaiuoli, the pedestrian high street of Florence. This street is one of the most elegant streets in the historic centre of Florence, and is a shopper's par-

adise. Turn left. Pedestrians have right of way, so cycle with care.

04 At the end of the high street, you will come to Piazza del Duomo. On your right will be the landmark 13th-century cathedral of Florence, Cathedral of Santa Maria del Fiore, and on your left, the iconic octagonal Battistero di San Giovanni, with similar marble facades. Explore at will, then leave the crowds behind through the narrow side street Via Ricasoli. Follow this street and you'll pass the Accademia Gallery where the

☕ Take a Break

Piazza della Repubblica has a couple of notable historic cafes worth stopping for. Even if you aren't hungry yet, have a coffee and one of the delicious pastries just so you can look at the elegant interior of **Caffè Gilli**. At over 270 years old, it's the oldest cafe in Florence, and the centuries of continuous trade have given it a somewhat royalty status on the Florentine cafe scene.

08 At the roundabout, turn right. Still following the cycle lane, continue down Viale Giovanni Verga until you come to another sporting complex, where you'll find the Museo del Calcio (Italian Football Museum), a must visit for football fans. There's bicycle parking just outside the entrance; remember to lock up.

09 From the museum, you'll follow the cycle lane on the main street, Via del Gignoro, towards the river. There are a couple of confusing junctions with multiple road diversions here, but as long as you keep to the red-painted cycle paths going in the general direction you'll be fine. Crossing the rail tracks again, you will eventually come to a small roundabout with a water fountain. Turn right here.

10 The cycle lane will take you along the main road; you'll notice the riverside after the small car park of Tuscany Hall. It is quieter and greener along the garden cycle paths but try not to get carried away and go too far, as you'll need to cross Ponte Giovanni da Verrazzano soon after passing the lovely riverside Ville Sull'Arno hotel. Turn right at the end of the bridge where there's a roundabout.

11 Ride along the cycle lane until you almost reach the next bridge, veer to the left and walk your bike through a series of pedestrian crossings until you come to Viale Michelangiolo. The road will gradually climb and curve towards Piazzale Michelangelo, where the best view of Florence rewards your efforts. Pause at Piazzale Michelangelo, where a bronze replica of *David* shares the panoramic view. There are usually markets where you can shop for souvenirs, and a cafe in La Loggia building for a coffee and cake. On each side of the piazza you'll find an iris garden and a rose garden, as well as a drinking fountain on the east side of the car park to fill your water bottle.

12 Take the steep winding road shared with cars back down to the street. Along the way, you'll see a layered water feature to your left and, at the bottom of the zigzag, an imposing a 1300s city gate, Porta San Niccolò. Pass these attractions onto the main road and turn left onto the cycle lane along the river. The cycle lane ends at Ponte alle Grazie, but the small road that continues along, with parked cars on each side, is cyclist friendly and drivers are generally careful.

13 Continue onwards; you'll have a view of the famous Ponte Vecchio on your

SKANDARAMANA/SHUTTERSTOCK ©

Piazzale Michelangelo

A Note on City Cycling

There are over 100km of bike paths in Florence, though the majority are outside the city centre or along the river, used mostly by local commuters to get to and from places. In the historic centre, narrow streets and busy squares make it difficult to build additional cycling infrastructure, but motorists are used to bikes and keeping safe just takes a little common road safety sense. Follow the flow of traffic (don't go against it) to make sure you enjoy your day on the bike; should you find yourself on a street heading against one-way traffic, walk your bike along that section.

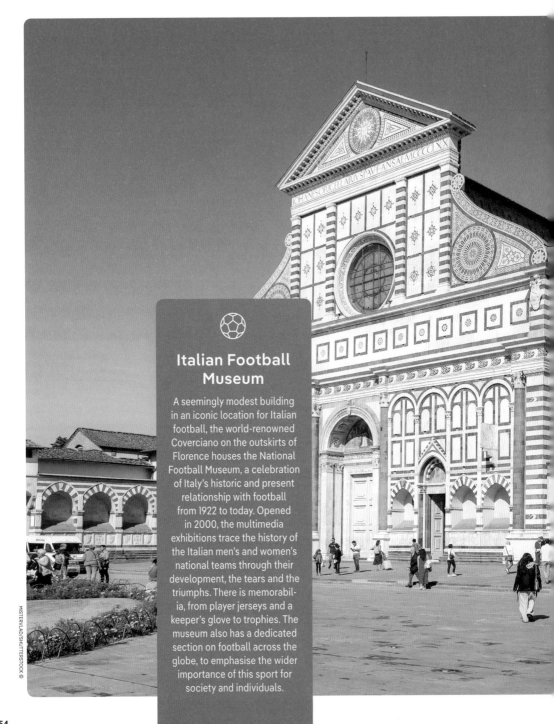

Italian Football Museum

A seemingly modest building in an iconic location for Italian football, the world-renowned Coverciano on the outskirts of Florence houses the National Football Museum, a celebration of Italy's historic and present relationship with football from 1922 to today. Opened in 2000, the multimedia exhibitions trace the history of the Italian men's and women's national teams through their development, the tears and the triumphs. There is memorabilia, from player jerseys and a keeper's glove to trophies. The museum also has a dedicated section on football across the globe, to emphasise the wider importance of this sport for society and individuals.

Basilica of Santa Maria Novella

right. Should you wish to stop for a photo, signal and carefully pull over onto the pedestrian path. Or simply continue cycling down this road, which turns into a smaller backstreet lined with shops. Pass an arch just as you approach Ponte Vecchio, then continue on Borgo S Jacopo, until a set of traffic lights where you turn right towards Ponte Santa Trinita.

14 Don't cross the bridge yet. Continue on the riverside street Lungarno Guicciardini, again sharing with light traffic, to Ponte alla Carraia, where you'll want to cross the river. Before you do, you might want to cycle a little beyond the bridge to a small platform on the river where there's a nice viewpoint of the little barrier cascade. At golden hour you'll often find groups of locals here sharing a bottle of vino. Return to Ponte alla Carraia after a brief stop and cross the river along the cycle lane.

15 The Monument to Carlo Goldoni, playwright and writer from Venice, who was considered the father of comedy in Italy, will greet you on the other side as you come to the end of the bridge. You will want to go straight in its direction, but this is a busy junction with cars and buses turning, so take care. Walk your bike across the road

TOP TIP:
'Mille e una bici' Bike Rentals (en.comune.fi.it) is a city bike-share scheme with hourly rates from €2 an hour, perfect for those only wanting to cycle a small part of this itinerary for a couple of hours. You'll find these bikes at the central railway station and Piazza Ghiberti.

towards Piazza Goldoni behind the monument, then along the narrow one-way street of Via del Moro, watching out for cars.

16 Follow the flow of traffic, noticing that Piazza Santa Maria Novella is approaching to your left through a series of one-way streets. From here you could walk your bike back to the starting point. Alternatively, continue to a junction with a column of the cross, where you will turn into Via dei Banchi to the left of the column; the traffic will finally be heading the right way. Turn left and onto the piazza, facing the Basilica of Santa Maria Novella.

☕ Take a Break

Towards the conclusion of the ride, **La Loggia** at Piazzale Michelangelo is a restaurant with terrace seating that serves Tuscan-style meals and an *aperitivo* menu of wine and cocktails and small plates. There's also a delicious dessert menu featuring sweet plates, from cheesecakes to gelato and, of course, the iconic tiramisu. It's the perfect place for a snack or a meal while admiring Florence from a height.

25

DELPIXART/GETTY IMAGES ©

Ciclopista del Trammino

DURATION	DIFFICULTY	DISTANCE	START/END
1.5hr	Easy	26km	Leaning Tower of Pisa

TERRAIN		Paved

Leaning Tower of Pisa

Get away from the bustling centre of Pisa and spend a day cycling to the seaside along an old railway line and one of Tuscany's newest cycleways – the Ciclopista del Trammino. Mostly traffic-free, the route follows Pisa's excellent network of cycle lanes to get out of the centre before passing through picturesque countryside along the Arno river. When you reach the Marina di Pisa, it's time to enjoy some great seafood and gelato. This ride is perfect for families and those who want a gentler tempo.

Bike Hire

Smile & Ride has a range of bikes for rent, from basic city bikes to race road bikes. Rates start at €7.50 an hour or €17 per day.

Starting Point

The official starting point is at the former Marina Trammino Station near Pisa Centrale train station. For this itinerary, you will start at the Leaning Tower of Pisa.

01 Start at the site for which the city is most famous, the base of the Leaning Tower of Pisa. From here, follow the small Via Santa Maria south all the way down to the river. The first half of this street is mostly only for pedestrians and bikes, while the second half is a road with parked cars on each side. You won't be the only cyclist on the road, and Italians are mostly used to sharing the road with cyclists, but nevertheless, take care. Turn right when you reach the river.

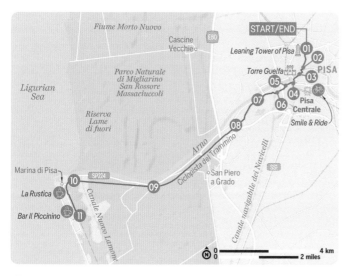

DEA/R. CARNOVALINI/GETTY IMAGES ©

Elevation (m)

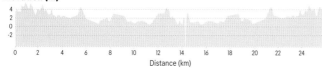

Distance (km)

02 Turn left to cross the Ponte Solferino then immediately turn right after the bridge to join a nice stretch of cycle lane that continues following the river and from where you have a view across to the historic part of Pisa.

03 The cycle lane turns at a junction where you'll see two remaining ancient gates of Pisa, with Torre Guelfa across the river, and the ruins of Porta della Degazia on your immediate right. Keep following the cycle lane as it wraps around the old bastion wall until you come to a small roundabout.

04 Using the second pedestrian crossing after the roundabout, cross onto a dedicated cycle lane in between two buildings. You have now officially navigated onto the Ciclopista del Trammino cycleway. Continue along as it takes you under a railway bridge.

05 You are still in Pisa's main urban centre. Keep going on the cycle lane. While a cycle lane exists, there are still several crossings marked by zebra strips that you need to make. Remember to walk your bicycle across the crossings as required by Italian law.

06 A small section of the cycle lane approaching the Navicelli Canal is painted red, as this is shared with pedestrians; slow down and give way if required.

About the Ciclopista del Trammino

The Ciclopista del Trammino was inaugurated in 2020, after years of planning for a dedicated cycleway connecting Pisa to its marina. The old railway line opened in 1892, departing from Marina Trammino station to Marina di Pisa train station (pictured above). The train, named *Stràsciapoveri*, made the 14km journey in a speedy 42 minutes! At the Marina di Pisa train station you can still see the old platform and tracks. The line closed in 1932 due to a decrease in demand. You'll find remains of the old railway along the route.

07 Continue along Via Livornese. This is the main road out of Pisa towards Livorno. Depending on the time of day, you may encounter traffic; but don't worry, soon you'll leave this behind.

08 After a final right turn off Via Livornese on the outskirts of Pisa, you will join a tree-lined, traffic-free cycleway. Breathe. You have now left the centre of Pisa behind.

09 For the next 8km, you'll be cycling along the most beautiful part of the cycleway. After an initial section where it runs parallel to a major road, the remaining ride will get quieter, and you will pedal along with shrubs and farmland on each side, passing a couple of settlements on the way. There will be a few points where the cycleway crosses a country road where the occasional car may be driving past, so take care when you come to these. On sunny weekends and during Italian school holidays, it can get quite busy here, but you will still find some quiet cycling moments in between.

10 Approaching Pisa's marina, the cycleway turns left through a pine forest. Continue with it until it finishes at the former Marina di Pisa train station, the official end of the cycleway.

11 Follow the mapped itinerary to return to Pisa from this point. However it is recommended you first take some time to explore the marina area at your leisure before heading back. From the disused train station, the sea is just one straight road (shared with cars) down on Via Cagliaritana. A lovely bike path along the beach is a way to return to the main part of the Ciclopista del Trammino cycleway, leading you to the port and a view of the old stilt fishing hut at the mouth of the Arno river. You can pick up the main cycleway, which will take you towards Pisa Centrale station to the former Marina Trammino Station, technically the official start of the Ciclopista del Trammino cycleway.

 **Take a Break**

Around the corner from Piazza Gorgona on the Marina di Pisa waterfront area, you'll find the friendly **Bar Il Piccinino**, where light meals such as sandwiches, salads and nibbles are accompanied by ocean views. It's a popular hangout for an *aperitivo* and can get rather busy in the afternoon. For a more substantial meal, head to **La Rustica,** a bit further towards the marina, which has a menu of pasta, pizza and fresh seafood dishes. Try the *fritto misto di mare* (mixed fried seafood), done as the locals like it.

MILOSK50/SHUTTERSTOCK ©

San Piero a Grado

San Piero a Grado

If time permits, take a detour to the village of San Piero a Grado to visit the Romanesque Catholic church built in the 11th century, which is recognised as a 'Messenger of Peace Monument' by the Unesco Clubs.

Particularly interesting are the stone carvings of faces and patterns on the walls and door frames, some of which seem to be medieval graffiti. The old bell tower was destroyed at the end of WWII by retreating German troops; after a few stop and start projects, reconstruction efforts restarted in 2019.

26

Orbetello Lagoon & Flamingos

DURATION	DIFFICULTY	DISTANCE	START/END
1.5hr	Easy	19km	Orbetello

TERRAIN	Paved on-road bike lane, quiet country roads

LUCIANO SALVATORE/SHUTTERSTOCK ©

Flamingos, Orbetello Lagoon

Tuscany is great for bike rides in general, but the biodiversity along the region's coast makes exploring on two wheels particularly special – even more so where flamingos are involved. You'll start in the small town of Orbetello, an ancient Etruscan settlement before the Romans, which occupies one of the most unique geolocations in Tuscany – a small strip of land that cuts through the Orbetello Lagoon. Along the route you'll enjoy birdlife and nature and mostly car-free paths. Look out for flocks of pink flamingos between autumn and spring.

Bike Hire

Located near Piazza Mario Cortesini, the starting point in Orbetello's town centre, family-run La Casa del Ciclo has been in the bicycle rental and repair business since 1937. Bike hire starts from €10 per day.

Starting Point

Start in the centre of Orbetello, at Piazza Mario Cortesini. If you aren't staying here and instead will arrive by train, the Orbetello Monte Argentario train station is about 3.5km away.

01 You're in the centre of Orbetello, on the lagoon known for the flocks of pink and white flamingos that come here each year in autumn and winter to nest. From the fountain in the middle of Piazza Mario Cortesini, cycle under the arches of the historic Porta Nuova, then immediately turn left through a car park onto Via Giamcomo Leopardi. At the end, you'll join a cross street with a cycle lane. Turn left onto the cycle lane.

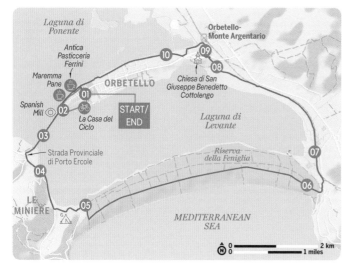

Elevation (m)

FOOTTOO/SHUTTERSTOCK ©

02 After about 100m, you'll have a nice view of the lagoon on your right. If you're lucky there might be a couple of flamingos and water birds around. Continue down this lovely stretch of cycle lane, which will eventually take you onto the causeway crossing the lagoon. There's an ancient Spanish mill on the lagoon just off to your right, which is a good opportunity for a photo stop.

03 Surrounded by water on both sides, cycling on a causeway so close to the water's surface is always an adventure. As you approach the end of the causeway, the cycle lane veers off to the right into a park. Don't follow it; instead, carefully

join the traffic on the road and make a left turn onto Strada Provinciale Porto Ercole. You'll be cycling with car traffic from now. As tempting as it looks, bicycles are not allowed on the pedestrian footpath on the left, so keep on the road and relax; motorists are mostly friendly to cyclists in these parts.

04 Follow this tree-lined road that runs along with the lagoon on your left-hand side. You'll pass the small village of Le Miniere before you arrive at the next intersection. Follow the direction of traffic and turn left, keeping the lagoon to your left and a campground to your right.

The Spanish Mill

The small ancient Spanish mill (pictured above) in the middle of the lagoon is the only surviving one of what was once a series of nine mills. The mills were built in the lagoon by the Sienese around the 15th century for defence purposes; they were later restored and converted during Spanish rule as a grinding mill for wheat and corn, using the power of the wind and the water's currents. The resulting products were then shipped back to land in small boats called *barchini*. In recent years, the remaining mill has become a symbol of Orbetello.

05 You will notice your surroundings starting to get greener. Ahead of you is the Feniglia nature reserve, a long stretch of pine forest flanked by the lagoon and the Mediterranean Sea. Explore the network of cycling paths at leisure, and check out the bird-watching towers on the lagoon or the beaches that extends along the length of the forest.

06 Emerging out of the forest on the other side is a bridge. Cross this bridge and follow the road curving to the left around a car park with a fence on the left. As you come to a T-junction with a stop sign, turn left here. While this road is narrow it's also one of the main thoroughfares in this area, so look twice for cars before turning. Don't worry, though, in a short while you'll be turning off this road.

07 After 150m, just before a small overhead rail bridge, look out for a gated path with a blue pedestrian and cycle sign to your left. Turn left onto this path. You are now on a traffic-free path following the railway line back to Orbetello.

08 As you approach town, the path becomes a traffic road again. The road ends where there's a disco venue with a large car park to your right. In front of you is a major road; you'll need to cross it very carefully, using the traffic lines on the ground as your guide, and turn left. You only want to be on this road for 20m before turning right off it at a small church named Chiesa di San Giuseppe Benedetto Cottolengo.

09 Cross the road again at the next junction where there's a small shopping centre with a car park. At this point, follow the flow of traffic to the right on Via Franco Baghini, then left on Via della Stazione to enter the start of the cycle lane on the left just before a car parking area.

10 At the next T-junction, turn right, keeping on the cycle lane. Once again, you have the beautiful lagoon to your left where you can try to spot water birds. Continue down this cycle lane until you are back in the town centre.

☕ Take a Break

Before you set off, purchase items for a picnic from **Antica Pasticceria Ferrini**, a lovely bakery, or **Maremma Pane**, a small local deli, to enjoy at the picnic tables in the forest, or on the beach, as there are no shops in the nature reserve. Alternatively, there's a restaurant opposite the Feniglia car park on the other side of the forest where you could stop for a meal or a coffee and a brownie. Check if it's open on the day you want to visit.

GIUSEPPE ZANONI/GETTY IMAGES ©

Orbetello Lagoon

Orbetello Lagoon Oasis Nature Reserve

While the flamingos are the obvious stars of the Orbetello Lagoon, it should in fact be the black-winged stilts that are credited for the creation of the Orbetello Lagoon Oasis Nature Reserve. A WWF project, the reserve was dedicated in 1971 after the discovery of a small colony of the black-winged stilts around the lagoon, a species originally believed to be extinct in Italy.

As a wetland reserve, this is bird-watching paradise, and observation towers inside the reserve as well as on land surrounding the lagoon allow visitors a glimpse into the life of the water birds.

27

Sentiero della Bonifica

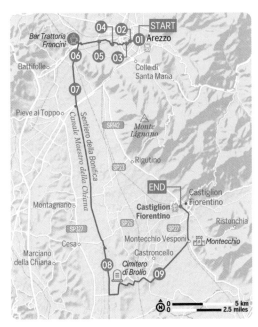

DURATION	DIFFICULTY	DISTANCE	START/END
4hr	Intermediate	40km	Arezzo/ Castiglion Fiorentino

TERRAIN	Paved on-road bike lane, shared roads, gravel path

Elevation (m)

The Sentiero della Bonifica (Reclamation Way) is a trail through a reclaimed valley, stretching along an ancient road used for the maintenance of the historic canal between Arezzo and Chiusi. The complete trail spans 60km, with access points along the way so cyclists can easily choose the sections they wish to do. There are also useful information boards with stories to tell, as well as water taps to fill up your bottles. From Arezzo, you'll be utilising the excellent cycle path network to reach the official trail before diverting along country roads to finish in Castiglion Fiorentino, from where you can return to your starting point by train.

Bike Hire

Epic Bike (epicbike.it) is a delivery and pick-up bike hire service in the Arezzo and surrounding areas. Rates start from €45 per day for a regular bike and €60 for an e-bike.

Starting Point

Start at the edge of a little park on the south side of Arezzo train station, accessed via a tunnel under the train tracks from the historic side of Arezzo.

01 From Arezzo train station, follow the cycle path to your right until the crossing. Walk your bike across the road to join the cycling path next to a small restaurant on Via del Duomo Vecchio, which ends after 60m. Continue onto this gravel path with a sign indicating 'Sentiero della Bonifica'.

02 You will come to a small junction with a set of steps in front of you and a snack bar; enter the gates to your left and follow the right

Olive grove near Arezzo

The Reclamation

For 500 years before the 1800s, the area between Arezzo and Chiusi was either a swamp or flooded under water, due to tectonic movements that shifted the flow of two historic rivers that flooded the valley between Arezzo and Chiusi. A reclamation project was the solution of hydraulic engineer Vittorio Fossombroni. First, a canal was constructed to allow the excess water to flow into the Arno near Arezzo. Then, land had to be raised, or reclaimed; the result is a highly fertile land with great access to water for farming, including vegetables, apple and pear orchards, grapes and olives.

fork all the way to where it meets a road. Continue down the road and turn right to join the traffic onto Via Paolo Toscanelli.

03 Coming up to a T-junction where the road ends, turn right again onto the busier Via Alcide De Gasperi. Don't worry, you'll be turning off it soon. A cycle lane awaits at the next T-junction, where you'll turn left. Follow this cycle lane as it veers left at the next turn to a crossing, curves back onto the road, then dips seamlessly under a large, round junction. Keep going until where the cycle lane requires you to cross to the other side of the road to continue. Walk your bike across, then on to the path with a park on your left and residential flats and car park on your right.

04 The cycle lane ends when it meets the road. Turn left and join the traffic. With a block of green space on your right, you'll only have a short ride to go before you join another shared pedestrian and cycle lane along Via Caduti di Cefalonia e Corfù; this time, turn right. Follow it to where it ducks under the elevated roads, where the cycle lane breaks before it is picked up again just across to your right. Keep cycling, until you come to Via Piero Calamandrei.

05 You are now on one of the major roads in and out of Arezzo. Turn left onto the cycle lane that's on the same side of the road. Watch out for cars coming in and out of driveways, as there are a few along this route. In 2km you'll come to a roundabout. Follow the cycle lane as it goes around it in the direction of traffic, then take the short gravel track to the entrance of the bridge where you'll carefully join the traffic. At the end of the bridge, carefully get off your bike, and walk across the pedestrian crossing towards Bar Trattoria Francini, where you can stop for a quick break.

06 Getting back on your bike, cycle past the buildings and take the small street on the left. A gravel path at the end of this street is the Reclamation Way where you'll spend most of the remainder of the ride. Turn right to join the route.

07 The first section of the gravel path is still open to local farm vehicle traffic, although it does become a shared pedestrian and cycle path. You'll be travelling about 20km of the trail, mostly without traffic. However, there are points where the path intersects with a road or requires you to cross to the other side of the canal, where you will

need to look twice for fast-driving cars before crossing.

08 Coming to the intersection with Strada Provinciale 27, turn left. The SP27 passes Brolio, one of the agricultural villages along the Reclamation Way. At the small cemetery – Cimitero di Brolio – on your left, turn right just after

PEGASOPHOTO/SHUTTERSTOCK ©

Montecchio castle

☕ Take a Break

Pack a light lunch, a few snacks and a full water bottle before you set off, as there are no shops along this itinerary. Or, stop at **Bar Trattoria Francini** just before you join the Reclamation Way. Have a quick coffee and grab a pastry here. There are several water fountains en route for refills, so don't be afraid to hydrate!

the zebra crossing, onto Via della Chiesa Brolio. This ends at a T-junction with SP27. Turn right.

09 Coming to a roundabout, continue straight (first exit) onto an unnamed road, whose tarmac dissolves into a gravel path after a couple of houses. At the end of this path, you'll see the castle of Montecchio

Arezzo's Interesting Characters

At the beginning of the Reclamation Way are two bronze figures, dedicated to two of Arezzo's special citizens, to your right outside a beautiful mansion. The seated woman is Angiolina Cipollini. Born in 1888, she used to beg for money on the main streets of Arezzo. Often teased by local boys, she never lost her humour and responded with good will. The Gold Man on the left represents a man whose son was lost during the war in Russia. He would dress in gold and stand in silence with his bicycle, waiting for his son to return.

appearing on a hilltop to your right. As you meet the main road beneath the castle, turn left. This last short stretch of the journey is on a main traffic thoroughfare; take extra caution. Follow the flow of traffic to enter the town of Castiglion Fiorentino, arriving at the train station to take the train back to Arezzo.

Also Try...

Elba

The Full Reclamation Way

DURATION	DIFFICULTY	DISTANCE
7hr	Difficult	60km

Those with ambition and energy could choose to cycle the full length of the Sentiero della Bonifica (Reclamation Way), all the way from Arezzo to Chiusi (or in reverse).

This will allow you to experience more of the points of interest in the reclaimed landscape of this valley. Not only was the area transformed by the water drainage work of the reclamation, but it was also a battle ground between various powers of Tuscany. Expect everything from 'defence' towers built for political claims to the land, to bridges and tunnels of brilliant engineering for manipulating the flow of water. Near Chiusi, Montepulciano Lake Nature Reserve displays what remains of the prehistoric swamp of the area; it's a good spot for bird-watching.

Elba Island Loop

DURATION	DIFFICULTY	DISTANCE
5hr	Intermediate	40km

Napoléon Bonaparte's place of exile, Elba can be reached by ferry from Piombino. With fabulous sea views and some of Italy's best beaches, the island is big enough for a full day of exploring by bike.

Starting from the main port of Portoferraio, there are various corners of the island you can explore. The cycling is mostly on quiet roads, and it's easy to pick one direction and create a route with a return loop. Parts of the island can be difficult due to the hilly terrain, but there's nothing too strenuous that requires heavy training. Alternatively, consider renting an e-bike to make it easier to visit some of the mountaintop lookouts that take in views of the beaches below.

WOJCIECH TCHORZEWSKI/SHUTTERSTOCK ©

Historic doors, Siena

The Volcano of Tuscany

DURATION	DIFFICULTY	DISTANCE
6hr	Difficult	40km

On the southern side of Tuscany is the dormant volcano Mt Amiata, the highest mountain in Italy at 1736m. This is a different kind of Tuscany to experience by bike.

Here it is primarily mountain-biking territory, but quiet roads also make leisure cycling a great way to explore. The leafy slopes of Amiata are delightful in autumn when locals are out with baskets full of nuts picked from the fields of chestnut trees. Those interested in the way people have lived with volcanoes in the past should ride to the mining town of Abbadia San Salvatore for a visit. At the end of a bike ride, a soak in the natural sulphuric baths at Bagni di San Filippo is just what tired legs need!

Gates of Siena

DURATION	DIFFICULTY	DISTANCE
1hr	Easy	12km

A city known for its association with the Palio, an ancient horse race between the *contradas* of Siena since the 17th century, has much history behind its city gates.

An itinerary where you can start from any gate you like, this is a gentle ride tracing the outer wall of Siena, visiting all 12 of the historic *porte* (doors), from the oldest Porta Romana and Pispini to the fortress linked to the powerful Medici family – the perfect way to learn about the history of the city. Finally, add on a loop around the sloped circuit of Piazza del Campo as a tribute to the Palio, which is raced on the same grounds twice each year.

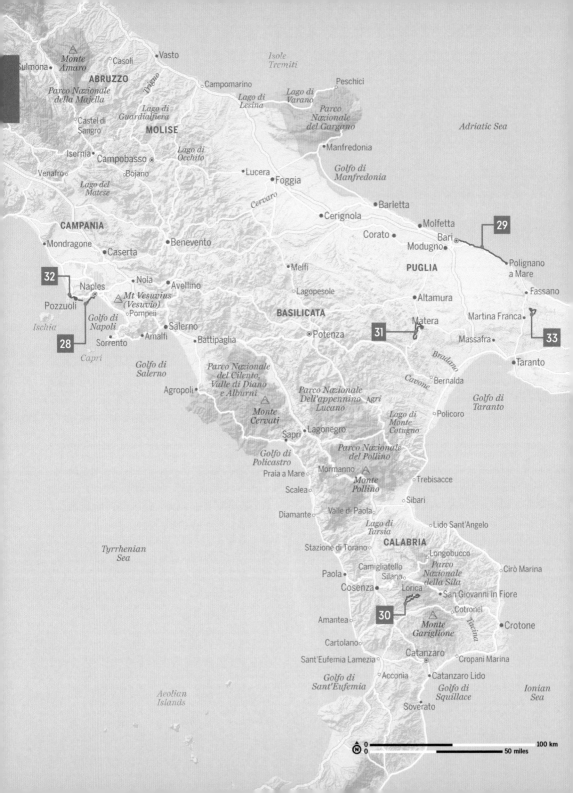

DYNAMOLAND/SHUTTERSTOCK ©

Roman ruins, Pozzuoli (p194)

Southern Italy

Explore

Southern Italy

The lower part of the Italian boot is often known for its wild coastlines, rugged landscape and famously disorderly traffic. However, things have changed, and the increasing popularity of cycling has changed the priorities around infrastructure and tourism development. Not only are cycle lanes slowly being introduced in its cities and towns, much of the region has also ramped up the focus on creating cycle tourism itineraries through some of the most beautiful parts of southern Italy. From coastal routes to forest paths, a bike ride here will give you the opportunity to discover some of the least visited areas of some of Italy's least visited regions.

Campania

Best known for the bustling city of Naples and the archaeological area of Pompeii, Campania has been luring tourists to its dramatic coast since the 18th century. A lack of modern cycling infrastructure can make a comfortable ride hard to find, especially in and out of Naples, but the high concentration of Roman ruins, the chance to witness fascinating landscapes complete with active volcanoes, and the beauty of its coastline all make up a fantastic bike-riding experience.

Puglia

An Apulian *trullo* is the postcard image of Puglia, the grey coned roofs a notable contrast to what is more popularly believed to be

'Italian architecture'. In fact, this small region on the heel end of the Italian boot is a region full of surprises – of ancient dwellings, fragile fishing villages, gorgeous clifftop towns with whitewashed houses, and rows upon rows of olive groves against the brilliant turquoise of the Adriatic Sea. A ride into the countryside is a peek into the soul of the region and a chance to learn about some of the unique Apulian history and heritage through its architecture and cuisine.

Basilicata

Positioned right on the border of two regions, Matera is often mistaken as an Apulian city. While the Unesco Heritage Site of Sassi di Matera was made

WHEN TO GO

The best time to plan a cycling trip in southern Italy is during spring when the days are bright and not yet too hot, or autumn when the hype of olive harvest activities is in full swing. Try to avoid July and August, which will be exceptionally hot and busy, and winter from December to February, when most hotels and services close for the season.

more famous as a filming location for Hollywood movies, at the same time, it is also a great base for a cycling adventure in Basilicata. There are various cycle routes from here to nature reserves and national parks, and the more adventurous can try a long ride to the sea. Cycling isn't easy with the undulating rugged hills but the experience will be worth the effort.

Calabria

Known as the region of two seas, flanked by the Adriatic and the Tyrrhenian, Calabria has always been a place of crossroads. While most use the region as a gateway to Sicily, there are good reasons why Calabria is a rising star on Italy's cycle tourism landscape. The brand-new long-distance Ciclovia dei Parchi (Parks Cycle Path) project aims to link the four national parks along the spine of the region. The first section of the planned 545km route has opened through Sila and Pollino national parks and is promoted as being the best cycling experience in the south.

WHERE TO STAY

Southern Italy's lack of international chain hotels is its charm. From family-run B&Bs to independent boutique hotels, this is a region to really soak up the legendary warmth of Italian hospitality. In and around Naples, you'll find the widest range of accommodation options, including luxury resorts along the coast. In Puglia, stay in a traditional *trulli* or *massarie* for an authentic experience of this unique region. While the coast may be tempting in Calabria, it is worth spending some time in Pollino National Park where you have easier access to the first finished stages of the Ciclovia dei Parchi, still in development.

WHAT'S ON

Napoli Bike Festival

(napolibikefestival.it) A weekend of bike rides, concerts and activities celebrates everything bicycle and promotes better cycling infrastructure in the city. Usually held annually in May.

Festival Valle d'Itria

(festivaldellavalleditria.it) A popular international music festival over two weeks in July/August in Puglia's Martina Franca.

Calabrian Food Festivals

In Calabria, regional cuisine is celebrated with a series of festivals across August to November. The most unusual is the **'Nduja Festival** in Spilinga in honour of the spicy spreadable sausage in August, while the town of Sant'Agata di Esaro is particularly atmospheric in November when it celebrates the **Chestnut Fair**.

TRANSPORT

Naples is southern Italy's largest gateway. To access the rest of the south, there's a good network of regional train and bus services between most major cities and towns. In most cases, bicycles can be taken on trains at a cost, with the exception of Puglia, where it's free to take bicycles on board.

Resources

Visit Campania (www.italia.it/en/campania) Information on sights and attractions across Campania.

Calabria Tourist Office (calabriastraordinaria.it/en) A good resource for events and suggested itineraries across Calabria.

Cycling in Puglia (viaggiare inpuglia.it/ideeDiViaggio.do) Has specific information on cycling around Puglia.

Cycling in Basilicata (basilicataturistica.it/en) Has a list of cycle routes around the region of Basilicata.

28

Posillipo & Parco Virgiliano

DURATION	DIFFICULTY	DISTANCE	START/END
2hr	Difficult	17km	Piazza del Plebiscito

TERRAIN	Paved cycle paths, cobblestone road, tarmac road

FRANCESCA SCIARPA/SHUTTERSTOCK ©

Parco Virgiliano

On the surface, Naples is a jumble of traffic chaos, but once out of the city centre, a lovely bike path takes you across to the side of Naples that is leafier and quieter. Then, after a steady climb along the coast, you'll visit the affluent district of Posillipo and enjoy the views from Parco Virgiliano. You'll be sharing the road with cars on this ride, and the narrow streets can force drivers to get rather close, but most drivers do look out for bikes on the road and will slow down or stop for you. There is a method to the Neapolitan madness!

Bike Hire

Bicycle House is a cafe and bike rental space inside the beautiful Galleria Principe di Napoli. Rentals are available by hourly or daily rates, starting from €6 an hour.

Starting Point

Start at Piazza del Plebiscito, Naples' largest square with the Palazzo Reale di Napoli on one side and the Basilica di San Francesco di Paola on the other.

01 From Piazza del Plebiscito, join the traffic on the short road leading to the sea where you will find the beginning of a cycle lane. Turn right onto this cycle lane that will take you along the seafront all the way to the other end of Naples, passing the imposing Castel dell'Ovo to your left and the brilliantly chaotic city centre to your right.

Elevation (m)

Distance (km)

02 The cycle lane ends at Mergellina wharf, and you'll need to walk your bike across the zebra crossing and very carefully join the traffic going in the same direction. There is a confusing junction here at the lights; make sure you're turning into Via Mergellina in the direction of Posillipo.

03 You know you are in the right neighbourhood when the tarmac becomes a stretch of badly patched cobbled road. Cycling with the busy but mostly friendly traffic, you'll climb this narrow street that runs along the coast through the affluent Posillipo district. Pedalling hard, you'll be rewarded with the increasingly beautiful view to your left as well as the beautiful villas and colourful houses in this part of Naples.

04 There are a couple of terraces with views towards Naples and beyond; where there are photo opportunities on the left, pull over and walk your bike across just to be safe. After a short stretch of badly maintained cobblestones, the street is smooth with a bitumen surface again. Continue on; you're not far from the park now.

05 Turn left onto Via Tito Lucrezio Caro, and the winding hill will take you to the gates of Parco Virgiliano. You'll come to a small gate first, the easiest entrance should you need to use the toilet, or cycle on and enter from the main entrance

Castel dell'Ovo

Just off the promenade at the waterfront, Castel dell'Ovo (pictured above) is the oldest castle on the coast in Naples. First built in the 1st century BCE, it was transformed and expanded through various wars and conquests, meaning there's very little of the original castle left. It's called the 'Egg Castle' (as its Italian name translates) because rumour has it that the Roman poet Virgil placed an egg inside the castle's foundations while it was being built, claiming that, should the egg ever break, the castle will also crumble and mark the end of the city of Naples.

at the top. Explore the park at leisure, and enjoy the wonderful views of the surrounds from the viewpoints in the park, then continue on the suggested return route.

06 Exiting the park, go straight on Viale Virgilio. You can stay on the road, which is likely to be quiet, or use the driveway on the right side of the road that turns into a cycle and pedestrian path after the houses on the right. The path ends at a small roadside restaurant where you'll need to rejoin the traffic. When you come to the small roundabout, turn left onto Via Alessandro Manzoni.

07 There's a bit more steady uphill riding to go as the road curves right, revealing a good view of the Bagnoli area below. This is your last climb before a long, winding descent. Next you'll follow this wider, better paved road with traffic back to Naples. Although drivers continue to be friendly to cyclists, they have a tendency to drive faster on this road, so take extra care. At a small roundabout, follow the road to the right onto Via Francesco Petrarca.

08 This lovely tree-lined road will open up after 500m and you'll enjoy views of Naples and the sea to your right as you effortlessly roll downhill with traffic. The descent is gradual to begin with but it gets quite steep after the halfway panoramic point to your right. Simply keep a grasp on your breaks and stay in your line of traffic and there should be no problems. When you come to a fork, take the downhill option.

09 After a narrow sharp turn the road ends around the point where the seaside cycle lane ended earlier today. Depending on the time of day, you might find a couple of fishers selling their catch on the sidewalk. Walk your bike across the road, and, perhaps, continue walking until you find the entrance back onto the cycle lane.

10 Join the cycle lane again to return all the way back to Piazza del Plebiscito. Now that you are back, take your time to enjoy the waterfront atmosphere, often lined with trinket sellers, buskers and sunbathers.

☕ Take a Break

There are a couple of fuelling stops in Parco Virgiliano. In a side gate just before you reach the main gate into the park, you'll find a small kiosk selling coffee and snacks. At the end of the path to your left, you'll also find public toilets. There's another kiosk just inside the main area of the park near the athletics tracks. The park makes a good place to rest, with benches to enjoy views of Mt Vesuvius in the distance.

STEFANO TAMMARO/SHUTTERSTOCK ©

Archaeological park, Posillipo

Posillipo's Roman Past

Originally known as Pausílypon, meaning 'escape from worry' in ancient Greek, the Posillipo district of Naples is an affluent neighbourhood full of restored historic homes and cliff-edge beaches. Upon seeing the area's beautiful prospect, the Romans built grand, sea-facing villas here, which over the centuries gradually faded. In more recent years, they have been restored as luxury residences.

There is a submerged archaeological park on the small Gaiola island off the cliffs from Posillipo, which contains evidence of it being a former Pausilypon Imperial Villa, belonging to Roman Emperor Augustus.

29

Ciclovia Adriatica: Bari to Polignano a Mare

DURATION	DIFFICULTY	DISTANCE	START/END
3hr	Intermediate	37km	Bari/Polignano a Mare

TERRAIN	Paved cycle path, on road

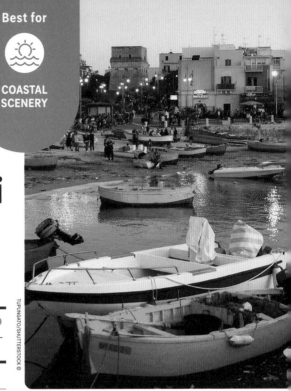

TUPUNGATO/SHUTTERSTOCK ©

Torre a Mare

A great way to experience the laid-back seaside of Puglia, this cycle route along the coast is part of the longer Ciclovia Adriatica cycle route that begins in northern Italy and ends at the tip of the Italian boot. On this itinerary, you'll cycle from bustling Bari through faded resort towns such as Mola di Bari before ending at beautiful Polignano a Mare, all the while enjoying the simmering Adriatic Sea by your side. Due to the length and the requirement to cycle mostly on road, it is suitable for those used to commuting by bike.

Bike Hire

Velo Service (veloservice.org) from the city centre of Bari has bike rentals starting at €15 per day for a leisure city bike to €35 for an e-bike.

Starting Point

The start point in front of Teatro Margherita on Piazza IV Novembre is not far from the bike hire location and Bari's tourist information point.

01 Start in front of Bari's Teatro Margherita on the edge of the old town near the wharf. From here, walk your bike across the zebra crossing on Piazza IV Novembre and towards a park with a statue of Giuseppe Massari. You can now join the on-road cycle lane that runs along the busy Lungomare Araldo di Crollalanza. Other than looking out for cars coming from side streets and buses pulling over at their stops, you should feel no pressure from the passing traffic here. Disappointingly the bike lane ends after just a kilometre;

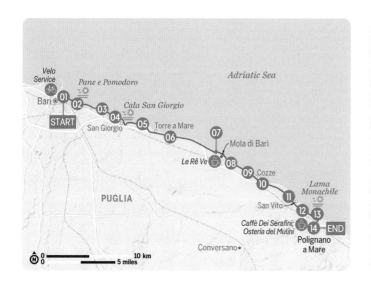

TOP TIP:

Travelling with your bike on trains in Puglia is free. Train carriages with bike racks are usually at either end of the train. Newer trains in Puglia also come with e-bike charging points, making exploring the region by any kind of bike easy and convenient.

Elevation (m)

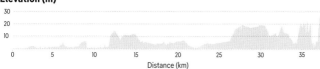

Distance (km)

nevertheless, continue along this coastal road, passing a series of grand administration buildings and a city park on your right. At the upcoming intersections, keep going straight while watching out for turning vehicles. You'll soon be out of the centre of Bari and the streets should become quieter.

02 White sandy beaches – the first with a quirky name Pane e Pomodoro (Bread and Tomato) – now follow on the left side of the road, where the road merges into Corso Trieste. There is a bike lane that runs behind the hedges along the beach, with an awkward access point through a narrow gate at a small round platform marked by a palm tree. If you miss it, con-

tinue on the road which, anyhow, is the easier option. Otherwise, follow this cycle lane until a large car park, where you'll want to exit and join the traffic by crossing the zebra crossing on foot.

03 The surrounds during the next few kilometres will feel rather dilapidated, but among some of the crumbling houses you might spot a couple of rundown *trulli*, the traditional houses of Puglia. Things get a little livelier when you approach San Giorgio. After a four-way junction and a small bridge beyond, turn left onto the minor Strade del Pantano and follow it as it weaves through residential houses before turning left again at Traversa III S Giorgio. Ride along and curve with it to the right as you arrive at

a small beach – Cala San Giorgio – with fishing boats.

04 The road along the coast of San Giorgio can be very busy on market days, as it's here that many fishers set up shop to sell their catch of the day right by the edge of the road. Locals come here by bike or car, and the atmosphere can be very exciting. However, many people double park for convenience and traffic can get chaotic – look out for any sudden movements while enjoying the bustling vibe that this little village radiates.

05 This coastal road will take you to the end of the village, where it will divert inland to enter the next town, Torre a Mare. If you like, turn

☕ Take a Break

There's a selection of cafes, bars and restaurants in Mola di Bari, which marks the approximate halfway point of the itinerary. Try **Le Rê Ve** on the street corner at the harbour end of Piazza XX Settembre. The outdoor seating will be particularly practical for the bikes and there is a good selection of bakery items (grab some packaged cookies to take on your journey) and cold drinks, as well as a menu of fish burgers. But unfortunately no coffee.

left into one of the side streets (the best one being Cristoforo Colombo) to check out this small waterfront town, and visit the lively harbour with the ancient gates to Bari. Otherwise, at the end of this stretch of road, you will come to a T-junction with Via Bari. Turn left here.

06 You are now cycling on a minor road parallel to the major highway. The road is well surfaced and the few cars that do drive on this road are mostly local traffic. About 2km from Torre a Mare, a cycle lane appears on the left side of the road at an exit point of the highway. Carefully join the cycle lane on the opposite side of the road, which will take you into the resort town of Mola di Bari. Observe where the cycle lane switches to the other side of the road a number of times, marked by a strip of red paint or zebra crossing, requiring you to cross over to continue. Cars do not always stop so take extra care when crossing.

07 Arriving in Mola di Bari, join the lovely but underused cycle path lined with palm trees along the waterfront. There's a small fishing wharf to your left and a small fortified castle to your right, making a nice photo stop. If you

have time, it might be worthwhile making a diversion to visit Palazzo Pesce, browse the narrow shopping streets and take a turn around the pretty Piazza XX Settembre with a fountain centrepiece where you can pause for a coffee in one of the surrounding cafes.

08 The cycle path with palm trees ends around the bend after the castle and you'll need to join the traffic again, but not for long. Just after passing the harbour to the left and a small roundabout decorated with an anchor on your right, you will turn left to continue along the coast, joining the red-painted cycle path in front of the Chapel of Holy Mary of Grace on Viale Unità D'Italia.

09 As there are no footpaths along this road, many pedestrians use this narrow cycle path as a way in and out of town. Show courtesy, alert early with a bell and pass slowly. The path will run for about 4km before ending at the town of Cozze. When it does, join the traffic, and turn left (third exit) at the large roundabout coming up.

10 Back on the minor road, take a few moments and look to your left to divert your eyes from the uninteresting

SABINO PARENTE/SHUTTERSTOCK ©

Mola di Bari

Mola di Bari

Mola di Bari's story dates back to the 13th century when it was an embarkation point for the crusaders. Over time it became a fishing village and a seaside resort, and a substantial agricultural and fishery industry remains. It's not uncommon to see elderly fishers mending their nets by their boats – it's their catch which the town lives to consume. The octopus is celebrated here and the annual Octopus Festival in July is widely anticipated; octopus is cooked using traditional methods, either gilled and stuffed in a sandwich or stewed.

Volare!

Of all the things and people Polignano a Mare could celebrate, it is Domenico Modugno that takes centre stage. This Italian singer of the popular song 'Volare' was born here in 1928, on a day when the strong winds of the Maestrale blew across this clifftop town. The town used to call him 'Mimi'.

You'll find photos of young Domenico on the wall inside Bar Supermago del Gelo, where he used to eat his ice cream, and on the edge of town by the sea is a bronze statue of the singer. It hasn't been an easy relationship though – for many years the town held a grudge against him for pretending he was from Sicily!

Domenico Modugno statue

highway. While you can't really see the sea from here, there are a few old farm buildings and *trulli* to be seen among the olive groves. As rural life fades and holiday resorts begin to appear, you know you are near. Keep going.

11 Past signs to the town of San Vito, where there's a large service station with a shop and cafe should you need anything, Polignano a Mare will start to appear on the horizon. You'll pass a big resort on your left with low white buildings and lush green lawns; continue a bit further, through a large intersection and turn left onto a side street marked as a no-through road.

12 The street ends at a small car park in front of a restaurant, where you'll find a gravel path to your right leading to a small beach. Follow it through, walk your bike across the sand, and join the narrow road in front of you. It's technically a driveway to the parking area of the couple of hotels and restaurants on each side; cycle with caution. At the top of this driveway, a delightful cycle and pedestrian path lined with wooden fences will take you into the heart of Polignano a Mare.

13 Enjoy the scenery of the wild sea and the view of the whitewashed houses built on the dramatic cliff of Polignano a Mare while you can because the cycle path ends shortly and you will need to rejoin traffic. Follow the flow of traffic on Via S Vito, taking it slow, as soon you'll come to the balcony of the town: a view of the most photographed Lama Monachile cove and beach on your left.

14 You're now in Polignano a Mare, and the cycle route will take you around the main sights of the historic centre, including a picturesque square and clifftop terraces for views of the caves. Feel free to divert from the itinerary and explore on your own; perhaps enjoy a seafood meal in one of the local restaurants or do some souvenir shopping before cycling through town and ending this excursion at the railway station for your train back to Bari.

☕ Take a Break

To really soak in the atmosphere of Polignano a Mare town, enjoy a meal at one of several quality restaurants serving local seafood to tame your post-ride hunger before your train home. **Osteria dei Mulini** is in a charming alley in the historic centre and serves traditional Puglian cuisine, predominantly featuring seafood. For a coffee, **Caffè Dei Serafini** on Piazza San Benedetto with a view of the sea offers great espresso and friendly service. The owner also has a good wine list should you feel it time to really relax.

30

Lago Arvo Loop

DURATION	DIFFICULTY	DISTANCE	START/END
2hr	Intermediate	28km	Lorica
TERRAIN		On road	

MARCO FINE/SHUTTERSTOCK ©

Lago Arvo

A scenic loop around Lake Arvo is a perfect way to discover the beauty of the Parco Nazionale della Sila (Sila National Park), Calabria's green heart. This stunning route starts and ends in the resort town of Lorica, weaving in and out of pine-forest-lined roads, always with views of the lake in sight. The lake is on the itinerary of Calabria's newly established long-distance cycle route, the Ciclovia dei Parchi. While the full course is on road shared with traffic, cycling is a popular activity here, so you won't encounter any issues.

Bike Hire

If you are staying in Lorica, local bike and tour operator Hitinero has bike rentals from €30 per day. Otherwise, rent a bike from Consenza and get here by coach, which can take bikes on board on limited services.

Starting Point

You could potentially start anywhere in Lorica. For a scenic start to the ride, begin at the east end of town on the road next to the lake.

01 You can start anywhere along the lake shore in Lorica, but the mapped route will begin on a bend in the road, outside a B&B on the east side of town. Follow the lovely paved road west along the lake, ignoring all turn-offs until the end.

02 This pretty lakeside road eventually meets the main Via Nazionale. Turn left onto the road, taking care to look both directions for traffic. You'll be following this main road for the

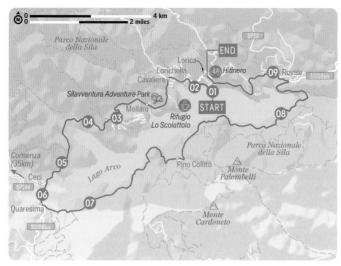

☑

TOP TIP:

There are no shops along the way, so it's best to shop in Lorica for picnic supplies to eat along the way. There are several points on the lake where you can deviate onto the hiking paths and stop for a break.

Elevation (m)

Distance (km)

remaining of the ride. The initial few kilometres will have you pass through the villages of Lorichella and Cavaliere. There are several side tracks that branch off from the main road, which leads to the lake side or hiking trails. Explore them if you wish, especially the tracks around Silavventura Adventure Park, then return to the main road to continue.

03 Although considered a main road, it's quiet most of the time. Greenery is all around you, which sometimes opens up to houses with vegetable patches between them. Around the 4km mark, there's a slight incline, with the steepest point coming up at Km 5. You are now on a hill looking down towards the lake, and all the climbing is

rewarded with a panoramic of the landscape.

04 Continue. The road deteriorates a little and becomes slightly narrower as you ride further away from the main urban areas on the lake. Look out for small natural spring water fountains on the roadside to your right for opportunities to fill your drink bottle.

05 There's more of an incline before a lovely straight descent approaching Ceci; here the landscape opens up to agriculture fields on both sides. Ignore the fork on entering Ceci and keep to the road on the left. You'll pass a couple of barn structures and a small electrical substation on your left as you

About Lago Arvo

Stretching 9km wide, Lago Arvo (Lake Arvo) is an artificial lake that has, since 1931, served as a dam generating hydroelectricity for the surrounding areas, but there's evidence of human settlement here since ancient times. Other than the tourist resort of Lorica and other nearby towns, villages surrounding the lake are mostly agricultural and cows can often be seen grazing on the grass along the lake's shore. The lake is rich with fish and the natural surroundings full of birds and wildlife; it's popular with hikers and those who come for water activities in summer.

continue on this route. Ignore the blue traffic sign indicating a turn-off to the right and continue straight ahead, following the brown tourist route of Parco Nazionale della Sila.

06 The next short stage of the road suddenly becomes better maintained, but unfortunately this doesn't last! At the next junction by the village Quaresima, turn left onto a secondary road and ride through this small farming community. You will pass an electricity tower on your left. The view is fantastic from this far-western end of the lake. Soak it in.

07 Now you are riding along the southern shore of the lake, with a stretch of uphill coming. Push on, and it levels down as the lake disappears behind the trees to your left. The road winds in and out of pine forests and lush meadows, leading you to the small, almost abandoned village of Pino Collito, with a crumbling farmhouse that greets you on a hairpin bend. There's a bit more climbing to do after the farmhouse, with a stretch of larch pines known as Giganti della Sila, the giants of Sila. Lining the road densely in parts, their presence can make a difference on a hot summer's day!

08 After following the road for a while, you'll find a lovely mansion appearing on your left. This is a good spot for a view, and between the trees you can almost see across to the opposite side of the lake where you began earlier in Lorica. After the mansion, take the left downhill road when you see a fork on your way. Follow it until it ends at a T-junction in Rovale, and turn left at the T onto Strada Statale 108bis in the direction of Lorica.

09 Cars can be travelling faster on this stretch of road, so listen for any passing vehicles as you cycle along. Follow the course of this road all the way into Lorica, ignoring a big turn off to your right leading into the forest. You'll pass a campsite surrounded by pine trees. Follow the sign pointing to Lorica, and enjoy the final leg of your bike ride.

☕ Take a Break

After the ride, a detour to **Rifugio Lo Scoiattolo** just outside Lorica is worthwhile. A popular spot for lunch and dinner, the menu of light antipasti plates and hearty pasta and meat dishes is served amid the forest on the lake.

LAPAS77/SHUTTERSTOCK ©

Sila National Park

The Pine Trees of Sila

Sila National Park is the oldest national park in Calabria, and is most associated with its protected forest of *pinus laricio* Poiret, the Calabrian Pine. There are nine biogenetic nature reserves in the park, two of which are dedicated to the protection of the Calabrian pine, tenderly nicknamed 'Giganti della Sila', the Giants of Sila. In a particular part of Sila, the ancient forest of pines date back to the 17th century, with some estimated to be over 350 years old and as tall as 45m. You'll encounter stretches of pine forest on your bike ride, although around the lake, you'll mostly find younger, regenerated pines.

31

San Giuliano & La Cripta del Peccato Originale

DURATION	DIFFICULTY	DISTANCE	START/END
3hr	Difficult	40km	Piazza Vittorio Veneto, Matera

TERRAIN		Tarmac and gravel roads

Elevation (m)

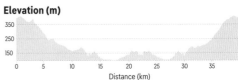

A ride through serene farmlands and a visit to the nature reserve of Lago di San Giuliano is a beautiful cycling experience, very different to the Unesco-protected Sassi di Matera. After the initial few kilometres of traffic, the quiet undulating country roads open up to blanket views of rural Basilicata, a landscape filled with birdsong during the warmer months. A visit to the Crypt of the Original Sin by bike is a bonus to this great day out. An e-bike is recommended to tackle the rise and fall of the landscape.

Bike Hire

Ferula Bike Shop is a friendly rental store near the Matera train station with a variety of bikes, including high-end road bikes and e-bikes. Rentals cost from €25 per day.

Starting Point

Piazza Vittorio Veneto is the main square with access points to Sassi di Matera. Adjacent to the roads leading out of Matera, it's also a good place to meet and purchase supplies for the ride.

01 From Piazza Vittorio Veneto, head north away from the pedestrian area and cautiously join the traffic on the corner where Via Roma bends into the one-way Via XX Settembre. Ride straight ahead onto Via XX Settembre, which is lined with street parking and loading zones. Depending on the time of day, this otherwise quiet street could be very busy with commercial activity, so watch out.

02 Continue until you pass a lovely park on your left, where a small road merges in from your right. There's a six-way roundabout coming

Piazza Vittorio Veneto, Matera

up, where you'll take the third exit (or second, if you discount the one-way street coming into the roundabout) onto Via Annunziatella. Take care on this popular commuter route in and out of Matera, lined with commercial shop fronts on both sides. At a fork, go left onto Via Nazionale.

03 Still on uneventful city streets, follow Via Nazionale until after the road flies over the highway below and turns into Viale dei Peucezi. At the next roundabout, turn left onto Via dei Dauni. Follow this road of mostly industrial traffic through two roundabouts until the larger roundabout marking the end of

Via dei Dauni. Turn right onto Via Gravina, once again full of Matera's industrial and farm traffic. After more small roundabouts, the road widens and splits into a large roundabout again. This time, turn left, onto Via Granulari.

04 You are now entering the farming area of Matera, by the looks of the tractors on sale along this road. Travel for about 280m, turn right onto Via delle Officine, then in another 100m, turn right onto a roundabout, where you'll take the left exit onto the main road (SP6) with olive groves and stone walls on your right and a beautiful outlook of the valley to your left.

05 Follow SP6 for a while, and notice it curves to the left after about 800m. Flanked by rows of olive trees, this is potentially a nice ride if there's no traffic to battle, although you will have only another 800m after the curve to go before turning onto a gravel country road to your left, Contrada Chiatamura, marked by a blue sign pointing to La Martella. Turn left here.

06 Although the road surface is not ideal, the ride gets easier and more pleasant now that the main roads out of Matera has been left behind. There should be little traffic now, with only the occasional local

☕ Take a Break

On the ride to the reserve there are no stopping points to buy supplies, so it's best to stock up in Matera for a picnic by the lake. **Il Buongustaio**, a small deli on the corner of Piazza Vittorio Veneto, is a top place to pick up quality local cheese, cured meats and a bottle of wine for the ride. **House of Bread** next door will satisfy you with bread, pastries, cookies and slices of pizza to complete the picnic platter.

farm vehicle requiring access, so relax and enjoy the views. You will be following this road all the way to its end, accompanied by olive groves, wheat fields and vegetable patches along the way.

07 You'll come to a junction with a major road after about 3km; cross with care and continue on the small road. From this point, the road deteriorates into gravel and mud, with the worst surface coming up just outside a cattle farm. After another couple of kilometres, the road ends at a T-junction. Turn right onto Strada Provinciale Papalione. This is a good road for panoramic views of the surrounding valley. With limited traffic, you can really enjoy the country air as you pedal all the way, mostly on a descent, to the Lake Giuliano Reserve. Keep following it as it bends and twists, until the final steep downhill, where you will see the lake shimmering on the horizon, takes you to the end of the road where you need to turn left.

08 The lake is now on your right, and you will soon be able to turn onto a signposted path leading to the reserve. Turn in, as it will be a chance to have a picnic break on the shores and enjoy the natural surrounds with a healthy population of birdlife around the reserve. If you wish, you could

end the ride here and turn back. Or, after you've had a fill of fresh lakeside air, continue on to see something very special. Return to the road and turn right. Follow it as it winds its way around the reserve and farms. This should be a quiet road, but watch out for tractors. Keep riding until you see an electrical substation and a road to your left. Turn left here.

09 This small road will lead you to the La Cripta del Peccato Originale (Crypt of the Original Sin), a special attraction of the Matera area outside the old city. On the way, notice a water reservoir on your right; this is one of the best places to look back towards the lake reserve. Continue and pass vineyards on your left and right before you come to Casal Dragone, an accommodation, restaurant and farm shop; stop for supplies if it's open. The path from here to the crypt is on steep, loose gravel, so it's a good idea to park your bike at the house and walk down. The time to visit the crypt has not been factored into the ride duration.

10 After visiting the crypt, start your return journey by tracing your route back to the end of the first farm track you came on. This time, instead of turning left back onto it, continue up Strada Provinciale Papalione as a short cut. You will come to

RENATO GRANIERI/ALAMY STOCK PHOTO ©

La Cripta del Peccato Originale

La Cripta del Peccato Originale

Discovered in 1963 by a group of local youths playing around in the area, the Crypt of the Original Sin is a rupestrian church inside a natural cave with religious frescoes dating back to the second half of the 8th century. Commonly known as 'the Sistine Chapel of rupestrian art', it's filled with biblical figures, the most treasured of which is a representation of the Virgin Mary dressed in the sumptuous clothing of the Byzantine empress, the Basilissa. As the name of the artist is unknown, the nickname 'flower painter' is used by locals to refer to the person behind these paintings.

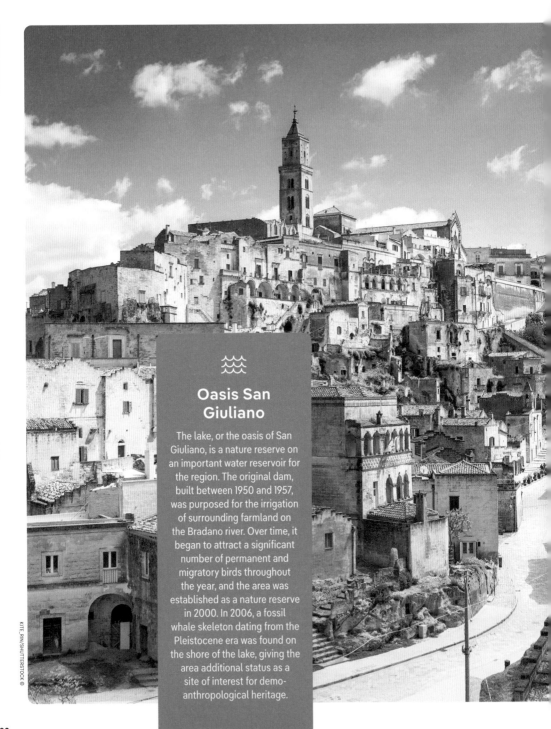

Oasis San Giuliano

The lake, or the oasis of San Giuliano, is a nature reserve on an important water reservoir for the region. The original dam, built between 1950 and 1957, was purposed for the irrigation of surrounding farmland on the Bradano river. Over time, it began to attract a significant number of permanent and migratory birds throughout the year, and the area was established as a nature reserve in 2000. In 2006, a fossil whale skeleton dating from the Pleistocene era was found on the shore of the lake, giving the area additional status as a site of interest for demo-anthropological heritage.

Matera

a junction with multiple entry and exits onto the road. Continue straight from here, and follow the flow of traffic to the right onto Via la Martella. You are now back in urban Matera so take extra caution as you cycle along with traffic.

11 On Via la Martella you will encounter two large roundabouts. Simply continue straight, keeping to the same road. After the second roundabout, there is an opportunity to cycle on the little side parking area along the shops. As you come to the end of it, turn right onto an unnamed road then turn left at the next crossroads, onto the residential Via degli Aragonesi.

12 There are a few twists and turns through dull neighbourhoods coming up as we try to avoid the main roads. At the end of Via degli Aragonesi, turn left onto Viale Italia, then take the next right. Follow it to the end, turn right at the T-junction then take an immediate left. You should now be on the smaller Via Ettore Maiorana (a larger road of the same name branches off on the right). Follow the road until the end where it meets the main road; turn right here.

13 Carefully navigate around the large roundabout, walk across the zebra

TOP TIP:

The return route to Matera is extremely hilly, so ask about the bike shop's pick-up service, where you and the bike can be picked up from the reserve at an additional cost, saving you the steep climb home.

crossings if you have to, and turn onto the tree-lined Via Alessandro Manzoni. After 200m, turn right onto Viale Giuseppe Parini, which becomes Via della Croce after an intersection with a small traffic island in the middle and a couple of cafes to your left and right. Continue up in the same direction until you meet the junction with Via Lupo Protospata, which opens up to Via Nazionale on your left.

14 You'll need to cross the small Via Lupo Protospata before turning right onto this now familiar road where you travelled from this morning. Follow it, with a small deviation to adhere to the one-way street system, back to Piazza Vittorio Veneto. It's now time for a post-ride coffee.

☕ Take a Break

Casal Dragone is a family-run *agriturismo* (farm-stay accommodation) en route to the Crypt of the Original Sin. The house you see is the old family farmhouse of five generations, which is now a B&B with an on-site restaurant serving light meals of pasta, omelettes and stuffed pizza made from the farm's own produce. Wine tasting packages are also available. Check if it's open on the day of your visit, as it's often closed during quiet seasons.

32

Best for

HISTORY

Roman Pozzuoli & Lago d'Averno

DURATION	DIFFICULTY	DISTANCE	START/END
1.5hr	Intermediate	17km	Piazza Bagnoli (Bagnoli)/Pozzuoli Solfatara train station

TERRAIN	On road, gravel path

ENRICO DELLA PIETRA/SHUTTERSTOCK ©

Miseno peninsula

Near Naples there's an intriguing area dotted by lakes and Roman curiosities. A ride along the coast between Bagnoli and Pozzuoli is a pleasant start to discovering this less-visited area, with a beautiful outlook to the sea, a feature that is consistent throughout the ride. Arriving at Pozzuoli, you'll discover Roman ruins similar to those found in Rome, evidence that Pozzuoli was once a significant Roman city. With the exception of the nature loop around Lago d'Averno, cycling infrastructure is unfortunately sparse; luckily most drivers will look out for cyclists on the road.

Bike Hire

You're best off renting a bike from Bicycle House in Naples and travelling by the train to Bagnoli.

Starting Point

Piazza Bagnoli is just 50m from Bagnoli train station by the beach. If you're not staying in the area, Bagnoli has regular train and metro services from Naples.

01 From Piazza Bagnoli, follow the coastal cobbled road shared with traffic in the northwest direction on Via di Pozzuoli. Continue in this direction, passing the bus terminal on your right, where the road is renamed Via Napoli. Enjoy the view towards the Miseno peninsula ahead of you. Reaching the end of the town, the road curves and travels along the coastline. Continue until you approach Pozzuoli.

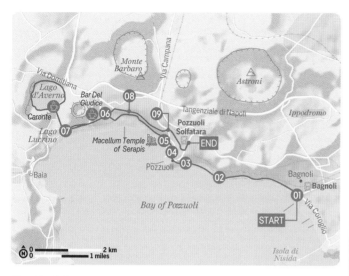

MAURIZIO DE MATTEI/SHUTTERSTOCK ©

Elevation (m)

50
30
10
0   2   4   6   8   10   12   14   16
Distance (km)

02 Keep following the traffic. You'll notice the start of a seafront promenade on your left as you get closer to the urban centre. After a pink building on your left is an entrance onto this promenade for bikes. This is a lovely stretch of the beach of Pozzuoli where you can stop for a break and some photo opportunities. At the end of the promenade turn right, then using the zebra crossing, walk your bike across to continue cycling on the road to the left.

03 Turn right onto one-way Via Salvatore Baglivo, a cobbled street just after a car park. When you reach the end of the street, turn left onto an even narrower one-way street and a short tunnel. Cycling through the tunnel is an experience!

04 Emerging from the tunnel, turn right onto cobbled Via Giovanni de Fraia. If you wish, you could walk around the pretty old harbourside village on your left before continuing. Note that cycling is not allowed in the village pedestrian areas. Otherwise, at the end of Via Giovanni de Fraia, turn left to follow Via A Maria Sacchini. The road splits just after the train station. Ignore the wide ascending ramp on your right and take the smaller road on the left towards a patch of Roman ruins.

Pozzuoli

Pozzuoli probably doesn't ring a lot of bells for the average tourist, but evidence suggests that it must have been an important Roman town, due to the existence of several ruins found in the area. Back then, Pozzuoli was called Puteoli. It is one of only four cities in the world to have two Roman amphitheatres, one of which, the Flavio amphitheatre, is the third largest in Italy. The smaller amphitheatre (pictured above) has been buried under modern buildings, although some arches can still be seen between the roads. The existence of a marketplace, baths and villas is another indication of the wealth of Puteoli during Roman times.

05 The Macellum Temple of Serapis is the ruins of a Roman public market, punctuated by three marble columns in between the bricked sections. After this brief photo stop, continue on the same road and follow it as it merges onto Via Nicola Fasano. Industrial areas cover the next couple of kilometres and traffic can get a little busy; stay on the side and keep cycling. Stay on Via Nicola Fasano until you pass under a low traffic bridge where the road turns into Via Raimondo Annecchino. You'll pass Arco Felice train station on the left, where the road veers right, ending at the junction with two traffic islands. Take extra care to turn left here, onto Via Miliscola.

06 Via Miliscola is a bustling road with a row of busy shops and cafes, which is a good place to stop if you wish to take a break. Continue along it until you notice the road broadens, splits and is joined by the exit of a tunnel. Take the ascending one-way street on the far right, allowing you to avoid the busiest part of Via Miliscola. Follow it until it meets the main road again at a small roundabout with multiple exits. Take the second exit on the right; you should have a small lake on your left.

07 When you arrive at a fork with a gate signed Parco del Laghi, continue on the road to the right. The road is lined with reeds until it ends at tranquil Lago d'Averno. A bike and walking trail circumnavigates the lake, which you'll ride by turning right to follow the gravel track.

08 On returning to the same point where you began, take the same road back to the main road, turn left onto Via Miliscola and follow it in reverse until you come to the junction with traffic islands. This time continue straight onto Via Campi Flegrei. After a short ride, Via Campi Flegrei flows towards the right where it is joined by another road coming down from the left. This is now a rather busy road, but pleasant with sweeping views of the sea on the right. A steady incline will take you to a viewpoint at the top.

09 At a busy roundabout with a palm tree, take the second exit onto Corso Nicola Terracciano. Visit the Roman amphitheatre coming up on the left, then follow the edge of the amphitheatre to the Pozzuoli Solfatara train station.

☕ Take a Break

Bar Del Giudice on Via Miliscola in Pozzuoli has been in business since 1953, and is credited for inventing the city's sweet pastry called the *procolino*. This is a perfect place to stop for a coffee. For a more substantial feed with a view, **Caronte** on the shore of Lago d'Averno has a simple menu of pasta and pizza dishes. For street food options, a small kiosk on the right side of the road before the amphitheatre sells a range of fried finger food.

Lago d'Averno

Lago d'Averno

Lago d'Averno (Lake Averno) is a volcanic crater lake that was considered by the Romans to be the gateway to hell, featuring as a synonym to death in much Roman literature. At the same time, the Romans also came here for leisure activities, and the ruins of a bath can still be seen on the east side of the lake. In April 2022 the lake famously turned a bright shade of pink, which caused an online sensation, generating both awe and worry. While the lake turns a tinge of red each year around the same time, due to a natural occurrence of algae releasing biochemicals in the water, the pink colour was usual!

33

Ciclovia Acquedotto Pugliese

DURATION	DIFFICULTY	DISTANCE	START/END
1hr	Easy	14km	Cisternino

TERRAIN		On road and gravel path

P TOMLINS/ALAMY STOCK PHOTO ©

Apulian aqueduct

Puglia is a land of *trulli*. These distinct houses of grey pointy roofs and whitewashed walls are the postcard of an Apulian experience and you'll encounter plenty on your ride along these country roads lined with olive groves and vineyards. In most parts, you'll be cycling on roads shared with traffic, making this ride more suitable for those used to commuting by bike. There's also a lovely stretch of the Ciclovia dell'acqua, a bike path that follows the Apulian aqueduct, a special part of Puglia's culture and heritage.

Bike Hire

MeBike Puglia in Cisternino is run by two enthusiastic locals. Rental prices for their fleet of e-bikes start at €25 per day, and varies based on duration and other needs.

Starting Point

Start at a small car park (easily reached from any part of the city) at the bottom of the stairs that take you up to Cisternino's popular terrace lookout: Belvedere Cisternino.

01 Starting from a small car park on Via Martina Franca in Cisternino, which has a lovely view of the surrounding Itria Valley, ride downhill until you come to a fork just after the Church of Santa Maria di Costantinopoli on your right. Turn right onto Via Benedetto Croce.

〰 Apulian Aqueduct

Despite being a coastal region, Puglia has always been known as arid. Roman poet Horace described his native land as having a 'thirst that rises to the stars'. As population grew in the area, the traditional method of rainwater collection was no longer sufficient. The lack of water required a modern solution that turned into one of the largest construction projects in Italy in the 20th century: the Apulian aqueduct. Construction of the full 2189km of aqueduct that brought freshwater to various parts of Puglia started in 1906 and was officially finished in 1939. Today parts of the aqueducts are still in use, bringing water to farmlands and rural villages.

Elevation (m)

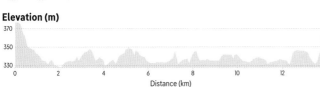

02 You are now on a secondary road without much of a shoulder, which is typical of Puglia. Follow this road as it changes name to Contrada Barbagiulo. Keep going until you come to a stop sign after a stretch of concrete walls to your right. Turn left here; you are still on Contrada Barbagiulo. Cross the railway tracks, then turn right at the fork at the end onto a narrower road.

03 You are now on a lovely unnamed country road flanked with stone walls and surrounded by olive trees. Follow it, ignoring all turn-offs until the end where you'll meet the line of railway tracks. Turn right towards the crossing, then cross at an opportune moment.

04 Turn left, the road immediately bends right, then left again. Follow it, passing a *trullo* immediately on your right and one among olives trees and a vineyard on your left. When the road comes to an obvious fork, turn right. Still on an unnamed road, continue with it as it curves left and right; you'll come to a cross junction with a gravel path. Turn right onto the gravel path. You are now on the Ciclovia dell'acqua, the Apulian aqueduct cycleway. For the next kilometres you'll enjoy traffic-free cycling.

05 The gravel path ends on a main road, where you will turn right and join the traffic for a short while, before turning left onto Via dei Trulli, a beautiful narrow road with vineyards, olive trees, a number of old *trulli* houses, and a sweeping view of the valley to your left.

06 Cycle through the commune of Figazzano. After a small roadside chapel and before the end of town, turn right onto Via del Parco, a narrow lane on an incline which will level out as it bends right. Follow it. You will come to a junction with a main road; cross carefully and continue on the narrow lane until a multi-Y fork. Follow to your right onto Contrada Figazzano.

07 Follow a series of left and right turns where the road eventually becomes a dirt track until it meets a tarmac road leading you back on the gravel bike path. Turn left and you'll be following the aqueduct cycle route southbound where the path ducks under the railway line and through beautiful Apulia countryside. Along the way, you'll cross Strada Provinciale 13, a main road, as well as two minor roads. Look twice both ways before crossing.

08 Coming up to the village of Portarino, turn left at the intersection. This unnamed street is lined with stone walls and you should see a *trullo* house coming up on your left and right just after turning. Keep following this narrow road until you come to the end in the village of San Salvatore. Turn left, then immediately turn right at the stop sign. After another cross junction, you'll come to a fork. Go left, and travel further until a larger fork in the road appears. Follow it to the left.

09 Passing more *trulli* houses, you will eventually come to a junction with a triangular roundabout in the middle. Follow the flow of traffic to turn left here. Follow it until a roundabout on the main road, Strada Provinciale 13. At the roundabout, turn right (the first exit) and travel with traffic for about 500m, then carefully turn left onto Via Martina Franca. This last stretch is a climb up as it curves right leading you back to Cisternino – hopefully you still have some energy left!

☕ Take a Break

Caffè della Valle is a small cafe popular with commuting tourists; it's near the village of Cervillo on Strada Provinciale 13, close to where you will cross the main road on the bike path the second time. The cafe has bike parking, outdoor seating and a good selection of pizza, *panzerrotti* and local-style sandwiches.

Alternatively, for something sweet, **Almond Pasticceria Artigianale** is an artisan bakery-cafe at the end of the road from San Salvatore, on the edge of Cisternino. Enjoy a cake or gelato in the lovely garden.

THEGRIMFANDANGO/SHUTTERSTOCK ©

Puglian *trulli*

Trulli of Puglia

The distinct shape of the *trulli* (or *trullo* in its singular form) is a feature on all Apulian landscapes. The grey pointy cones and the rounded whitewashed walls can be spotted among the olive groves and vineyards of the Istria Valley. The style dates back to the Messapians, a group of tribes who settled in the region during the Iron Age; today the oldest *trulli* still standing are several thousand years old.

The *trulli* design is based on self-sufficiency, with double-walled insulation allowing the house to be cool in summer and warm in winter. Today the *trulli* are mostly used as farm storage or tourist accommodation, which makes a unique experience to a visit to Puglia.

Also Try...

Pollino National Park, Calabria

The Easternmost Point of Italy

DURATION	DIFFICULTY	DISTANCE
1hr	Easy	12km

From the seaside town of Otranto, ride south to enjoy the beauty of Puglia's Salento Coast, flanked by farm fields and landscapes dotted with ancient defence towers that once alerted in sequence any attacks from the east.

It's one direct route before the white lighthouse – the easternmost point of Italy – comes into sight. Keen cyclists can continue onto the town of Porto Badisco for more views of the dramatic coves and pretty beaches this stretch of coastline is known for. Return by the same route, stopping to visit Cava di Bauxite as you get closer to Otranto. Traffic will be sparse, but the road surface won't be great, so much swerving around potholes will be required.

The Calabrian Coast

DURATION	DIFFICULTY	DISTANCE
1hr	Intermediate	14km

The beautiful coastline of Calabria is much celebrated for its cross-cultural heritage and wild rugged landscape.

While cycling along the entire coast is achievable, the stretch between Scilla and Bagnara is less busy with traffic and easily accessed by train. Both towns boast beautiful beaches and ancient sights, and the ride along the coastal road hanging on the edge of the cliff is as spectacular as it sounds. Along the way you will see derelict houses wedged between rocks and seaside mansions. This is a route popular with road cyclists, although you'll also encounter leisure cyclists enjoying an active day out. Cycle with caution as the rocky surrounds make it more difficult for cars to see you on the road.

Porto Badisco, Puglia

Ciclovia dei Parchi della Calabria

DURATION	DIFFICULTY	DISTANCE
4hr	Difficult	34km

The Ciclovia dei Parchi in Calabria is a cycle route of 545km down the national parks of Calabria (Aspromonte, Sila, Pollino and Serre), passing quaint villages and stunning nature.

A small recommended section begins at the hilltop village of Laino Borgo. You will cross into Laino Castello before arriving at Mormanno, where you should taste the famous filled biscuits called *bocconotti*. From here it's onwards through a fragrant lavender farm before a steep incline up Serra mountain. The descent into medieval Morano Calabro is the thrilling finale. Steep climbs give this route its difficult rating, but those who accept the challenge will be rewarded with laid-back Calabrian hospitality, brilliant nature and a look into the region's historic past.

Porcida Island

DURATION	DIFFICULTY	DISTANCE
2hr	Intermediate	20km (or more)

Shadowed by its bigger sister, Ischia, Porcida is a small island with brightly coloured houses and offers a great day out from Naples and surrounds, particularly on a bike.

There are no specific routes to take on Porcida, simply follow your curiosity to discover its many corners. As a general guide, make sure you include Corricella, the island's oldest village and the one with the most colourful palette in its houses, and the island of Vivara, a nature reserve accessed via a bridge from Porcida. Lastly, take one more good look at Porcida from Terra Murata, the medieval village that looks out to the sea. For easeful navigation up and down Porcida's narrow streets, hiring of an e-bike is recommended.

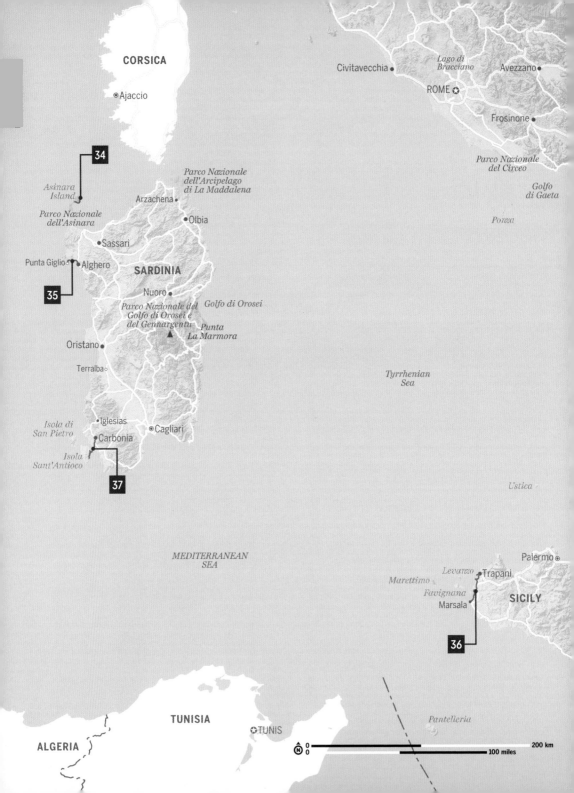

CORSICA

Ajaccio

34

Asinara
Island

Parco Nazionale
dell'Asinara

Parco Nazionale
dell'Arcipelago
di La Maddalena

Arzachena

Olbia

Punta Giglio

Alghero

Sassari

SARDINIA

35

Nuoro

Golfo di Orosei

Parco Nazionale del
Golfo di Orosei e
del Gennargentu

Punta
La Marmora

Oristano

Terralba

Isola di
San Pietro

Iglesias

Cagliari

Carbonia

Isola
Sant'Antioco

37

MEDITERRANEAN
SEA

Civitavecchia

Lago di
Bracciano

Avezzano

ROME

Frosinone

Parco Nazionale
del Circeo

Golfo
di Gaeta

Ponza

Tyrrhenian
Sea

Ustica

Palermo

Levanzo

Trapani

Marettimo

Favignana

Marsala

SICILY

36

TUNISIA

TUNIS

ALGERIA

Pantelleria

N 0
0

200 km

100 miles

STEFANO ZACCARIA/SHUTTERSTOCK ©

Cala d'Oliva (p209), Asinara

The Islands

Explore

The Islands

Italy's largest islands – Sicily and Sardinia – are known for the inviting clear waters of their wonderful coastlines. And while there is plenty of that, crossing the Mediterranean to explore these islands guarantees a memorable experience that includes much more than just pristine beaches – here archaeological treasures blend with lush nature, regional cuisine bursts with unique flavours and every journey on two wheels is a continuous surprise. Climb along cliffs dropping into the ocean on a mountain bike, or roam the empty roads of uninhabited islands once closed to the public – whatever route you choose, you'll be rewarded with spectacular scenery.

Sicily

The largest island in the Mediterranean, Sicily boasts a cultural and historical heritage that incorporates Italian, Greek, Arab and Spanish influences into its food, its architecture and its dialect. Such a rich tradition is complemented by natural elements that range from the dark slopes of Mt Etna, continental Europe's largest volcano, to the crystal-clear waters touching places like Favignana, off the western coast. Exploring Sicily on a bike means taking in the best of both worlds, riding from city to city through unparalleled scenery along the coastline or in the interior. The small towns of the Val di Noto in eastern Sicily offer some of the most impressive architecture in the region, while the winding streets of Palermo or the rolling hills of Erice are worthy alternatives to the relaxing beach resorts. While the infrastructure for cyclists is far from well developed – cycling lanes are few and far between – many secondary roads see little traffic and allow for peaceful riding between sights. The heat during summer months can get unbearable, but thanks to its mild winters and warm springs, Sicily makes for an ideal off-season cycling destination.

Sardinia

It's not uncommon to meet people taking a few weeks off to ride along the whole 1897km of Sardinia's coastline, the longest in all of Italy. You can't really blame long-distance cyclists –

WHEN TO GO

Both Sicily and Sardinia see a huge influx of tourists during summer – avoid July and August if you'd rather have the coasts for yourself. Peak holiday season also means extreme temperatures, which can make longer cycling trips far from pleasurable. Plan your trip in spring or autumn for best climate conditions.

travelling on a bike on the island of Sardinia means riding along panoramic routes for days on end, from rural countryside to historic cities. The mountainous interior drops into picturesque farmland at a lower elevation to reach picture-perfect beaches, glistening oceans and precipitous cliffs as the land merges with the water. Opportunities to discover the traces left by the ancient Nuragic or Roman civilisations mix with the breathtaking scenery that attracts so many during summer months. For those not wanting to take on the challenge of a grand tour of the island, shorter routes abound. Roads have well-maintained surfaces and are mostly traffic-free, especially during the low season. An increasing number of dedicated cycling lanes have been built in recent years, and further inland, trails wind their way through the beautiful Mediterranean forests, passing through narrow valleys and ancient ruins. Cycling Sardinia is a unique opportunity to explore a beautiful part of Italy. No matter how much time you have, you'll always find something to do.

TRANSPORT

Trains are a cheap – albeit slow – way to move around both Sicily and Sardinia. Not all trains allow for carrying bikes on board; look for the bicycle symbol when booking tickets on trenitalia.com. In Sardinia, buses run by ARST have space available for bikes; ask the driver. The surcharge for taking bikes on trains is €3.50; ARST buses require an extra ticket to bought for carrying the bike on board.

 WHAT'S ON

Cavalcata Sarda

If you find yourself in northwestern Sardinia on the second to last Sunday of May, stop by Sassari to check out the Cavalcata Sarda, a traditional celebration where horse riders perform daring parades and acrobatic stunts in the city's streets.

GiroSardegna

(girosardegna.it) Sardinia's first long-distance cycling race is held each year in April. Its longest itinerary runs for 438km.

 WHERE TO STAY

Both Sicily and Sardinia offer options for every budget and taste, from seaside campsites to luxurious holiday beach resorts. Hostels are typically present only in larger cities or in the more popular destinations, while camping is only allowed in designated areas. In places like Asinara island, accommodation is only available between April and October. Prices can double during summer months, when most visitors arrive to make the most of the islands' beaches; avoiding peak holiday season will save you some money and free you from crowds.

Resources

Sardegna Ciclabile
(sardegnaciclabile.it) Showcases complete cycling itineraries in Sardinia, including elevation profiles, detailed maps, and sights along the way.

Parco Ciclistico Etna
(parcociclisticoetna.com) Contains information on possible routes to follow around Mt Etna, Italy's highest active volcano, in eastern Sicily.

34

Best for

WILDLIFE

Asinara Island

DURATION	DIFFICULTY	DISTANCE	START/END
3hr	Intermediate	20km	Cala Reale

TERRAIN	Mostly paved, some sections unpaved

Asinara

Positioned at Sardinia's northwestern tip, Asinara island emerges shyly from the deep-blue waters of the Mediterranean, offering a peaceful retreat to a population of feral donkeys, wild horses and lively goats that inhabit its sunburnt landscape. For well over a century the island has been closed to the public, functioning first as a penal colony and then as a maximum security prison for Italy's most infamous criminals. From cycle paths that run across the barely inhabited island, traces of this past are still visible.

Bike Hire

In Porto Torres, E-bike Asinara (ebikeasinara.it) provides mountain bikes and e-bike rentals starting at €20 and €35 per day. Taking the bike on the ferry costs €3 each way. Guided tours are available.

Starting Point

Ferries run year-round from Porto Torres on Sardinia to Cala Reale in approximately 1½ hours. This is your starting point for the route. Tickets cost €17.50 both ways.

01 Take the first ferry from Porto Torres and you'll reach the small port of Cala Reale, in the central part of Asinara, just in time to start your cycle across the northern part of this sun-bleached island. Ferries depart Porto Torres at 8.30am and reach Cala Reale port at around 10am. The main structure welcoming you in Cala Reale, was once the summer residence of the royal Savoy family, who ruled over the Kingdom of Sardinia before the unification of Italy in 1861. Take some time to explore the nearby Austro-Hungarian chapel, then

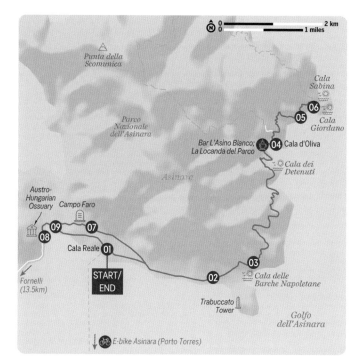

Elevation (m)

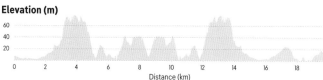

pedals to face the long incline leading towards Cala d'Oliva. The twisting road climbs up on the ridge offering exceptional views of the surrounding scenery. The ascent is worth the effort; after reaching the highest point (71m) after approximately 3km, you'll be refreshed by the dry, salty air hitting your cheeks as you ride downhill all the way to Cala d'Oliva, visible in the distance.

04 A group of low white houses will appear as you approach the settlement of Cala d'Oliva, nestled between two rocky beaches. During the high season you'll find a couple of restaurants, a hotel, a world-class diving centre and a hostel here, although Cala d'Oliva's tourism industry is both limited and relatively recent. When it was turned into a maximum security prison in 1885, Asinara's population moved to Sardinia proper and left Cala d'Oliva in the hands of the authorities that later erected the bunker where ill-famed mafia boss Totò Riina would eventually be held captive. Take some time to explore the whitewashed hamlet and the former prison. Make sure to pay a visit to the workshop of wood sculptor Enrico Mereu, said to be the island's only permanent resident, then continue north along the coast.

05 This stretch is known as the Sentiero del Faro (Lighthouse Route) and runs from Cala d'Oliva all the way to the Faro di Punta dello Scorno – the northernmost tip of the island. A mountain bike is essential for this section and some experience will come in handy,

head east along the coast in the direction of Trabuccato, past the eerie, terracotta-coloured Sanitary Station, which hosted thousands of sick prisoners during WWI.

02 The initial stretch of the itinerary runs parallel to the Sentiero dell'Asino Bianco (White Donkey Route) walking path, and you'll soon understand why. Small, friendly, albinistic Asinara donkeys roam freely around the scattered buildings that once formed the local hospital-slash-prison. Within minutes you'll pass by

the promontory where you'll see the lone Trabuccato Tower, which dates back to the 17th century, keeping watch over the turquoise bays east and west. There is a side track leading to the tower if you want to take a closer look, but otherwise continue northward keeping the coast on your right.

03 Past the promontory and the tower you'll reach the tempting Cala delle Barche Napoletane, a white sandy beach worth taking a break for. Dip your toes in its clear waters then get your feet back on the

Take a Break

With next to no permanent residents on the island, Asinara can't claim much of a restaurant scene. Two eateries are found on the itinerary covered in this guide, both in Cala d'Oliva, although they operate only during the high season. **La Locanda del Parco** prepares fine seafood dishes and offers accommodation to those who wish to stay overnight on the island. **Bar L'Asino Bianco** is a cafe where you'll find quick lunches and sandwiches to be enjoyed with a side of mesmerising ocean views.

as there are large rocks on the ground. Your destination here is not the lighthouse – which began functioning in 1859 – but rather Cala Sabina and Cala Giordano, two pristine coves found approximately 2km from Cala d'Oliva. If you choose to cut your trip short – perhaps due to an extended freshly caught seafood lunch in Cala d'Oliva – you can skip to step 9.

06 One of the most beautiful beaches on Asinara has to be earned. To get to Cala Sabina (also known as Cala dei Ponzesi) you'll follow the uneven path amid the bushy Mediterranean vegetation growing up from the coast. Cala Sabina will welcome you with its transparent waters hugged by sand and juniper shrubs behind a hill sloping down into the sea. Here you'll find picnic tables, ideally positioned to enjoy a packed lunch with a view. Steps away is Cala Giordano, a lesser-known but equally mesmerising beach offering a quiet refuge on those rare summer days when Cala Sabina is too busy. From here you can turn back and return to Cala d'Oliva.

07 Once you get back to the main track it's all smooth sailing to Cala d'Oliva and then Trabuccato. Take the winding cliffside road you travelled on earlier, circling Cala dei Detenuti (Inmates Cove) and Cala d'Oliva's watchtower. Ride past Trabuccato's prison cells until you see a split on the road, just before the sign marking the entrance into Cala Reale. Take the unpaved track on the right. Ride behind Cala Reale on the island's interior to the graveyard of Campo Faro. Watch out for grey and white donkeys crossing the path, take a look at the old post office and then move onward towards the lagoon. You'll ride beside a wide grassy plain near where wild horses come to rest, and then across the flat body of water populated by herons and flamingos.

08 The final leg of the itinerary will take you back to one of the darkest times of Asinara's history. Shortly after the lagoon you'll encounter a straight, white side path leading to a cross-shaped building. This is the Austro-Hungarian Ossuary, a religious complex built in the 1930s at the request of the Austrian government as a space to

ELISA LOCCI/SHUTTERSTOCK ©

Asinara donkey

Asinara Donkeys

Small in size and covered in white fur, the free-roaming indigenous donkeys of Asinara are known all over Italy but their origin remains uncertain. Legends abound – ask around and you'll hear stories of shipwrecks and transcontinental trade between rulers. In all likelihood, these animals were simply indigenous grey donkeys that developed a form of albinism that spread across the island over time. It's often thought that the name Asinara comes from the word donkey, *asino* in Italian. However, Asinara is actually derived from the Latin term *sinuaria*, given by Romans and meaning 'bent', to reflect the jagged profile of the island's coastline.

The Austro-Hungarian Chapel

During WWI, Asinara was transformed into a concentration camp for tens of thousands of Austro-Hungarian prisoners of war who had been captured in the Balkans during the conflict with Serbian forces. With the Austro-Hungarian forces expanding in 1915, the Italian government agreed to move 30,000 prisoners captured by the Serbian allies to Asinara. Many died of cholera, and those who survived quickly developed depression due to the desert island's lack of stimuli. To keep busy, the prisoners built the 4.5m by 4.5m chapel that is still found in Cala Reale today. The chapel's lunette was decorated by Hungarian prisoner György Nemess.

give Austro-Hungarian prisoners of war a dignified burial. The structure contains the remains of over 7000 people who had died in the penal colony during WWI and were initially buried in mass graves. The ossuary is closed to the public, but you can peek through the glass door to see the 18 glass cases housing the prisoners' bones.

09 Make a stop at Cala dell'Ossario, opposite the Austro-Hungarian Ossuary, for one final swim before returning to Cala Reale and completing the circuit. On the way back, cross the lagoon once again and take the main road on the right, passing the Cala Reale church and the animal rescue centre where injured sea turtles are given a second life. Push a little further and you'll reach your starting point at the visitor centre; by the time you get there the former royal palace will be kissed by the warm, setting sun. The last ferry to Porto Torres departs from the Cala Reale port at 4.30pm or 5.30pm during the low season (October to April), and at 6pm

TOP TIP:

Stock up on water and supplies in Porto Torres before heading to Asinara, especially if you're travelling in the low season. There is a CRAI supermarket near the port in Via Mare 24, which opens at 8am.

during the rest of the year. Check schedules at delcomar.it.

If you are riding your own bike or don't need to be back in Porto Torres on the same day, consider crossing the whole island all the way south to Fornelli, where ferries depart to Stintino. This will add an additional hour of riding to the itinerary. Stintino is located 28km north of Porto Torres and 55km from Alghero.

 Take a Break

When cycling through Asinara remember to bring your own supplies, as tourist infrastructure is mostly non-existent, especially from October to April. Luckily, there are plenty of hard-to-beat picnic spots, where you can stop and enjoy a break surrounded by nature and wild donkeys. During the summer months the heat can be scorching – bring plenty of water. Also, leave no trace behind.

Austro-Hungarian Chapel

35

Best for

COASTAL SCENERY

Alghero to Punta Giglio

DURATION	DIFFICULTY	DISTANCE	START/END
3hr	Intermediate	35km	Alghero

TERRAIN	Mostly paved, some sections unpaved

ARKADY ZAKHAROV/SHUTTERSTOCK ©

Alghero

From the sand-coloured fortress embracing the historic centre of Alghero, a fantastic bike ride will take you to Fertilia and then Punta Giglio along a seaside cycling path that enters a natural reserve where exceptional views of both Alghero and Capo Caccia await. Visit one of Sardinia's ancient *nuraghi*, then continue into a protected forest once used as an anti-aircraft base during WWII. Scenery, culture and adrenaline come together on the breezy, watchtower-dotted coast of northwestern Sardinia.

Bike Hire

Raggi di Sardegna (algherorentabike.com) operates in the heart of Alghero and provides both mountain bikes and e-bikes for hire. The friendly staff are ready to help you with any tips you might need.

Starting Point

The cycling lane starts just outside Alghero's fortress by the port, near a sign that commemorates the passage of revolutionary Giuseppe Garibaldi in the city.

01 Hop on your mountain bike in the historic core of Alghero and ride out in the early morning, passing the ancient towers and defensive cannons that adorn the city centre. Head towards the port where sailboats line up one after the other and join the cycling path that you'll notice running parallel to the water in the direction of Fertilia, a small settlement outside of Alghero. While the flat, straight path might tempt you to build up speed, be careful as pedestrians often seem unaware that it's a dedicated cycling route. Especially in the vicinity of Alghero, where the route runs next to pop-

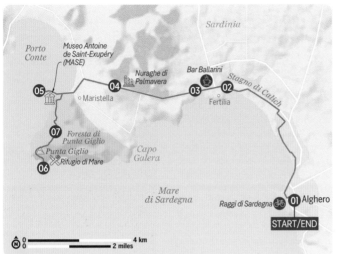

Elevation (m)

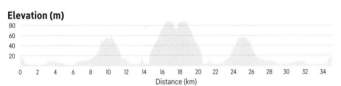

ular beaches and seafront cafes, the path can be mistaken for a sidewalk. Ride out of the city past the pastel-coloured hotels.

02 Welcoming you into Fertilia is a yellow bridge from which you'll notice the ruins of an ancient Roman bridge stretching into the water. This relic once spanned 24 arches across the Calich pond, but in the 1930s approximately half of it was destroyed. Turn right after the new yellow bridge to visit the tiny archaeological park and take a few steps on the 2000-year-old structure left here by the Romans.

03 Cross Fertilia and continue following the cycling path that runs next to the forest on the right-hand side

of the main road. Continue for 3.5km all the way to the quintessentially Sardinian Nuraghe di Palmavera, an incredible archaeological site worth visiting on your way to Punta Giglio. The stone-built complex is believed to have been erected starting from around 1500 BCE, later growing to become a settlement consisting of more than 150 huts.

04 As you leave the Palmavera site behind, the long, straight road slopes down until a roundabout, where the cycling lane ends. Take the left in the direction of Maristella and ride beside the Hotel Porto Conte. Continue straight until you reach the watchtower facing the Capo Caccia. The watchtower contains the Museo Antoine de

The Catalan Language

As you roam the streets of Alghero and its surroundings, you may notice that many street signs carry text in two languages – Italian and Catalan. The dominant Catalan presence in Alghero dates back to the early 14th century, when the Aragonese colonisers formed an enclave in the area of Alghero, uniting the region with the crown of Aragon. Public offices reserved for Catalans were opened and many Sardinians expelled. Since then ancient Catalan is one of the indigenous languages of northwestern Sardinia, spoken only within the municipality of Alghero.

Saint-Exupéry (MASE), an exhibition space dedicated to the French pilot and writer and author of *The Little Prince*. Antoine de Saint-Exupéry arrived in Sardinia in 1944 and spent several months living in a villa overlooking the Bay of Porto Conte. The MASE Museum traces the events that marked Saint-Exupéry's life before, during and after his stay in Alghero, through documents, photographs and interactive installations.

05 Turn back and ride on the same road you came from for 700m. On your right you will see a fence marking the entrance to the Foresta di Punta Giglio nature reserve. Take the gravel path leading towards Punta Giglio and start your climb to the tip of the promontory. This is the most challenging part of the route – you will have to climb up to 120m altitude. The limestone promontory of Punta Giglio is home to numerous animal and plant species. The first part of the trail twists and turns amid marine pine trees until you reach the highest point where the vegetation gets lower and dwarf palm trees and juniper shrubs are hit by the sunshine.

06 Continue until you see Rifugio di Mare, the restaurant and guesthouse positioned on top of the promontory. You can leave your bike by the structure and continue on foot to reach Punta Giglio, a few minutes further up. Along the white gravel path you will see a series of circular military fortifications, used to spot incoming enemy planes during WWII. You can enter the structure and climb up to the roof for a spectacular view of Alghero, on your left, and Capo Caccia, on your right.

07 To get back, retrace your steps following the same path you climbed earlier. A refreshing downhill trail will take you back to the entrance of the park, where you can take a right and ride back to the roundabout. Take a right once again and continue straight all the way to Alghero, past the Calich pond and into the historic centre of the city.

☕ Take a Break

Located by a roundabout between Fertilia and the Nuraghe di Palmavera complex, **Bar Ballarini** makes for an ideal refuelling spot on your way out from Alghero or on the way back. The menu is composed of a long list of stuffed focaccias and freshly caught seafood dishes to be enjoyed on the sunny terrace. Traditional desserts such as *seadas* (light pastry filled with cheese and honey) are also available as well as great espresso to get you going after a generous lunch.

Nuraghie di Palmavera (p215)

◎

What is a Nuraghe?

A *nuraghe* is a type of ancient megalithic structure found in Sardinia, originally built by the Nuragic civilisation that inhabited the island during the Bronze Age. Thousands of such mysterious tower-like structures are scattered around the island, adorning the landscape. Historians and archaeologists still debate the origin and purpose of these ancient castles, but they are generally believed to have served as defensive fortifications. They may have also had religious or ceremonial functions, as well as being used for other practical purposes such as grain storage. Today *nuraghi* are an important part of Sardinia's cultural heritage.

36

Through Trapani's Salt Pans to Marsala

DURATION	DIFFICULTY	DISTANCE	START/END
3hr	Easy	39km	Trapani/ Marsala

TERRAIN		Paved

Elevation (m)

Along the western coast of Sicily, in Italy's deep south, some of the country's most important salt pans expand between two historic cities opening onto the Mediterranean. Cycling from Trapani to Marsala through the island's mirror-like flats, between ancient mills and past flocks of flamingos, is a full immersion in unparalleled scenery best enjoyed at a slow pace. History and nature blend across two protected reserves, taking you from the 'city of two seas' to one of Sicily's renowned wine regions, where a sweet reward awaits after a ride.

Bike Hire

Mercé and Bike Shop Noleggiamo both operate in central Trapani, offering city bikes and mountain bikes for hire. Call in advance to book your bike in the high season.

Starting Point

Start your trip on the southern edge of Trapani's historic centre. Anywhere near the port – Piazza Garibaldi, for instance – makes for a good take-off spot.

01 Few natural elements are needed to produce salt – sea water, wind, sunshine and low rainfall. These resources abound in the province of Trapani and they are also some of the essential ingredients of a great cycling trip. Looking out over the Egadi Islands, historic Trapani offers a mix of ancient castles and baroque architecture encircled by nature reserves and long, sandy beaches. Before setting out to explore the coast and the salt pans, it's worth taking a peek inside the spectacular Cattedrale di San Lorenzo and visiting the archaeological museum housed inside the Torre di Ligny, a defensive structure dating back

Best for

FOOD

Windmill and salt pans near Marsala

to the 17th century that is now home to artefacts recovered from the Mediterranean seabed. Once you're done touring the city, fuel up with an espresso or *granita di caffè* and a freshly made *cannolo* (ricotta-filled fried pastry shells) at Pasticceria La Rinascente, two minutes north of Trapani's port, then jump on your bike to start your journey south towards Marsala. From the port, head east taking Viale Regina Elena and then Via Ammiraglio Staiti.

02 Continue until reaching Via Libica, leaving the historic city centre behind. Ride to the roundabout and continue straight onto Strada Pro-

vinciale 21, the main road you will be following on and off all the way to your destination. Here, right after the roundabout, you'll enter the magic landscapes formed by Trapani's salt pans – a timeless place where shallow, geometrical ponds expand in their stillness on both sides of the path.

03 Shortly after exiting Trapani's core you'll reach the Riserva Naturale Saline di Trapani e Paceco, a protected natural area covering nearly 10 sq km. The path cuts through artificial basins that have been used to extract salt for centuries. It's believed that Phoenicians were already collecting salt here as early

as the 5th century BCE, although the distinctive mills you'll see reflected on the thin layer of water covering the ground are much more recent. Salt trading became a pillar of the local economy in the Middle Ages during Sicily's Aragonese period and has continued to this day. The Saline di Trapani e Paceco reserve was established in 1995, becoming a biodiversity hot spot. Landscape and wildlife photographers will want to stop at the panoramic viewpoint located in the middle of two basins, especially during the early-morning hours. About 240 bird species use the salt flats to rest between flights throughout the year – telephoto lenses will come in handy here.

☕ Take a Break

Located steps away from Nubia's Museo del Sale, the restaurant **La Torre di Nubia** makes for an ideal lunch spot outside of Trapani. Open for lunch and dinner, this seaside eatery serves generous portions of dishes that elevate local produce such as pistachios and freshly caught fish. The menu changes often, so ask the staff for a recommendation based on the season. If available, try the typical *busiate* pasta served with swordfish, prawns or mussels. Tasty vegetarian options are also available.

04 Make a short detour from Strada Provinciale 21 to head towards Nubia, where you'll find Trapani's great Museo del Sale. The local salt museum is housed inside an ancient *baglio* – a 17th-century, stone-built farm topped by a six-sail windmill – and showcases artefacts, photographs and documents tracing the history of salt extraction and trading in Trapani. From working tools such as the *ruzzoli*, once used to flatten the soil, or the *cattedri*, used for the salt's transportation, the exhibits will help you put the scenery into context. Even if the museum is closed – as it may be during the winter – its traditional architecture makes it worth a stop.

05 Continue cycling on the narrow roads that run parallel to Strada Provinciale through Salina Grande, then rejoin the main road to reach Palma and then Marausa. At this point you'll be approximately halfway to Marsala; if you're looking to break the itinerary, take a right and ride for less than 3km to Lido di Marausa, where a long, sandy beach will welcome you with views of the Egadi Islands of Favignana and Levanzo, not far off the coast. Both islands, easily reached from Trapani, are well worth a visit – especially if you happen to be in Sicily during shoulder season when temperatures are ideal and

beaches are still free from crowds. Once you pass Marausa you'll find Trapani's tiny airport.

06 Past the airstrips, take a right and reach the coast. Ride along the Baia dei Fenici, a popular beach during summer months, and enter the Riserva Naturale Isole dello Stagnone di Marsala. One of the earliest nature reserves to be established in Sicily, the Stagnone – literally, the big pond – encompasses a calm, transparent body of water that divides the mainland from Isola Grande and three other islands – Mozia, Santa Maria and Schola – forming this archipelago. Like the Riserva Naturale Saline di Trapani e Paceco, the Stagnone also forms an oasis for dozens of migratory bird species that can be seen lazily hovering over the shallow waters. Depending on the season, you might spot mighty herons, ducks, marsh harriers and even ospreys looking for food during their travels. Ferries travelling to the island of Mozia – colonised by the Phoenicians as early as the 8th century BCE – depart every half-hour from the Contrada Spagnola area and take 15 minutes. Functioning as an open-air archaeological museum, the island has an entry ticket of €9, which can be purchased once you arrive at the port. It is worth parking your bike on the

Vineyards, Marsala

Marsala Wine

The product Marsala is most famous for outside of Sicily is the rich, nutty fortified wine that the city has been producing for over two centuries. Marsala wine – made from a blend of different grape varieties, including Grillo, Catarratto and Inzolia – comes in different styles and its denomination is protected by law, meaning it can only be made in this corner of Sicily and nowhere else. Marsala wine can be dry, semi-dry and sweet, and can be aged from one year to over 30. One of the best-known styles is Marsala *perpetuo*, where the wine is continuously blended with older vintages to create a consistent yet complex flavour.

Favignana

As you cycle between Trapani and Marsala, an island will emerge from the ocean about 7km from the coastline. It is the island of Favignana, the largest of the Egadi Archipelago, where pristine beaches, hidden coves and spectacular cliffs form the wonderful geography of this Sicilian gem. If time allows, it's worth taking a day or more to explore Favignana. During high season, regular hydrofoils and ferries depart daily from the ports of both Trapani and Marsala. Around Favignana's port there are many restaurants and cafes where you can stop for lunch, while resorts and B&Bs are scattered throughout the island if you want to spend the night.

mainland and reserving a couple of hours to walk around Mozia to visit its ancient necropolis and the Whitaker museum, where you can learn about the fascinating history of this Sicilian treasure trove.

07 At this point Marsala is getting close. As you ride along the coast, you'll notice the sea starting to quiver, set in motion by the wind that now blows freely no longer impeded by Isola Grande. Kitesurfers take advantage of the waves off the Contrada Spagnola road, which you can follow until reentering Strada Provinciale 21, leading directly into Marsala's historic heart.

08 You won't have to travel for long in Marsala to find an excuse to celebrate reaching your destination. Right after entering the city of Marsala from its northern border you'll have the opportunity to taste one of the products the city is most proud of – the aptly named Marsala fortified wine. The Cantine Pellegrino has been operating continuously since 1880 and runs tours and tastings in its winery located by the Parco Salinella, parallel to Strada Provinciale 21. If you started your trip in the morning it should be early enough to go for a tasting session (but late enough to justify a drink or two!).

TOP TIP:

One of the unexpected traditional foods you will find in Trapani is couscous, a dish that originated in North Africa but has become one of the staples of local cuisine. Served with seafood, couscous *alla trapanese* can be found on menus in pretty much every trattoria in town.

09 If you started your ride in Trapani's Piazza Garibaldi you may, for the sake of consistency, want to end the trip at Marsala's Porta Garibaldi, the stone archway in the heart of the city. Here, on 11 May 1860, revolutionary Giuseppe Garibaldi disembarked with the Expedition of the Thousand, opening the way for the Unification of Italy. After reaching the centre of town you can ride back to Trapani the way you came (the return train does not have a carriage for bikes), or continue cycling along the coast all the way to Mazara del Vallo, 24km south, in approximately 1½ hours.

☕ Take a Break

A short distance from the Riserva Naturale Isole dello Stagnone di Marsala, you can find **MammaColette's** homey restaurant and B&B welcoming you with its inviting outdoor terrace. Kitesurfers, cyclists and holidaymakers all come here to eat fresh, homemade food cooked up daily based on the availability of ingredients. If available, try the stuffed cuttlefish – one of the delights of Trapani's coast. The restaurant sits next to Marsala's kitesurfing club, in case you decide to test your skill on the Mediterranean waves before a hearty meal.

Favignana

37

Carbonia to Sant'Antioco

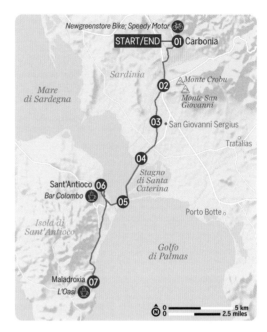

FABIANO CADDEO GORENE/ALAMY STOCK PHOTO ©

DURATION	DIFFICULTY	DISTANCE	START/END
3.5hr	Easy	42km	Carbonia

TERRAIN		Paved

Elevation (m)

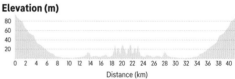

Welcome to Sulcis, a land of ancient traditions, breathtaking landscapes and rich history located in the southwestern part of Sardinia. Embraced by the Mediterranean waters, this little-known corner of Italy is traversed by a cycling path that was completed in 2020 after four years of work. The path connects the Fascist-era mining town of Carbonia with the island of Sant'Antioco via tranquil landscapes that blend the dry countryside filled with prickly pear cactuses with cliffs dropping into blue ocean waters. A favourite spot for divers and kitesurfers, Sant'Antioco calls for slow exploration.

Bike Hire

The Newgreenstore Bike shop and Speedy Motor can rent mountain bikes upon request in Carbonia. Make sure to give them a call in advance to check availability.

Starting point

The cycling lane runs parallel to the SS126 road. From central Carbonia you can take Via Aspromonte and you will see the path once you reach the roundabout.

01 A one-hour train ride from Cagliari takes you directly into the heart of Carbonia, the main urban centre in the Sulcis region of Sardinia. As you enter the town, you will notice its rationalist architecture made of simple geometrical shapes and symmetrical patterns. The style, typical of the Fascist era, is part of the historical heritage of the city – Carbonia was built almost from scratch in the 1930s to house the workers employed in the nearby Serbariu coal mine. From the main square, Piazza Roma, head

Historic mine, Carbonia

Carbonia's Coal Museum

To learn more about the history of Carbonia, it's worth visiting the city's Museo del Carbone, dedicated to the history of the Serbariu coal mine and its workers. Operating from 1937 to 1964, the main mine in the region drove the birth and growth of Carbonia, a city whose name literally means 'coal city'. Inside the museum you can join an underground tour during which you'll take a look at the machinery used to extract the mineral and visit an exhibition that looks at the working conditions of the miners who moved to Carbonia. Book tours ahead at museodelcarbone.it.

west towards Strada Statale 126, the main road that runs by the city. Take Via Aspromonte and as you reach the roundabout at the end of the street you should see the red cycling path running beside the road.

02 The initial stretch of this itinerary might not look very exciting – the road leaving the city tends to be heavily trafficked and the cycling path runs through an industrial area. But be patient – in a matter of minutes you will reach the open countryside and be surrounded by greenery. Follow the straight, flat path in the direction of the small settlement of San Giovanni Sergius. Two mountains – Monte Crobu and Monte San Giovanni – will accompany you on your left as you exit Carbonia.

03 After 7 easy kilometres you will reach San Giovanni Sergius. The cycling lane runs next to the town through a shaded section lined with trees and then a series of gardens fenced off by prickly pear cactuses. After passing San Giovanni Sergius, the path turns to the right; follow the route towards Sant'Antioco and you will soon find yourself surrounded by the water on both sides.

04 Connecting Sardinia's mainland with the island of Sant'Antioco is a thin stretch of land that runs between the open sea and the mirror-like Stagno di Santa Caterina, a flat body of water populated by a variety of birds. The protected area is home to pink flamingos, white herons, gulls and many other animals that can be spotted feeding on the shallow waters of the lagoon, partly occupied by the Sant'Antioco salt pans. On the opposite side you have the bay facing Sant'Antioco, which can be seen on the promontory in the distance. The weather conditions make the area an ideal kitesurfing spot.

05 After a break to check out the many species that populate the lagoon, continue until the bridge that leads into Sant'Antioco proper. The cycling path ends here. Next to the new bridge, you'll notice the remains of the ancient Roman bridge – known locally as Ponti Mannu – which used to connect the island known in antiquity as Sulci with the mainland, following the road that led all the way to Cagliari. The bridge has been restored multiple times over the course of the past century and now sits on dry land next to its modern counterpart.

06 Past the bridge take a right to reach Sant'Antioco's main square, an open piazza dotted with cafes facing the small port and the bay. Stop here to take a break in one of the square's terraces and after refuelling turn back to head towards the southern part of the island. Leave Sant'Antioco behind and ride on the quiet asphalt road past some storehouses and

ESKIMO/ALAMY STOCK PHOTO ©

Sant'Antioco

☕ Take a Break

Right on Sant'Antioco's *lungomare* (seafront promenade), **Bar Colombo** feeds hungry cyclists in front of the island's marina, preparing sandwiches, light bites and *aperitivo* cocktails served with finger food on its sunny terrace by the water. Open all day and busy during summer evenings, this little cafe will get you going for the remaining leg of the journey. Once you get to Maladroxia, you can recharge the batteries with a fresh fruit salad or an Ichnusa beer from **L'Oasi** cafe, located right by the beach.

farms that dot the eastern coast for approximately 9km.

07 Your destination is Maladroxia – a heavenly beach where fine sand is met by the turquoise waters of the Mediterranean. The road splits at Km 26, just before you enter Maladroxia; make sure to take a left unless you want to climb up Monte S'Arraigraxiu. Return

The Ancient Sulky

Archaeologists consider Sant'Antioco to be one of the oldest cities in Sardinia, due to findings demonstrating that the island was already permanently inhabited thousands of years ago. The discovery of ceramics of Phoenician origin dating back to approximately 800 BCE has led researchers to believe that Sant'Antioco – originally known as Sulky – had already developed its urban core back then. Thanks to its fertile interior and its seafood-rich surroundings, the island attracted a stable population earlier that much of the rest of Sardinia, developing as one of the most important trading centres in the Mediterranean.

to Carbonia, following the same route in the opposite direction. Or if you feel like continuing, you can keep riding along the coast (off the mapped itinerary) – the beautiful beaches of Coaquaddus and Turri await 4km and 5.5km respectively past Maladroxia, with spectacular views from Torre Canai. These beaches are popular in summer, but visit off season and you'll likely have them for yourself.

Also Try...

Bosa, Sardinia

Alghero to Bosa

DURATION	DIFFICULTY	DISTANCE
3.5hr	Intermediate	44km

After exploring the area of Punta Giglio near Alghero, consider heading south to get the most out of northwestern Sardinia.

The western coastline of the island is marked by a long, panoramic road that stretches from Alghero to Bosa, a colourful town in the province of Oristano. While the ride requires some stamina – due to a climb to 650m altitude about midway – the views that will accompany you for the duration of the journey make every moment worth it. When it's time to return to Alghero you can carry your bike on one of the ARST buses that connect Sardinian cities.

Pista Altomontana Etna

DURATION	DIFFICULTY	DISTANCE
3hr	Intermediate	36km

Reaching 3357m above sea level, Mt Etna is continental Europe's highest active volcano. Cycling on its slopes is no easy task, but if you're keen for an uphill challenge there are many options available to immerse yourself in the lava-covered nature of Sicily's Etna.

The Pista Altomontana runs around the volcano on a dirt track at an average altitude of 1700m, with many huts along the way that you can use if you decide to stay the night. The itinerary starts in Serra La Nave, reached by car via the SP92 road from Nicolosi, and is best explored during the summer months when the snow melts and uncovers century-old lava flows.

Modica, Sicily

Favignana Island

DURATION	DIFFICULTY	DISTANCE
2.5hr	Easy	33km

Cycling is the best way to see the island of Favignana (p222), off Sicily's western coast. Favignana is mostly flat and there are plenty of bike rental services on the island, making it accessible to everyone.

The road running along the coast stretches for approximately 33km, and while you can technically complete the loop starting and ending at the island's port in a couple of hours, it's worth stopping frequently to visit the many idyllic beaches that Favignana is famous for. Highlights include Cala Rossa, the best-known cove on the island, Cala Bue Marino and Cala Azzurra – natural swimming pools where you can spend hours on end.

Ragusa to Modica

DURATION	DIFFICULTY	DISTANCE
2hr	Intermediate	28km

A road filled with ups and downs will allow you to explore some of the late-baroque treasures of the Val di Noto listed as Unesco's World Heritage Sites in Sicily's Ragusa and Modica.

Visit the iconic Piazza del Duomo where the San Giorgio Cathedral stands, and the historic district of Ibla, the oldest part of Ragusa, then take off following the secondary road running along the Irminio river, into the lush valley leading to Modica. There awaits more stunning architecture, including the Duomo di San Pietro, the Cattedrale di San Giorgio and the Church of San Giovanni Evangelista.

Arriving

Italy's major cities are well connected by air to the EU, the UK and the rest of the world, as well as by train connections into bordering Austria and France and sea links to nearby countries, including France, Croatia and Greece. If you're travelling from outside Europe, you're likely to be landing in Rome, where an extensive network of internal express and regional rail connections can get you easily elsewhere in the country.

Travelling with a Bike

Travelling with a bike can take the hassle out of hiring one locally, but can also be an inconvenience and expensive in some cases. No matter what size, bicycles must be packed in travel boxes when flying or taking the non-regional trains around Italy. You will need to disassemble the bike for packing so give yourself plenty of time to practise and get it right. While you may consider it an essential item at home, never pack CO_2 cartridges. You'll lose them at security. There are no shortage of bike shops in Italy so better to purchase them when you are there!

While the bike is in the box, it will be considered luggage. Due to its size, extra charges will apply on flights and some train and long-distance coach services. Bike boxes are considered special luggage and are collected at the oversized luggage collection point at airports.

Rail Transfers

Rome Fiumicino Airport has train connections to the city and beyond. Fares cost from €8 one way.

Milan Malpensa Airport is the gateway for the north. Train fare to Milan is €13 one way.

Bari Bari Airport has a direct train to Bari Centrale (€5 one way).

Florence Florence's Amerigo Vespucci Airport has tram services to the central station (€1.50, additional for large suitcases).

ENTERING ITALY

If you're travelling from a country in the Schengen Area, there are no border checks other than the sign that indicates you have entered Italy. You will need your passport otherwise.

SIM CARD

You'll notice SIM card kiosks at the airport but you're likely to get a better deal at a mobile provider's store with pre-paid SIM options. Bring your passport as you might be asked for it.

CASH

Most credit and debit cards are widely accepted, but it's still a good idea to carry some cash in small denominations, especially in small towns and villages.

TAXIS

If you take a taxi from your point of arrival, make sure it's a certified metered taxi from a taxi stand and avoid any driver who approaches you to ask if you need a taxi.

Getting Around

DRIVING IN ITALY

A road trip in Italy can be exciting and terrifying at the same time. Away from major highways, roads are generally narrow and at times confusing. Be sure to check the conditions and rules with the car hire company before setting off.

Public Transport

You can easily travel between Italian cities using the extensive train and long-distance bus network around the country. If you plan to use the train a lot over a period of time, consider purchasing a suitable travel pass.

Bikepacking

Are you in a region for a while? Consider leaving some luggage with your hotel (or luggage storage) and give bikepacking a go. Slowly making your way by bike is a great way to discover hidden corners of a destination.

Connecting Trains

At the point of purchasing your train ticket, you'll be advised on whether you need to change trains during your journey. Always check the platform you need to change to, as it might be on the other side of the station.

FRIENDLY WARNINGS

In Italy, roads are narrow and there may not be enough space for cars to pass you with wide berth. It is common that cars will give a quick honk just before they pass you, whether you are walking or cycling. Don't be put off. This is a courtesy gesture to let you know they are just behind you, so don't make any sudden changes in your direction. Likewise, if you are passing pedestrians while cycling, give them a couple of rings to alert them in the same way.

Accommodation

BIKE HOTELS

In order to capitalise on the increasing popularity of cycle tourism in Italy, many hotels are claiming to welcome cyclists. Before you book, ask exactly what the hotel offers, as sometimes hotels advertised to be 'bike friendly' merely have a couple of bike racks for bicycle parking with no other facilities. A true cycling hotel will have a secure bike storage, with tools for repairs, tyre pumps and wash area, as well as a water source where you can fill up drink bottles. Most will also have staff who are cycling enthusiasts and willing to offer their wisdom on local routes and other recommendations.

HOW MUCH FOR A NIGHT IN...

Three-bedroom holiday villa in Tuscany €250

Double room in an *agriturismo* in Sicily €90

Rifugio accommodation from €50

Agroturismi

There has been a recent boom in *agriturismo* initiatives, providing tourist accommodation on farms. This is a great option for those looking for a slower, more rustic Italian experience, with opportunities for travellers to join cooking workshops or be closer to nature. Rooms are usually offered on half-board basis, which gives you a chance to sample the excellent meals made from the farm's own produce.

Rifugi

Rifugi (mountain huts) are a popular accommodation choice in the Italian Alps for those looking for a rustic mountain experience. Simple rooms with simple meals are the key; rooms are offered on a half-board basis, drinks extra. It is recommended to book well ahead. *Rifugio* seasons are dependent on the weather conditions.

Palazzi

All around Italy, many old *palazzi* (palaces) are being restored and converted into luxury accommodation. These *palazzi* were the pride of many Italian aristocrats, and proprietors will gladly tell you the history of these beautiful buildings, often with stories of family drama and romantic scandals.

Monasteries & Convents

For something different, it is possible to stay in monasteries and convents that provide lodging for travellers, many of which are in remote and quiet locations. As rules and curfews apply to those staying with the monks and the nuns, the experience won't be suitable for everyone. This accommodation option isn't always advertised so enquire at local tourist offices.

TRULLI

Unique to the region of Puglia, many *trulli* (circular stone-built houses) have been converted into self-catering accommodation for tourists. From studio units to five-bedroom properties, it is worth considering staying in one of these beautiful, ancient structures when in the region. Most are located in rural areas, although in the town of Alberobello there are plenty in the centre.

Bikes

HOW MUCH TO HIRE A...

Road/ Gravel/ Mountain Bike
from €40/day

Touring Bike
from €10/day

E-Bike
from €20/day

Bike Rental

Cycle tourism is a big thing in Italy, and in almost every city and town there's at least one shop renting bikes. They're generally independent small businesses run by locals, and you'll find they are the best people to ask for local insights into cycling routes and road conditions around the area. Some accommodation, especially those located in places with a strong link to cycling events or heritage, will also have bikes either free for guests to use or to rent at a small price.

Another option when in a city is to check out the local bike-share schemes. Cities like Rome, Florence and Milan have ready-to-hire street bikes paid by the hour, some with e-bike options.

E-Bikes

E-bikes are big business these days, their popularity increasing even among local populations. In the very narrow streets of Italy, this is a bonus, allowing for easier rides in the mountainous regions and relief for the legs on the brilliantly scenic hills that are ubiquitous to the Italian landscape. Therefore, you'll find that almost all bike rentals will have some e-bikes available. In fact, some bike rentals only specialise in e-bikes.

Charging an e-bike at the end of the day is easy. Often the batteries are portable and can be charged using a normal electrical outlet. You will find some charging stations for e-bikes along a city's network of cycle lanes or at petrol stations, or ask a bike shop.

OTHER GEAR

All bike rentals in Italy will come with a mini hand pump, a repair kit and a lock. Other accessories such as helmets, GPS devices, bike trailers, rear racks and panniers may be available for an additional charge. Water bottles are generally for sale for hygiene reasons.

Health & Safe Travel

INSURANCE

In general, most comprehensive travel insurance will cover leisure cycling but not specialised cycling such as cycle touring or downhill mountain biking. Check the policy wording and make sure additional cover is purchased should you wish to include extensive cycling as part of your trip.

Emergencies

If you have an issue with your bike, call your provider or head to the nearest cycle store for help. If you are injured or engaged in an accident, call the European-wide emergency number 112.

Weather

Italian summers can get very intense and heat stroke is a serious health threat, especially if you are outdoors and cycling. Prevention is key. Drink plenty of cool water and avoid caffeine and too much sugar. Should you feel unwell, stay under the shade and place something cool at the back of your neck. Getting worse? Seek medical treatment.

Security

Like most places, bike theft is rife in cities and major towns in Italy, but less so in country villages. Your bike rental should come with a lock. Park and lock the bike at a dedicated bike rack, and thread the lock through its frame. Choose a location where you can occasionally keep an eye on it while you are out and about.

BIKE BREAKDOWN

Always ask for a contact number (a mobile number linked to a messaging service) from your bike rental shop, if not already offered. The rental service will assist with persons and bike retrieval if the breakdown is due to a problem with the bike (and not as the result of an accident caused by you).

Responsible Travel

Climate Change

It's impossible to ignore the impact we have when travelling, and the importance of making changes where we can. Lonely Planet urges all travellers to engage with their travel carbon footprint. There are many carbon calculators online that allow travellers to estimate the carbon emissions generated by their journey; try resurgence.org/resources/carbon-calculator.html. Many airlines and booking sites offer travellers the option of offsetting the impact of greenhouse gas emissions by contributing to climate-friendly initiatives around the world. We continue to offset the carbon footprint of all Lonely Planet staff travel, while recognising this is a mitigation more than a solution.

RESOURCES

Italy's National Tourist Board
italia.it/en
Up-to-date information on all regions of Italy.

Komoot
komoot.com
A cycling and hiking route-sharing website.

Trenitalia
trenitalia.com
Italy's railway network website.

EAT LOCAL

Find the Italian food of your dreams by eating in local restaurants that promote regional, seasonal cuisine and wines, often coming directly from producers within the town itself.

BUY LOCAL

Another fridge magnet doesn't make a great souvenir. Instead try to buy something direct from local artisans and craftspeople and take home a unique piece of Italian culture.

WATER

Tap water is safe to drink. Water fountains can be found near town squares or on the side of cycling tracks, so bring your own reusable bottle. Water not suitable for drinking will be labelled *acqua non potabile*.

Nuts & Bolts

CURRENCY: EURO (€)

Opening Hours

We've provided high-season opening hours. Hours decrease in winter.

Banks 8.30am–1.30pm and 2.45–4.30pm Monday to Friday

Bars & Cafes 7.30am–8pm, sometimes to 1am or 2am

Restaurants noon–3pm and 7.30–11pm (later in summer)

Shops 9am–1pm and 3.30–7.30pm (or 4–8pm) Monday to Saturday. In cities some shops stay open all day. Some shops close Monday.

Traditionally, Italians enjoy a long lunch break. Outside major cities, expect shops and services to be closed for two to three hours during the middle of the day. As a consolation, they do open until later in the evening.

ELECTRICITY

Type C
220V/50Hz

Type L
220V/50Hz

Cash & Cards

Businesses in Italian cities and most tourist towns will accept card and contactless payments, with Visa and MasterCard most commonly accepted, and Apple/Google Pay methods growing in popularity. If you're shopping in an independent store, you may get a discount if you offer to pay in cash.

While cities have embraced cashless payments, always carry some cash when visiting towns and villages, where small businesses might not be as obliging. Try to pay as close to the price as possible and avoid paying in large denominations, as some places might not carry sufficient change.

Tipping

Tipping is appreciated but not mandatory in Italy, and is offered as a compliment to the service received. It's common to offer a tip of a few euros up to 10% of the value of the bill in a restaurant, but not expected in a bar for a quick coffee.

TOILETS

There are public toilets in cities, parks, train stations and petrol stations, but expect to pay from 50¢ to as much as €1.50. If you're stopping for a coffee at a bar, toilets are generally free to use.

SMOKING

Smoking in public indoor spaces in Italy has been banned since 2005. In 2021 Milan became the first city to introduce an outdoor smoking ban (which is being rolled out in stages until 2025).

HOW MUCH FOR A...

Cornetto (croissant)
€1–2

Glass of wine
from €3

Two scoops of gelato
from €2.50

Rides by Difficulty

Index

Behind the Scenes

Send us your feedback

We love to hear from travelers – your comments help make our books better. We read every word, and we guarantee that your feedback goes straight to the authors. Visit **lonelyplanet. com/contact** to submit your updates and suggestions. Note: We may edit, reproduce and incorporate your comments in Lonely Planet products such as guidebooks,websites and digital products, so let us know if you don't want your comments reproduced or your name acknowledged. For a copy of our privacy policy visit lonelyplanet. com/privacy.

ACKNOWLEDGMENTS

Digital Model Elevation Data
Contains public sector information licensed under the Open Government Licence v3.0 website http://www.nationalarchives .gov.uk/doc/open-government-licence/version/3/

Cover photograph Cyclist in Tuscany, Uwe Moser/Getty Images ©

THIS BOOK

This book was researched and written by Amy McPherson, Margherita Ragg and Angelo Zinna. It was produced by the following:

Destination Editor Amy Lynch

Product Editor Kate James

Book Designer Virginia Moreno

Cartographers Vojtěch Bartoš, Eve Kelly, Alison Lyall

Cover Researcher Marc Backwell

Assisting Editors Janet Austin, Alice Barnes-Brown, Melanie Dankel, Adriana Gallina, Gabrielle Innes

Series Product Development Marc Backwell, Ania Bartoszek, Fergal Condon, Amy Lynch, Katerina Pavkova